Hands-On Automated Machine Learning

A beginner's guide to building automated machine learning systems using AutoML and Python

Sibanjan Das
Umit Mert Cakmak

BIRMINGHAM - MUMBAI

Hands-On Automated Machine Learning

Commissioning Editor: Amey Varangaonkar
Acquisition Editor: Varsha Shetty
Content Development Editor: Tejas Limkar
Technical Editor: Sayli Nikalje
Copy Editor: Safis Editing
Project Coordinator: Manthan Patel
Proofreader: Safis Editing
Indexer: Aishwarya Gangawane
Graphics: Tania Dutta
Production Coordinator: Aparna Bhagat

First published: April 2018

Production reference: 1250418

Published by Packt Publishing Ltd.
Livery Place
35 Livery Street
Birmingham
B3 2PB, UK.

ISBN 978-1-78862-989-8

www.packtpub.com

`mapt.io`

Mapt is an online digital library that gives you full access to over 5,000 books and videos, as well as industry leading tools to help you plan your personal development and advance your career. For more information, please visit our website.

Why subscribe?

- Spend less time learning and more time coding with practical eBooks and Videos from over 4,000 industry professionals

- Improve your learning with Skill Plans built especially for you

- Get a free eBook or video every month

- Mapt is fully searchable

- Copy and paste, print, and bookmark content

PacktPub.com

Did you know that Packt offers eBook versions of every book published, with PDF and ePub files available? You can upgrade to the eBook version at `www.PacktPub.com` and as a print book customer, you are entitled to a discount on the eBook copy. Get in touch with us at `service@packtpub.com` for more details.

At `www.PacktPub.com`, you can also read a collection of free technical articles, sign up for a range of free newsletters, and receive exclusive discounts and offers on Packt books and eBooks.

Contributors

About the authors

Sibanjan Das is a business analytics and data science consultant. He has extensive experience in implementing predictive analytics solutions in business systems and IoT. An enthusiastic and passionate professional about technology and innovation, he has loved wrangling with data since the early days of his career. He has a master's in IT with a major in business analytics from Singapore Management University, and holds several industry certifications such as OCA, OCP, and CSCMS.

I dedicate my writing to my father Dr. M. N. Das, mother, grandparent, sisters, brothers, and brothers-in-law. Also, to my wife and son, Sachit, for their love and care. They motivated me to do what I always wanted to do. The list of people who inspire me is long. I want to thank them all for their endless encouragement and kind support.

Umit Mert Cakmak is a Data Scientist at IBM, where he excels at helping clients to solve complex data science problems, from inception to delivery of deployable assets. His research spans across multiple disciplines beyond his industry and he likes sharing his insights at conferences, universities, and meet-ups.

First and foremost, my heartiest thanks to my mother and father, for their true love, support, and I am grateful for the lessons that they have taught me. I would like to dedicate my writings to my family, friends, colleagues, and all the great people who relentlessly work to make the world a better place.

About the reviewers

Brian T. Hoffman has developed and deployed data science solutions for 20 years, in fields such as drug discovery, biotech, software, and sales. After obtaining his PhD in drug discovery from University of North Carolina, Chapel Hill, he completed his postdoctoral fellowship in developing new ML techniques with the National Institutes of Health. He has a passion for determining how data can help improve business decisions, and has managed international teams of scientists implementing data science solutions for companies ranging from startups to Fortune 100.

Packt is searching for authors like you

If you're interested in becoming an author for Packt, please visit authors.packtpub.com and apply today. We have worked with thousands of developers and tech professionals, just like you, to help them share their insight with the global tech community. You can make a general application, apply for a specific hot topic that we are recruiting an author for, or submit your own idea.

Table of Contents

Preface

Dear reader, welcome to the world of automated **machine learning (ML)**. **Automated ML (AutoML)** is designed to automate parts of ML. The readily available AutoML tools make the tasks of data science practitioners easier and are being well received in the advanced analytics community. This book covers the foundations you need to create AutoML modules, and shows how you can get up to speed with them in the most practical way possible.

You will learn to automate different tasks in the ML pipeline, such as data preprocessing, feature selection, model training, model optimization, and much more. The book also demonstrates how to use already available automation libraries, such as auto-sklearn and MLBox, and how to create and extend your own custom AutoML components for ML.

By the end of this book, you will have a clearer understanding of what the different aspects of AutoML are, and will be able to incorporate the automation tasks using practical datasets. The knowledge you get from this book can be leveraged to implement ML in your projects, or to get a step closer to winning an ML competition. We hope that everyone who buys this book finds it worthy and informative.

Who this book is for

This book is ideal for budding data scientists, data analysts, and ML enthusiasts who are new to the concept of AutoML. Machine learning engineers and data professionals who are interested in developing quick machine learning pipelines for their projects will also find this book useful.

What this book covers

Chapter 1, *Introduction to AutoML*, creates a foundation for you to dive into AutoML. We also introduce you to various AutoML libraries.

Chapter 2, *Introduction to Machine Learning Using Python*, introduces some machine learning concepts so that you can follow the AutoML approaches easily.

Chapter 3, *Data Preprocessing*, provides an in-depth understanding of different data preprocessing methods, what can be automated, and how to automate it. Feature tools and auto-sklearn preprocessing methods will be introduced here.

Chapter 4, *Automated Algorithm Selection*, provides guidance on which algorithm works best on which kind of dataset. We learn about the computational complexity and scalability of different algorithms, along with methods to decide the algorithm to use based on training and scoring time. We demonstrate auto-sklearn and how to extend it to include new algorithms.

Chapter 5, *Hyperparameter Optimization*, provides you with the required fundamentals on automating hyperparameter tuning a for variety of variables.

Chapter 6, *Creating AutoML Pipelines*, explains stitching together various components to create an end-to-end AutoML pipeline.

Chapter 7, *Dive into Deep Learning*, introduces you to various deep learning concepts and how they contribute to AutoML.

Chapter 8, *Critical Aspects of ML and Data Science Projects*, concludes the discussion and provides information on various trade-offs on the complexity and cost of AutoML projects.

To get the most out of this book

The only thing you need before you start reading is your inquisitiveness to know more about ML. Apart from that, prior exposure to Python programming and ML fundamentals are required to get the best out of this book, but they are not mandatory. You should have Python 3.5 and Jupyter Notebook installed.

If there is a specific requirement for any chapter, it is mentioned in the opening section.

Download the example code files

You can download the example code files for this book from your account at www.packtpub.com. If you purchased this book elsewhere, you can visit www.packtpub.com/support and register to have the files emailed directly to you.

You can download the code files by following these steps:

1. Log in or register at www.packtpub.com.
2. Select the **SUPPORT** tab.
3. Click on **Code Downloads & Errata**.
4. Enter the name of the book in the **Search** box and follow the onscreen instructions.

Once the file is downloaded, please make sure that you unzip or extract the folder using the latest version of:

- WinRAR/7-Zip for Windows
- Zipeg/iZip/UnRarX for Mac
- 7-Zip/PeaZip for Linux

The code bundle for the book is also hosted on GitHub at `https://github.com/PacktPublishing/Hands-On-Automated-Machine-Learning`. In case there's an update to the code, it will be updated on the existing GitHub repository.

We also have other code bundles from our rich catalog of books and videos available at `https://github.com/PacktPublishing/`. Check them out!

Download the color images

We also provide a PDF file that has color images of the screenshots/diagrams used in this book. You can download it here: `https://www.packtpub.com/sites/default/files/downloads/HandsOnAutomatedMachineLearning_ColorImages.pdf`.

Conventions used

There are a number of text conventions used throughout this book.

`CodeInText`: Indicates code words in text, database table names, folder names, filenames, file extensions, pathnames, dummy URLs, user input, and Twitter handles. Here is an example: "As an example, let's use `StandardScaler` from the `sklearn.preprocessing` module to standardize the values of the `satisfaction_level` column."

A block of code is set as follows:

```
{'algorithm': 'auto',
 'copy_x': True,
 'init': 'k-means++',
 'max_iter': 300,
 'n_clusters': 2,
 'n_init': 10,
 'n_jobs': 1,
 'precompute_distances': 'auto',
 'random_state': None,
 'tol': 0.0001,
 'verbose': 0}
```

Any command-line input or output is written as follows:

```
pip install nltk
```

Bold: Indicates a new term, an important word, or words that you see onscreen. For example, words in menus or dialog boxes appear in the text like this. Here is an example: "You will get a NLTK Downloader popup. Select **all** from the **Identifier** section and wait for installation to be completed."

 Warnings or important notes appear like this.

 Tips and tricks appear like this.

Get in touch

Feedback from our readers is always welcome.

General feedback: Email `feedback@packtpub.com` and mention the book title in the subject of your message. If you have questions about any aspect of this book, please email us at `questions@packtpub.com`.

Errata: Although we have taken every care to ensure the accuracy of our content, mistakes do happen. If you have found a mistake in this book, we would be grateful if you would report this to us. Please visit `www.packtpub.com/submit-errata`, selecting your book, clicking on the Errata Submission Form link, and entering the details.

Piracy: If you come across any illegal copies of our works in any form on the Internet, we would be grateful if you would provide us with the location address or website name. Please contact us at `copyright@packtpub.com` with a link to the material.

If you are interested in becoming an author: If there is a topic that you have expertise in and you are interested in either writing or contributing to a book, please visit `authors.packtpub.com`.

Reviews

Please leave a review. Once you have read and used this book, why not leave a review on the site that you purchased it from? Potential readers can then see and use your unbiased opinion to make purchase decisions, we at Packt can understand what you think about our products, and our authors can see your feedback on their book. Thank you!

For more information about Packt, please visit `packtpub.com`.

Introduction to AutoML

1

The last decade, if nothing else, has been a thrilling adventure in science and technology. The first iPhone was released in 2007, and back then all of its competitors had a physical integrated keyboard. The idea of touchscreen wasn't new as Apple had similar prototypes before and IBM came up with Simon Personal Communicator in 1994. Apple's idea was to have a device full of multimedia entertainment, such as listening to music and streaming videos, while having all the useful functionalities, such as web and GPS navigation. Of course, all of this was possible with access to affordable computing power at the time that Apple released the first generation iPhone. If you really think about the struggles that these great companies have had in the last 20 years, you can see how quickly technology came to where it is today. To put things into perspective, 10 years after the release of first generation iPhones, today your iPhone, along with others, can track faces and recognize objects such as animals, vehicles, and food. It can understand natural language and converse with you.

What about 3D printers that can print organs, self-driving cars, swarms of drones that fly together in harmony, gene editing, reusable rockets, and a robot that can do a backflip? These are not stories that you read in science fiction books anymore, and it's happening as you read these lines. You could only imagine this in the past, but today, science fiction is becoming a reality. People have started talking about the threat of **artificial intelligence (AI)**. Many leading scientists, such as Stephen Hawking, are warning officials about the possible end of humankind, which could be caused by AI-based life forms.

AI and **machine learning (ML)** reached their peak in the last couple of years and are totally stealing the show. The chances are pretty good that you have already heard about the success of ML algorithms and great advancements in the field over the last decade. The recent success of Google's AlphaGo showed how far this technology can go when it beat Ke Jie, the best human Go player on Earth. This wasn't the first time that ML algorithms beat humans in particular tasks such as image recognition. When it comes to fine-grained details, such as recognizing different species of animals, these algorithms have often performed better than their human competitors.

These advancements have created a huge interest in the business world. As much as it sounds like an academic field of research, these technologies have huge business implications and can directly impact your organizations financials.

Enterprises from different industries want to utilize the power of these algorithms and try to adapt to the changing technology scene. Everybody is aware that people who figure out how to integrate these technologies into their businesses will lead the space, and the rest are going to have a hard time catching up.

We will explore more of such examples in the book. In this book, we will be covering the following topics:

- Scope of machine learning
- What AutoML is
- Why use AutoML and how it helps
- When to use AutoML
- Overview of AutoML libraries

Scope of machine learning

Machine learning and predictive analytics now help companies to focus on important areas, anticipating problems before they happen, reducing costs, and increasing revenue. This was a natural evolution after working with **business intelligence** (**BI**) solutions. BI applications were helping companies to make better decisions by monitoring their business processes in an organized manner, usually using dashboards that have various **key performance indicators** (**KPIs**) and performance metrics.

BI tools allow you to dig deeper into your organizations historical data, uncover trends, understand seasonality, find out irregular events, and so on. They can also provide real-time analytics where you can set up some warnings and alerts to manage particular events better. All of these things are quite useful, but today businesses need more than that. What does that mean? BI tools allow you to work with historical and near real-time data, but they do not provide you with answers about the future and don't answer questions such as the following:

- Which machine in your production line is likely to fail?
- Which of your customers will probably switch to your competitor?
- Which company's stock price is going up tomorrow?

Businesses want to answer these kinds of questions nowadays, and it pushes them to search for suitable tools and technologies, which brings them to ML and predictive analytics.

You need to be careful though! When you are working with BI tools, you are more confident about the results that you are going to have, but when you are working with ML models, there's no such guarantee and the ground is slippery. There is definitely a huge buzz about AI and ML nowadays, and people are making outrageous claims about the capabilities of upcoming AI products. After all, computer scientists have long sought to create intelligent machines and occasionally suffered along the way due to unreal expectations. You can have a quick Google search about *AI winter* and learn more about that period. Although the advancements are beyond imagination and the field is moving quickly, you should navigate through the noise and see what the actual use cases are that ML really shines in and they can help you to create a value for your research or business in measurable terms.

In order to do that, you need to start with small pilot projects where:

- You have a relatively easier decision making processes
- You know your assumptions well
- You know your data well

The key here is to have a well-defined project scope and steps that you are going to execute. Collaboration between different teams is really helpful in this process, that's why you should break silos inside your organization. Also, starting small doesn't mean that your vision should be small too. You should always think about scalability in the future and slowly gear up to harness the big data sources.

There are a variety of ML algorithms that you can experiment with, each designed to solve a specific problem with their own pros and cons. There is a growing body of research in this area and practitioners are coming up with new methods and pushing the limits of this field everyday. Hence, one might get easily lost with all the information available out there, especially when developing ML applications since there are many available tools and techniques for every stage of the model building process. To ease building ML models, you need to decompose a whole process into small pieces. **Automated ML (AutoML)** pipelines have many moving parts such as feature preprocessing, feature selection, model selection, and hyperparameter optimization. Each of these parts needs to be handled with special care to deliver successful projects.

You will hear a lot about ML concepts throughout the book, but let's step back and understand why you need to pay special attention to AutoML.

As you have more tools and technologies in your arsenal to attack your problems, having too many options usually becomes a problem itself and it requires considerable amount of time to research and understand the right approach for a given problem. When you are dealing with ML problems, it's a similar story. Building high-performing ML models contains several carefully-crafted small steps. Each step leads you to another and if you do not drop the balls on your way, you will have your ML pipeline functioning properly and generalize well when you deploy your pipeline in a production environment.

The number of steps involved in your pipeline could be large and the process could be really lengthy. At every step, there are many methods available, and, once you think about the possible number of different combinations, you will quickly realize that you need a systematic way of experimenting with all these components in your ML pipelines.

This brings us to the topic of AutoML!

What is AutoML?

AutoML aims to ease the process of building ML models by automating commonly-used steps, such as feature preprocessing, model selection, and hyperparameters tuning. You will see each of these steps in detail in coming chapters and you will actually build an AutoML system to have a deeper understanding of the available tools and libraries for AutoML.

Without getting into the details, it's useful to review what an ML model is and how you train one.

ML algorithms will work on your data to find certain patterns, and this learning process is called **model training**. As a result of model training, you will have an ML model that supposedly will give you insights/answers about the data without requiring you to write explicit rules.

When you are using ML models in practice, you will throw a bunch of numerical data as input for training the algorithm. The output of the training process is a ML model that you can use to make predictions. Predictions can help you to decide whether your server should be maintained in the next four hours based on its current state, or whether a customer of yours is going to switch to your competitor or not.

Sometimes the problem you are solving will not be well-defined and you will not even know what kind of answers you are looking for. In such cases, ML models will help you to explore your dataset, such as identifying a cluster of customers that are similar to each other in terms of behavior or finding the hierarchical structure of stocks based on their correlations.

What do you do when your model comes up with clusters of customers? Well, you at least know this: customers that belong to the same cluster are similar to each other in terms of their features, such as their age, profession, marital status, gender, product preferences, daily/weekly/monthly spending habits, total amount spent, and so on. Customers who belong to different clusters are dissimilar to each other. With such an insight, you can utilize this information to create different ad campaigns for each cluster.

To put things into a more technical perspective, let's understand this process in simple mathematical terms. There is a dataset X, which contains n examples. These examples could represent customers or different species of animals. Each example is usually a set of real numbers, which are called **features**, for example if we have a female, 35 year old customer who spent $12000 at your store, you can represent this customer with the following vector (0.0, 35.0, 12000.0). Note that the gender is represented with *0.0*, this means that a male customer would have *1.0* for that feature. The size of the vector represents the dimensionality. Since this is a vector of size three, which we usually denote by m, this is a three-dimensional dataset.

Depending on the problem type, you might need to have a label for each example. For example, if this is a supervised learning problem such as binary classification, you could label your examples with 1.0 or 0.0 and this new variable is called **label** or **target** variable. The target variable is usually referred to as y.

Having x and y, an ML model is simply a function, f, with weights, w (model parameters):

$$f(x; w)$$

Model parameters are learned during the training process, but there are also other parameters that you might need to set before training starts, and these parameters are called **hyperparameters**, which will be explained shortly.

Features in your dataset usually should be preprocessed before being used in model training. For example, some of the ML models implicitly assume that features are distributed normally. In many real-life scenarios this is not the case, and you can benefit from applying feature transformations such as log transformation to have them normally distributed.

Once feature processing is done and model hyperparameters are set, model training starts. At the end of model training, model parameters will be learned and we can predict the target variable for new data that the model has not seen before. Prediction made by the model is usually referred to as $\hat{y}$:

$$\hat{y} = f(x; w)$$

What really happens during training? Since we know the labels for the dataset we used for training, we can iteratively update our model parameters based on the comparison of what our current model predicts and what the original label was.

This comparison is based on a function called **loss function** (or cost function), $L(\hat{y}, y)$. Loss function represents the inaccuracy of predictions. Some of the common loss functions you may have heard of are square loss, hinge loss, logistic loss, and cross-entropy loss.

Once model training is done, you will test the performance of your ML model on `test` data, which is the dataset that has not been used in the training process, to see how well your model generalizes. You can use different performance metrics to assess the performance; based on the results, you should go back to previous steps and do multiple adjustments to achieve better performance.

At this point, you should have an overall idea of what training an ML model looks like under the hood.

What is AutoML then? When we are talking about AutoML, we mostly refer to automated data preparation (namely feature preprocessing, generation, and selection) and model training (model selection and hyperparameter optimization). The number of possible options for each step of this process can vary vastly depending on the problem type.

AutoML allows researchers and practitioners to automatically build ML pipelines out of these possible options for every step to find high-performing ML models for a given problem.

The following figure shows a typical ML model life cycle with a couple of examples for every step:

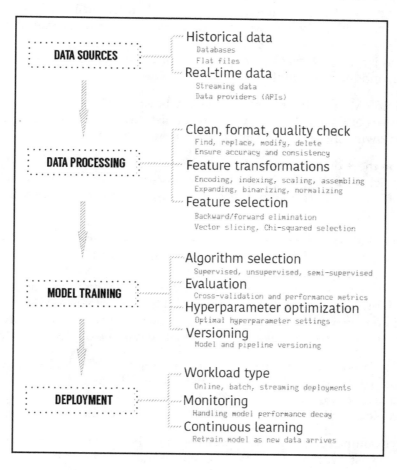

Data can be ingested from various sources such as flat files, databases, and APIs. Once you are able to ingest the data, you should process it to make it ready for ML and there are typical operations such as cleaning and formatting, feature transformation, and feature selection. After data processing, your final dataset should be ready for ML and you will shortlist candidate algorithms to work. Shortlisted algorithms should be validated and tuned through techniques such as cross-validation and hyperparameter optimization. Your final model will be ready to be operationalized with suitable workload type such as online, batch and streaming deployment. Once model is in production, you need to monitor its performance and take necessary action if needed such as re-training, re-evaluation, and re-deployment.

Once you are faced with building ML models, you will first do research on the domain you are working on and identify your objective. There are many steps involved in the process which should be planned and documented in advance before you actually start working on it. To learn more about the whole process of project management, you can refer to CRISP-DM model (https://en.wikipedia.org/wiki/Cross-industry_standard_process_for_data_mining), project management is crucially important to deliver a successful application, however, it's beyond the scope of this book.

In terms of building ML pipelines, you will usually have multiple data sources, such as relational databases or flat files, where you can get historical data. You can also have streaming data flowing into your systems from various resources.

You will work on these data sources to understand which of them could be useful for your particular task, then you will proceed to the data processing step where you will do lots of cleaning, formatting, and data quality checks followed by feature transformations and selection.

When you decide that your dataset is ready to be fed into ML models, you will need to think about working with one or more suitable ML models. You will train multiple models, evaluate them, and search for optimal hyperparameter settings. Versioning at this point will help you to keep track of changes. As a result of your experimentation, you will have a performance ML pipeline with every step optimized for performance. The best performing ML pipeline will be the one you would like to test drive in a production environment and that's the point where you would like to operationalize it in the deployment step.

Operationalizing an ML pipeline means that you need to choose a deployment type. Some of the workloads will be for batch processing the data you have in databases, and in that case you need batch deployment. Others could be for processing real-time data provided by various data providers, where you will need streaming deployment.

If you carefully examine each of these steps, especially the options in data processing and training steps are vast. First you need to select appropriate methods and algorithms, then you should also fine-tune hyperparameters for selected methods and algorithms for them to best perform for your given problem.

Just to give a simple example, let's assume that you are done with the steps up to model training step, you need to select a set of ML models to experiment. To make things simpler, let's say the only algorithm you would like to experiment with is k-means, it's just about tuning its parameters.

A k-means algorithm helps to cluster similar data points together. The following code snippet uses the scikit-learn library and you can install it using pip (http://scikit-learn.org/stable/install.html), don't worry if you don't understand every line:

```
# Sklearn has convenient modules to create sample data.
# make_blobs will help us to create a sample data set suitable for
clustering
from sklearn.datasets.samples_generator import make_blobs

X, y = make_blobs(n_samples=100, centers=2, cluster_std=0.30,
random_state=0)

# Let's visualize what we have first
import matplotlib.pyplot as plt
import seaborn as sns

plt.scatter(X[:, 0], X[:, 1], s=50)
```

The output of the preceding code snippet is as follows:

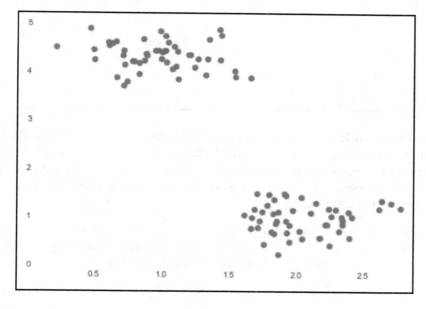

You can easily see that we have two clusters on the plot:

```
# We will import KMeans model from clustering model family of Sklearn
from sklearn.cluster import KMeans

k_means = KMeans(n_clusters=2)
```

```
k_means.fit(X)
predictions = k_means.predict(X)

# Let's plot the predictions
plt.scatter(X[:, 0], X[:, 1], c=predictions, cmap='brg')
```

The output of the preceding code snippet is as follows:

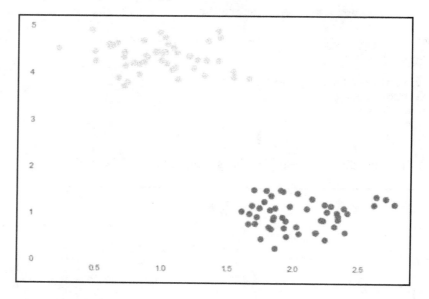

Nice! Our algorithm worked as we expected. Astute readers may have noticed that there was an argument named n_clusters for the k-means model. When you provide this value to the k-means algorithm, it will try to split this dataset into two clusters. As you can guess, k-means's hyperparameter in this case is the number of clusters. The k-means model needs to know this parameter before training.

Different algorithms have different hyperparameters such as depth of tree for decision trees, number of hidden layers, learning rate for neural networks, alpha parameter for Lasso or C, kernel, and gamma for **Support Vector Machines (SVMs)**.

Let's see how many arguments the k-means model has by using the get_params method:

```
k_means.get_params()
```

The output will be the list of all parameters that you can optimize:

```
{'algorithm': 'auto',
 'copy_x': True,
```

```
'init': 'k-means++',
'max_iter': 300,
'n_clusters': 2,
'n_init': 10,
'n_jobs': 1,
'precompute_distances': 'auto',
'random_state': None,
'tol': 0.0001,
'verbose': 0}
```

In most real-life use cases, you will neither have resources nor time for trying each possible combination with the options of all steps considered.

AutoML libraries come to your aid at this point by carefully setting up experiments for various ML pipelines, which covers all the steps from data ingestion, data processing, modeling, and scoring.

Why use AutoML and how does it help?

There are a lot of ML tutorials on the internet, and usually the sample datasets are clean, formatted, and ready to be used with algorithms because the aim of many tutorials is to show the capability of certain tools, libraries, or **Software as a Service (SaaS)** offerings.

In reality, datasets come in different types and sizes. A recent industry survey done by Kaggle in 2017, titled *The State of Data Science and Machine Learning,* with over 16,000 responses, shows that the top-three commonly-used datatypes are relational data, text data, and image data.

Moreover, messy data is at the top of the list of problems that people have to deal with, again based on the Kaggle survey. When a dataset is messy and needs a lot of special treatment to be used by ML models, you spend a considerable amount of time on data cleaning, manipulation, and hand-crafting features to get it in the right shape. This is the most time-consuming part of any data science project.

What about selection of performant ML models, hyperparameter optimization of models in training, validation, and testing phases? These are also crucially-important steps that can be executed in many ways.

When the combination of right components come together to process and model your dataset, that combination represents a ML pipeline, and the number of pipelines to be experimented could grow very quickly.

For building high-performing ML pipelines successfully, you should systematically go through all the available options for every step by considering your limits in terms of time and hardware/software resources.

 AutoML systems help you to define robust approaches to automatically constructing ML pipelines for a given problem and effectively execute them in order to find performant models.

When do you automate ML?

Once you are confident with building ML pipelines, you will realize that there are many mundane routines that you have to perform to prepare features and tuning hyperparameters. You also will feel more confident with certain methods, and you will have a pretty good idea of what the techniques are that would work well together with different parameter settings.

In between different projects, you gain more experience by performing multiple experiments to evaluate your processing and modeling pipelines, optimizing the whole workflow in an iterative fashion. Managing this whole process can quickly get very ugly if you are not organized from the beginning.

 Necessity of AutoML arises out of these difficult situations, when you are dealing with many moving parts and a great number of parameters. These are the situations where AutoML can help you focus on the design and implementation details in a structured manner.

What will you learn?

Throughout this book, you will learn both theoretical and practical aspects of AutoML systems. More importantly, you will practice your skills by developing an AutoML system from scratch.

Core components of AutoML systems

In this section, you will review the following core components of AutoML systems:

- Automated feature preprocessing

- Automated algorithm selection
- Hyperparameter optimization

Having a better understanding of core components will help you to create your mental map of AutoML systems.

Automated feature preprocessing

When you are dealing with ML problems, you usually have a relational dataset that has various types of data, and you should properly treat each of them before training ML algorithms.

For example, if you are dealing with numerical data, you may scale it by applying methods such as min-max scaling or variance scaling.

For textual data, you may want to remove stop-words such as *a*, *an*, and *the*, and perform operations such as stemming, parsing, and tokenization.

For categorical data, you may need to encode it using methods such as one-hot encoding, dummy coding, and feature hashing.

How about having a very high number of features? For example, when you have thousands of features, how many of them would actually be useful? Would it be better to reduce dimensionality by using methods such as **Principal Component Analysis (PCA)**?

What if you have different formats of data, such as video, audio, and image? How do you process each of them?

For example, for image data, you may apply some transformations such as rescaling the images to common shape and segmentation to separate certain regions.

There is an abundance of feature preprocessing methods, and ML algorithms will perform better with some set of transformations. Having a flexible AutoML system in your arsenal will allow you to experiment with different combinations in a smart way, which will save you much needed time and money in your projects.

Automated algorithm selection

Once you are done with feature processing, you need to find a suitable set of algorithms for training and evaluation.

Every ML algorithm has an ability to solve certain problems. Let's consider clustering algorithms such as k-means, hierarchical clustering, spectral clustering, and DBSCAN. We are familiar with k-means, but what about the others? Each of these algorithms has application areas and each might perform better than others based on the distributional properties of a dataset.

AutoML pipelines can help you to choose the right algorithm from a set of suitable algorithms for a given problem.

Hyperparameter optimization

Every ML algorithm has one or many hyperparameters and you are already familiar with k-means. But it is not only ML algorithms that have hyperparameters, feature processing methods also have their hyperparameters and those also need fine-tuning.

Tuning hyperparameters is crucially important to a model's success and AutoML pipeline will help you to define a range of hyperparameters that you would like to experiment with, resulting in the best performing ML pipeline.

Building prototype subsystems for each component

Throughout the book, you will be building each core component of AutoML systems from scratch and seeing how each part interacts with each other.

Having skills to build such systems from scratch will give you a deeper understanding of the process and also inner workings of popular AutoML libraries.

Putting it all together as an end–to–end AutoML system

Once you have gone through all the chapters, you will have a good understanding of the components and how they work together to create ML pipelines. You will then use your knowledge to write AutoML pipelines from scratch and tweak them in any way that would work for a set of problems that you are aiming to solve.

Overview of AutoML libraries

There are many popular AutoML libraries, and in this section you will have an overview of commonly used ones in the data science community.

Featuretools

Featuretools (`https://www.featuretools.com/`) is a good library for automatically engineering features from relational and transactional data. The library introduces the concept called **Deep Feature Synthesis (DFS)**. If you have multiple datasets with relationships defined among them such as parent-child based on columns that you use as unique identifiers for examples, DFS will create new features based on certain calculations, such as summation, count, mean, mode, standard deviation, and so on. Let's go through a small example where you will have two tables, one showing the database information and the other showing the database transactions for each database:

```python
import pandas as pd

# First dataset contains the basic information for databases.
databases_df = pd.DataFrame({"database_id": [2234, 1765, 8796, 2237, 3398],
"creation_date": ["2018-02-01", "2017-03-02", "2017-05-03", "2013-05-12",
"2012-05-09"]})

databases_df.head()
```

You get the following output:

	creation_date	database_id
0	2018-02-01	2234
1	2017-03-02	1765
2	2017-05-03	8796
3	2013-05-12	2237
4	2012-05-09	3398

The following is the code for the database transaction:

```python
# Second dataset contains the information of transaction for each database
id
db_transactions_df = pd.DataFrame({"transaction_id": [26482746, 19384752,
48571125, 78546789, 19998765, 26482646, 12484752, 42471125, 75346789,
```

```
16498765, 65487547, 23453847, 56756771, 45645667, 23423498, 12335268,
76435357, 34534711, 45656746, 12312987],
            "database_id": [2234, 1765, 2234, 2237, 1765, 8796, 2237,
8796, 3398, 2237, 3398, 2237, 2234, 8796, 1765, 2234, 2237, 1765, 8796,
2237],
            "transaction_size": [10, 20, 30, 50, 100, 40, 60, 60, 10,
20, 60, 50, 40, 40, 30, 90, 130, 40, 50, 30],
            "transaction_date": ["2018-02-02", "2018-03-02",
"2018-03-02", "2018-04-02", "2018-04-02", "2018-05-02", "2018-06-02",
"2018-06-02", "2018-07-02", "2018-07-02", "2018-01-03", "2018-02-03",
"2018-03-03", "2018-04-03", "2018-04-03", "2018-07-03", "2018-07-03",
"2018-07-03", "2018-08-03", "2018-08-03"]})

db_transactions_df.head()
```

You get the following output:

	database_id	transaction_date	transaction_id	transaction_size
0	2234	2018-02-02	26482746	10
1	1765	2018-03-02	19384752	20
2	2234	2018-03-02	48571125	30
3	2237	2018-04-02	78546789	50
4	1765	2018-04-02	19998765	100

The code for the entities is as follows:

```
# Entities for each of datasets should be defined
entities = {
"databases" : (databases_df, "database_id"),
"transactions" : (db_transactions_df, "transaction_id")
}

# Relationships between tables should also be defined as below
relationships = [("databases", "database_id", "transactions",
"database_id")]

print(entities)
```

You get the following output for the preceding code:

```
{'databases': (   creation_date  database_id  database_size
0     2018-02-01        2234             50
1     2017-03-02        1765            120
2     2017-05-03        8796            100
3     2013-05-12        2237             30
4     2012-05-09        3398             30, 'database_id'), 'transactions': (   database_id transaction_date  transaction_id  transaction_size
0     2234        2018-02-02       26482746          10
1     1765        2018-03-02       19384752          20
2     2234        2018-03-02       48571125          30
3     2237        2018-04-02       78546789          50
4     1765        2018-04-02       19998765         100
5     8796        2018-05-02       26482646          40
6     2237        2018-06-02       12484752          60
7     8796        2018-06-02       42471125          60
8     3398        2018-07-02       75346789          10
9     2237        2018-07-02       16498765          20
10    3398        2018-01-03       65487547          60
11    2237        2018-02-03       23453847          50
12    2234        2018-03-03       56756771          40
13    8796        2018-04-03       45645667          40
14    1765        2018-04-03       23423498          30
15    2234        2018-07-03       12335268          90
16    2237        2018-07-03       76435357         130
17    1765        2018-07-03       34534711          40
18    8796        2018-08-03       45656746          50
19    2237        2018-08-03       12312987          30, 'transaction_id')}
```

The following code snippet will create feature matrix and feature definitions:

```
# There are 2 entities called 'databases' and 'transactions'

# All the pieces that are necessary to engineer features are in place, you
can create your feature matrix as below

import featuretools as ft

feature_matrix_db_transactions, feature_defs = ft.dfs(entities=entities,
relationships=relationships,
target_entity="databases")
```

The following output shows some of the features that are generated:

database_id	database_size	SUM(transactions.transaction_size)	STD(transactions.transaction_size)	MAX(transactions.tr
1765	120	190	31.124749	
2234	50	170	29.474565	
2237	30	340	35.433819	
3398	30	70	25.000000	
8796	100	190	8.291562	

Generated features using databases and transaction entities

You can see all feature definitions by looking at the following `features_defs`:

```
feature_defs
```

The output is as follows:

```
[<Feature: database_size>,
 <Feature: SUM(transactions.transaction_size)>,
 <Feature: STD(transactions.transaction_size)>,
 <Feature: MAX(transactions.transaction_size)>,
 <Feature: SKEW(transactions.transaction_size)>,
 <Feature: MIN(transactions.transaction_size)>,
 <Feature: MEAN(transactions.transaction_size)>,
 <Feature: COUNT(transactions)>,
 <Feature: DAY(creation_date)>,
 <Feature: YEAR(creation_date)>,
 <Feature: MONTH(creation_date)>,
 <Feature: WEEKDAY(creation_date)>,
 <Feature: NUM_UNIQUE(transactions.DAY(transaction_date))>,
 <Feature: NUM_UNIQUE(transactions.YEAR(transaction_date))>,
 <Feature: NUM_UNIQUE(transactions.MONTH(transaction_date))>,
 <Feature: NUM_UNIQUE(transactions.WEEKDAY(transaction_date))>,
 <Feature: MODE(transactions.DAY(transaction_date))>,
 <Feature: MODE(transactions.YEAR(transaction_date))>,
 <Feature: MODE(transactions.MONTH(transaction_date))>,
 <Feature: MODE(transactions.WEEKDAY(transaction_date))>]
```

This is how you can easily generate features based on relational and transactional datasets.

Auto-sklearn

Scikit-learn has a great API for developing ML models and pipelines. Scikit-learn's API is very consistent and mature; if you are used to working with it, *auto-sklearn* (http://automl.github.io/auto-sklearn/stable/) will be just as easy to use since it's really a drop-in replacement for scikit-learn estimators.

Let's see a little example:

```
# Necessary imports
import autosklearn.classification
import sklearn.model_selection
import sklearn.datasets
import sklearn.metrics
from sklearn.model_selection import train_test_split
```

```
# Digits dataset is one of the most popular datasets in machine learning
community.
# Every example in this datasets represents a 8x8 image of a digit.
X, y = sklearn.datasets.load_digits(return_X_y=True)

# Let's see the first image. Image is reshaped to 8x8, otherwise it's a
vector of size 64.
X[0].reshape(8,8)
```

The output is as follows:

```
array([[ 0.,  0.,  5., 13.,  9.,  1.,  0.,  0.],
       [ 0.,  0., 13., 15., 10., 15.,  5.,  0.],
       [ 0.,  3., 15.,  2.,  0., 11.,  8.,  0.],
       [ 0.,  4., 12.,  0.,  0.,  8.,  8.,  0.],
       [ 0.,  5.,  8.,  0.,  0.,  9.,  8.,  0.],
       [ 0.,  4., 11.,  0.,  1., 12.,  7.,  0.],
       [ 0.,  2., 14.,  5., 10., 12.,  0.,  0.],
       [ 0.,  0.,  6., 13., 10.,  0.,  0.,  0.]])
```

You can plot a couple of images to see how they look:

```
import matplotlib.pyplot as plt

number_of_images = 10
images_and_labels = list(zip(X, y))

for i, (image, label) in enumerate(images_and_labels[:number_of_images]):
    plt.subplot(2, number_of_images, i + 1)
    plt.axis('off')
    plt.imshow(image.reshape(8,8), cmap=plt.cm.gray_r,
interpolation='nearest')
    plt.title('%i' % label)

plt.show()
```

Running the preceding snippet will give you the following plot:

Splitting the dataset to train and test data:

```
# We split our dataset to train and test data
X_train, X_test, y_train, y_test = train_test_split(X, y, random_state=1)

# Similarly to creating an estimator in Scikit-learn, we create
AutoSklearnClassifier
automl = autosklearn.classification.AutoSklearnClassifier()

# All you need to do is to invoke fit method to start experiment with
different feature engineering methods and machine learning models
automl.fit(X_train, y_train)

# Generating predictions is same as Scikit-learn, you need to invoke
predict method.
y_hat = automl.predict(X_test)

print("Accuracy score", sklearn.metrics.accuracy_score(y_test, y_hat))
# Accuracy score 0.98
```

That was easy, wasn't it?

MLBox

MLBox (`http://mlbox.readthedocs.io/en/latest/`) is another AutoML library and it supports distributed data processing, cleaning, formatting, and state-of-the-art algorithms such as LightGBM and XGBoost. It also supports model stacking, which allows you to combine an information ensemble of models to generate a new model aiming to have better performance than the individual models.

Here's an example of its usage:

```
# Necessary Imports
from mlbox.preprocessing import *
from mlbox.optimisation import *
from mlbox.prediction import *
import wget
```

```
file_link =
'https://apsportal.ibm.com/exchange-api/v1/entries/8044492073eb964f46597b4b
e06ff5ea/data?accessKey=9561295fa407698694b1e254d0099600'
file_name = wget.download(file_link)

print(file_name)
# GoSales_Tx_NaiveBayes.csv
```

The `GoSales` dataset contains information for customers and their product preferences:

```
import pandas as pd
df = pd.read_csv('GoSales_Tx_NaiveBayes.csv')
df.head()
```

You get the following output from the preceding code:

	PRODUCT_LINE	GENDER	AGE	MARITAL_STATUS	PROFESSION
0	Personal Accessories	M	27	Single	Professional
1	Personal Accessories	F	39	Married	Other
2	Mountaineering Equipment	F	39	Married	Other
3	Personal Accessories	F	56	Unspecified	Hospitality
4	Golf Equipment	M	45	Married	Retired

Let's create a `test` set from the same dataset by dropping a `target` column:

```
test_df = df.drop(['PRODUCT_LINE'], axis = 1)

# First 300 records saved as test dataset
test_df[:300].to_csv('test_data.csv')

paths = ["GoSales_Tx_NaiveBayes.csv", "test_data.csv"]
target_name = "PRODUCT_LINE"

rd = Reader(sep = ',')
df = rd.train_test_split(paths, target_name)
```

The output will be similar to the following:

```
reading csv : GoSales_Tx_NaiveBayes.csv ...
cleaning data ...
CPU time: 0.48662495613098145 seconds

reading csv : test_data.csv ...
cleaning data ...
CPU time: 0.43369483947753906 seconds

> Number of common features : 4

gathering and crunching for train and test datasets ...
reindexing for train and test datasets ...
dropping training duplicates ...
dropping constant variables on training set ...

> Number of categorical features: 3
> Number of numerical features: 1
> Number of training samples : 2842
> Number of test samples : 300

> You have no missing values on train set...

> Task : classification
Personal Accessories        762
Camping Equipment           662
Mountaineering Equipment    550
Golf Equipment              440
Outdoor Protection          428
Name: PRODUCT_LINE, dtype: int64

encoding target ...
```

`Drift_thresholder` will help you to drop IDs and drifting variables between `train` and `test` datasets:

```
dft = Drift_thresholder()
df = dft.fit_transform(df)
```

You get the following output:

```
computing drifts ...
CPU time: 0.2360689640045166 seconds

> Top 10 drifts

('PROFESSION', 0.20745484400656822)
('MARITAL_STATUS', 0.14729533192587363)
('AGE', 0.10706075533661741)
('GENDER', 0.028074126202205063)

> Deleted variables : []
> Drift coefficients dumped into directory : save
```

`Optimiser` will optimize the hyperparameters:

```
opt = Optimiser(scoring = 'accuracy', n_folds = 3)
opt.evaluate(None, df)
```

You get the following output by running the preceding code:

```
No parameters set. Default configuration is tested

##################################################### testing hyper-parameters... #####################################################

>>> NA ENCODER :{'numerical_strategy': 'mean', 'categorical_strategy': '<NULL>'}

>>> CA ENCODER :{'strategy': 'label_encoding'}

>>> ESTIMATOR :{'strategy': 'LightGBM', 'boosting_type': 'gbdt', 'colsample_bytree': 0.8, 'learning_rate': 0.05, 'max_bin': 255, 'max_dept
h': -1, 'min_child_samples': 10, 'min_child_weight': 5, 'min_split_gain': 0, 'n_estimators': 500, 'nthread': -1, 'num_leaves': 31, 'object
ive': 'binary', 'reg_alpha': 0, 'reg_lambda': 0, 'seed': 0, 'silent': True, 'subsample': 0.9, 'subsample_for_bin': 50000, 'subsample_fre
q': 1}


MEAN SCORE : accuracy = 0.0570060141068
VARIANCE : 0.00237658458727 (fold 1 = 0.0558482613277, fold 2 = 0.0548523206751, fold 3 = 0.0603174603175)
CPU time: 87.54920411109924 seconds

0.057006014106759734
```

The following code defines the parameters of the ML pipeline:

```
space = {
        'ne__numerical_strategy':{"search":"choice", "space":[0]},
        'ce__strategy':{"search":"choice",
                "space":["label_encoding","random_projection",
"entity_embedding"]},
        'fs__threshold':{"search":"uniform", "space":[0.01,0.3]},
        'est__max_depth':{"search":"choice", "space":[3,4,5,6,7]}
        }

best = opt.optimise(space, df,15)
```

The following output shows you the selected methods that are being tested by being given the ML algorithms, which is LightGBM in this output:

```
################################################## testing hyper-parameters... ##################################################

>>> NA ENCODER :{'numerical_strategy': 0, 'categorical_strategy': '<NULL>'}

>>> CA ENCODER :{'strategy': 'entity_embedding'}

>>> FEATURE SELECTOR :{'strategy': 'l1', 'threshold': 0.1672857583300912}

>>> ESTIMATOR :{'strategy': 'LightGBM', 'max_depth': 6, 'boosting_type': 'gbdt', 'colsample_bytree': 0.8, 'learning_rate': 0.05, 'max_bi
n': 255, 'min_child_samples': 10, 'min_child_weight': 5, 'min_split_gain': 0, 'n_estimators': 500, 'nthread': -1, 'num_leaves': 31, 'objec
tive': 'binary', 'reg_alpha': 0, 'reg_lambda': 0, 'seed': 0, 'silent': True, 'subsample': 0.9, 'subsample_for_bin': 50000, 'subsample_fre
q': 1}
```

You can also see various measures such as accuracy, variance, and CPU time:

```
MEAN SCORE : accuracy = 0.0724861302631
VARIANCE : 0.00306694867935 (fold 1 = 0.0684931506849, fold 2 = 0.0759493670886, fold 3 = 0.0730158730159)
CPU time: 48.87372016906738 seconds
```

Using `Predictor`, you can use the best model to make predictions:

```
predictor = Predictor()
predictor.fit_predict(best, df)
```

You get the following output:

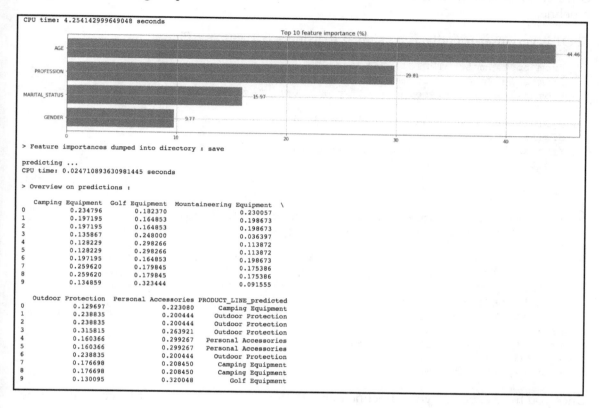

```
CPU time: 4.254142999649048 seconds
```

```
> Feature importances dumped into directory : save

predicting ...
CPU time: 0.024710893630981445 seconds

> Overview on predictions :

   Camping Equipment  Golf Equipment  Mountaineering Equipment  \
0           0.234796        0.182370                  0.230057
1           0.197195        0.164853                  0.198673
2           0.197195        0.164853                  0.198673
3           0.135867        0.248000                  0.036397
4           0.128229        0.298266                  0.113872
5           0.128229        0.298266                  0.113872
6           0.197195        0.164853                  0.198673
7           0.259620        0.179845                  0.175386
8           0.259620        0.179845                  0.175386
9           0.134859        0.323444                  0.091555

   Outdoor Protection  Personal Accessories  PRODUCT_LINE_predicted
0            0.129697              0.223080        Camping Equipment
1            0.238835              0.200444       Outdoor Protection
2            0.238835              0.200444       Outdoor Protection
3            0.315815              0.263921       Outdoor Protection
4            0.160366              0.299267     Personal Accessories
5            0.160366              0.299267     Personal Accessories
6            0.238835              0.200444       Outdoor Protection
7            0.176698              0.208450        Camping Equipment
8            0.176698              0.208450        Camping Equipment
9            0.130095              0.320048           Golf Equipment
```

TPOT

Tree-Based Pipeline Optimization Tool (TPOT) is using genetic programming to find the best performing ML pipelines, and it is built on top of scikit-learn.

Once your dataset is cleaned and ready to be used, TPOT will help you with the following steps of your ML pipeline:

- Feature preprocessing
- Feature construction and selection
- Model selection
- Hyperparameter optimization

Once TPOT is done with its experimentation, it will provide you with the best performing pipeline.

TPOT is very user-friendly as it's similar to using scikit-learn's API:

```
from tpot import TPOTClassifier
from sklearn.datasets import load_digits
from sklearn.model_selection import train_test_split

# Digits dataset that you have used in Auto-sklearn example
digits = load_digits()
X_train, X_test, y_train, y_test = train_test_split(digits.data,
digits.target,
                                            train_size=0.75,
test_size=0.25)

# You will create your TPOT classifier with commonly used arguments
tpot = TPOTClassifier(generations=10, population_size=30, verbosity=2)

# When you invoke fit method, TPOT will create generations of populations,
seeking best set of parameters. Arguments you have used to create
TPOTClassifier such as generations and population_size will affect the
search space and resulting pipeline.
tpot.fit(X_train, y_train)

print(tpot.score(X_test, y_test))
# 0.9834
tpot.export('my_pipeline.py')
```

Once you have exported your pipeline in the Python `my_pipeline.py` file, you will see the selected pipeline components:

```
import numpy as np
import pandas as pd
from sklearn.model_selection import train_test_split
from sklearn.neighbors import KNeighborsClassifier

# NOTE: Make sure that the class is labeled 'target' in the data file
tpot_data = pd.read_csv('PATH/TO/DATA/FILE', sep='COLUMN_SEPARATOR',
dtype=np.float64)
features = tpot_data.drop('target', axis=1).values
training_features, testing_features, training_target, testing_target =\
            train_test_split(features, tpot_data['target'].values,
random_state=42)


exported_pipeline = KNeighborsClassifier(n_neighbors=6,
```

```
    weights="distance")

exported_pipeline.fit(training_features, training_target)
results = exported_pipeline.predict(testing_features)
```

This is it!

Summary

By now, you should have an overall idea of what automated ML is and why you need to be familiar with ML pipelines.

You have reviewed the core components of AutoML systems and also practiced your skills using popular AutoML libraries.

This is definitely not the whole list, and AutoML is an active area of research. You should check out other libraries such as Auto-WEKA, which also uses the latest innovations in Bayesian optimization, and Xcessive, which is a user-friendly tool for creating stacked ensembles.

For now, this is enough of magic! You should start working on your own masterpiece and in the following chapters, you will be building an AutoML system of your own!

Introduction to Machine Learning Using Python

2

The last chapter introduced you to the world of **machine learning** (**ML**). In this chapter, we will develop the ML foundations that are required for building and using **Automated ML** (**AutoML**) platforms. It is not always clear how ML is best applied or what it takes to implement it. However, ML tools are getting more straightforward to use, and AutoML platforms are making it more accessible to a broader audience. In the future there will undoubtedly be a higher collaboration between man and machine.

The future of ML may require people to prepare data for its consumption and identify use cases for implementation. More importantly, people are needed to interpret the results and audit the ML system—whether they are following the right and best approaches to solving a problem. The future looks pretty amazing, but we need to build that future; that's what we are going to do in this book. In this chapter, we will walk you through the following topics:

- Machine learning process and its different types
- Supervised learning—regression and classification
- Unsupervised learning—clustering
- Ensembles—bagging, boosting, and stacking
- Inferring tasks based on data
- Task-specific evaluation metrics

We understand that a single chapter is not enough to learn and practice ML. There are already many excellent books and materials available on ML where you can find a detailed discussion on each of the mentioned topics. You can see some recommendations in the *Other Books You May Enjoy* section of our Back Matter. The objective of this chapter is to provide you with an overview of the different ML techniques and discuss some of its essential aspects that are necessary to work on the subsequent chapters.

So, machines are excited to learn. Are you ready to help them? Hold on tight. Let's first look at what machine learning is!

Technical requirements

All the code examples can be found in the Chapter 02 folder in GitHub.

Machine learning

Machine learning dates back to centuries. It was born from the theory that computers can learn without being programmed to perform specific tasks. The iterative aspect of ML is essential as the machines need to adapt themselves to new data always. They need to learn from the historical data, optimize for better computations, and also generalize themselves to provide proper results.

We all are aware of rule-based systems, where we have a set of predefined conditions for a machine to execute and provide the results. How great will it be when machines learn these patterns by themselves, deliver the results, and explain the rules that it discovered; this is ML. It is a broader term used for various methods and algorithms that are used by machines to learn from the data. As a branch of **artificial intelligence** (**AI**), the ML algorithms are quite often used to discover hidden patterns, establish a relationship, and also to predict something.

Machine learning relies on some formatted inputs, and it provides a result based on the task. The input format is specific to the type of ML technique used and also to the algorithm considered. This specific representation of input data is termed **features** or **predictors**.

Machine learning process

How do we learn? When we were studying in school or university, we were taught by our teachers. We learned from their teachings (training). At the end of the term, we needed to take a test (testing), which was basically to validate our knowledge. The scores we obtained decided our fate (evaluation). Usually, the evaluation was carried out by considering a threshold to pass (baseline). The scores determined whether we needed to retake the subject or were ready to move to the next level (deployment).

This is exactly how a machine learns as well. The words in the brackets are the terminology used by ML professionals. However, this is just one of the ways through which we, and the machines, learn. This is a typical supervised learning method. People sometimes learn from experience as well, and this is unsupervised learning. Let's study some more details about these learning methods.

Broadly we have two categories of ML algorithms as described earlier—supervised and unsupervised learning. There are a few other types, such as reinforcement learning, transfer learning, and semi-supervised learning, which are less often used and so are not in the scope of this book.

Supervised learning

As the name suggests, the learning process is supervised based on a specified target/outcome.

The objective of supervised ML models is to learn and discover the patterns that can correctly predict the outcome. In case of supervised learning, there is always a labeled historical dataset with a target attribute. All attributes other than the target are termed as **predictors/features**.

The target can be a continuous numeric attribute, a binary attribute indicating yes/no decisions, or a multi-class attribute with more than two outcomes. Based on the target, the model identifies a pattern, establishes a relationship between the predictors, and then uses the derived recipe to predict unknown targets in a new independent dataset.

Many ML algorithms fall into this class of learning methods, such as linear and logistics regression, decision trees, random forest, and **Support Vector Machines** (**SVMs**), to name a few.

To identify and select the most suited algorithm for a job is the most critical task in an ML project. This is also an essential section that requires significant attention while creating an AutoML system. There are various factors that govern this selection process and they will be covered at length in this book.

Unsupervised learning

Similarly, in the case of unsupervised learning, there is no target attribute. The objective of unsupervised learning is to identify patterns by deducing structures and the relations of the features in the input dataset. It can be used to discover rules that collectively define a group, such as topic generation, partitioning—such as customer segmentation or determining the internal structure of the data such as gene clustering. Examples of unsupervised learning algorithms include association rule mining and clustering algorithms.

It is quite essential to know about different learning algorithms before creating an AutoML system. Before using an algorithm, it is critical to understand its triple **W—What** it is, **Where** is it used, and by **What** method it can be implemented.

In the following sections, we will question different algorithms for their triple W, which will aid in creating a robust AutoML system.

Linear regression

Let's begin our triple W session with linear regression first.

What is linear regression?

It is the traditional and most-used regression analysis. It is studied rigorously and used widely for practical purposes. Linear regression is a method for determining the relationship between a dependent variable (y) and one or more independent variables (x). This derived relationship can be used to predict an unexplained y from observed x's. Mathematically, if x is an independent variable (commonly known as the predictor) and y is a dependent variable (also known as the target), the relationship is expressed as follows:

$$y = mx + b + \epsilon$$

Where m is the slope of line, b is the intercept of the best-fit regression line, and ϵ is the error term that is a deviation of the actual and predicted values.

This is the equation for simple linear regression, as it involves only one predictor (x) and one target (y). When there are multiple predictors involved to predict a target, it is known as **multiple linear regression**. The term *linear* suggests there is a fundamental assumption that the underlying data exhibits a linear relationship.

Let's create a scatter plot between two variables: **Quantity Sold** and **Revenue** of a product. We can infer from the plot that there is some positive relationship between these two variables, that is when the quantity of the products sold surged, the revenue went up. However, we can't establish a relationship between them to predict revenue from the quantity sold:

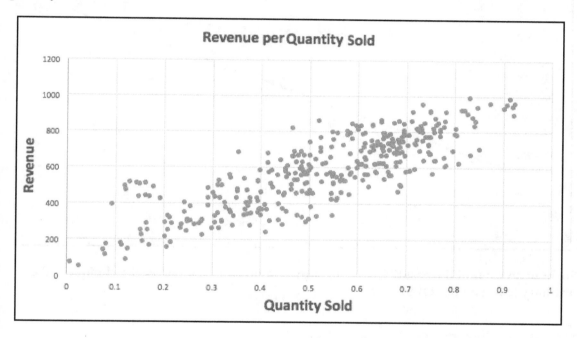

If we extend our previous scatter plot and add a trend line to it, we see the line of best fit. Any data points that lie on this line are flawlessly predicted values. As we move away from this line, the reliability of the prediction decreases:

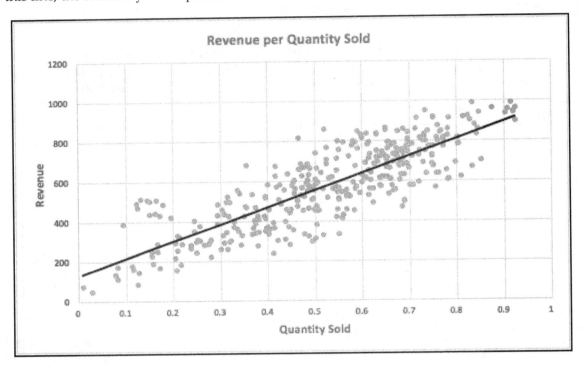

So, how do we find the best fit line? The most common and widely used technique is the **ordinary least square (OLS)** estimate.

Working of OLS regression

The OLS `LinearRegression` method is the most straightforward approach to fit a function to the data. It finds the best-fit line by minimizing the **sum of squared errors (SSE)** of the data. The SSE is the sum of the deviations of actual values from the mean. However, as always, the simplicity comes with a price. The price to pay for an excellent OLS method is adhering to its several fundamental assumptions.

Assumptions of OLS

All of these assumptions about the data should hold true to reap the benefits of the OLS regression techniques:

- **Linearity**: The true underlying relationship between X and Y is linear.
- **Homoscedastic**: The variance of residuals must be constant. The residual is the difference between the observed value and predictive value of the target.
- **Normality**: The residuals/errors should be normally distributed.
- **No or little multicollinearity**: The residuals/errors must be independent.

OLS is also affected by the presence of outliers in the data. Outlier treatment is necessary before one proceeds with linear regression modeling using OLS linear regression.

Where is linear regression used?

Linear regression has many practical use cases, and most of them fall into one of the following two broad kinds:

- If the goal is either a prediction or forecasting, it can be used to build a predictive model to a recognized dataset of dependent and independent values
- If the goal is to determine the strength of a relationship between the target and predictor variables, it can be applied to quantify the change in Y for a given value of X

By which method can linear regression be implemented?

We can create a linear regression model in Python by using scikit-learn's `LinearRegression` method. As this is the first instance where we are going to discuss implementing a model using Python, we will take a detour from our discussion of the algorithm and learn some essential packages that are required to create a model in Python:

- `numpy`: It is a numeric Python module used for mathematical functions. It provides robust data structures for effective computation of multi-dimensional arrays and matrices.

- `pandas`: It provides the DataFrame object for data manipulation. A DataFrame can hold different types of values and arrays. It is used to read, write, and manipulate data in Python.
- `scikit-learn`: It is an ML library in Python. It includes various ML algorithms and is a widely used library for creating ML models in Python. Apart from ML algorithms, it also provides various other functions that are required to develop models, such as `train_test_split`, model evaluation metrics, and optimization metrics.

We need to first import these required libraries into the Python environment before creating a model. If you are running your code in a Jupyter notebook, it is necessary to declare `%matplotlib inline` to view the graph inline in the interface. We need to import the `numpy` and `pandas` packages for easy data manipulation and numerical calculations. The plan for this exercise is to create a linear regression model, so we need to also import the `LinearRegression` method from the scikit-learn package. We will use scikit-learn's example `Boston` dataset for the task:

```
%matplotlib inline
import numpy as np
import pandas as pd
from sklearn.linear_model import LinearRegression
import matplotlib.pyplot as plt
from sklearn.datasets import load_boston
```

Next, we need to load the `Boston` dataset using the following command. It is a dictionary, and we can examine its keys to view its content:

```
boston_data = load_boston()
boston_data.keys()
```

The output of the preceding code is as follows:

```
Out[2]: dict_keys(['data', 'target', 'feature_names', 'DESCR'])
```

The `boston_data` has four keys that are self-explanatory on the kinds of values they point. We can retrieve the data and the target values from the keys `data` and `target`. The `feature_names` key holds the names of the attribute and `DESCR` has the description of each attribute.

It is always good practice to look at the data size first before processing the data. This helps to decide whether to go with the full data or use a sample of it, and also to infer how long it might take to execute.

The `data.shape` function in Python is an excellent way to view the data dimensions (rows and columns):

```
print(" Number of rows and columns in the data set ",
boston_data.data.shape)
print(boston_data.feature_names)
```

The output of the preceding code is as follows:

```
Number of rows and columns in the data set  (506, 13)
['CRIM' 'ZN' 'INDUS' 'CHAS' 'NOX' 'RM' 'AGE' 'DIS' 'RAD' 'TAX' 'PTRATIO'
 'B' 'LSTAT']
```

Next, we need to convert the dictionary to a DataFrame. This can be accomplished by calling the `DataFrame` function of the `pandas` library. We use `head()` to display a subset of records to validate the data:

```
boston_df =pd.DataFrame(boston_data.data)
boston_df.head()
```

 A DataFrame is a collection of vectors and can be treated as a two-dimensional table. We can consider DataFrame as having each row correspond to some observation and each column to some attribute of the observation. This makes them extremely useful for fitting to a ML modeling task.

The output of the preceding code is as follows:

Out[4]:

	0	1	2	3	4	5	6	7	8	9	10	11	12
0	0.00632	18.0	2.31	0.0	0.538	6.575	65.2	4.0900	1.0	296.0	15.3	396.90	4.98
1	0.02731	0.0	7.07	0.0	0.469	6.421	78.9	4.9671	2.0	242.0	17.8	396.90	9.14
2	0.02729	0.0	7.07	0.0	0.469	7.185	61.1	4.9671	2.0	242.0	17.8	392.83	4.03
3	0.03237	0.0	2.18	0.0	0.458	6.998	45.8	6.0622	3.0	222.0	18.7	394.63	2.94
4	0.06905	0.0	2.18	0.0	0.458	7.147	54.2	6.0622	3.0	222.0	18.7	396.90	5.33

The column names are just numeric indexes and don't give a sense of what the DataFrame implies. So, let us assign the `feature_names` as the column names to the `boston_df` DataFrame to have meaningful names:

```
boston_df.columns = boston_data.feature_names
```

Once again, we check a sample of `boston` house rent data, and now it describes the columns better than previously:

```
boston_df.head()
```

The output of the preceding code is as follows:

Out[5]:

	CRIM	ZN	INDUS	CHAS	NOX	RM	AGE	DIS	RAD	TAX	PTRATIO	B	LSTAT
0	0.00632	18.0	2.31	0.0	0.538	6.575	65.2	4.0900	1.0	296.0	15.3	396.90	4.98
1	0.02731	0.0	7.07	0.0	0.469	6.421	78.9	4.9671	2.0	242.0	17.8	396.90	9.14
2	0.02729	0.0	7.07	0.0	0.469	7.185	61.1	4.9671	2.0	242.0	17.8	392.83	4.03
3	0.03237	0.0	2.18	0.0	0.458	6.998	45.8	6.0622	3.0	222.0	18.7	394.63	2.94
4	0.06905	0.0	2.18	0.0	0.458	7.147	54.2	6.0622	3.0	222.0	18.7	396.90	5.33

In linear regression, there has to be a DataFrame as a target variable and another DataFrame with other features as predictors. The objective of this exercise is to predict the house prices, so we assign PRICE as the target attribute (Y) and the rest all as predictors (X). The PRICE is dropped from the predictor list using the drop function.

Next, we print the intercept and coefficients of each variable. The coefficients determine the weight and contribution that each predictor has on predicting the house price (target Y). The intercept provides a constant value, which we can consider to be house price when all of the predictors are absent:

```
boston_df['PRICE'] = boston_data.target
X = boston_df.drop('PRICE', axis=1)
lm = LinearRegression()
lm.fit(X, boston_df.PRICE)
print("Intercept: ", lm.intercept_)
print("Coefficient: ", lm.coef_)
```

The output of the preceding code is as follows:

```
Intercept:  36.4911032804
Coefficient:  [ -1.07170557e-01    4.63952195e-02    2.08602395e-02    2.68856140e+00
  -1.77957587e+01    3.80475246e+00    7.51061703e-04   -1.47575880e+00
   3.05655038e-01   -1.23293463e-02   -9.53463555e-01    9.39251272e-03
  -5.25466633e-01]
```

It is not clear from the earlier screenshot which coefficient belongs to what predictors. So, we tie the features and coefficients together using the following code:

```
pd.DataFrame(list(zip(X.columns, lm.coef_)),columns=
['features','estimatedCoefficients'])
```

The output of the preceding code is as follows:

Out[9]:

	features	estimatedCoefficients
0	CRIM	-0.107171
1	ZN	0.046395
2	INDUS	0.020860
3	CHAS	2.688561
4	NOX	-17.795759
5	RM	3.804752
6	AGE	0.000751
7	DIS	-1.475759
8	RAD	0.305655
9	TAX	-0.012329
10	PTRATIO	-0.953464
11	B	0.009393
12	LSTAT	-0.525467

Next, we calculate and view the mean squared error metric. For now, let us think of it as the average error the model has in predicting the house price. The evaluation metrics are very important for understanding the dynamics of a model and how it is going to perform in a production environment:

```
lm.predict(X)[0:5
mseFull = np.mean((boston_df.PRICE - lm.predict(X)) ** 2)
print(mseFull)
```

The output of the preceding code is as follows:

```
21.897779217687486
```

We created the model on the whole dataset, but it is essential to ensure that the model we developed works appropriately on different datasets when used in a real production environment. For this reason, the data used for modeling is split into two sets, typically in a ratio of 70:30. The most significant split is used to train the model, and the other one is used to test the model developed. This independent test dataset is considered as a *dummy production environment* as this was hidden from the model during its training phase. The test dataset is used to generate the predictions and evaluate the accuracy of the model. Scikit-learn provides a `train_test_split` method that can be used to split the dataset into two parts. The `test_size` parameter in the function indicates the percentage of data that is to be held for testing. In the following code, we split the dataset into `train` and `test` sets, and retrain the model:

```
#Train and Test set
from sklearn.model_selection import train_test_split
X_train, X_test, Y_train, Y_test = train_test_split(X, boston_df.PRICE,
test_size=0.3, random_state=42)
print(X_train)
```

As we have used `test_size=0.3`, 70% of the dataset will be used for creating `train` set, and 30% will be reserved for the `test` dataset. We follow the same steps as earlier to create a linear regression model, but now we would use only the training dataset (`X_train` and `Y_train`) to create the model:

```
lm_tts = LinearRegression()
lm_tts.fit(X_train, Y_train)
print("Intercept: ", lm_tts.intercept_)
print("Coefficient: ", lm_tts.coef_)
```

The output of the preceding code is as follows:

```
Intercept:  31.6821485821
Coefficient:  [ -1.32774155e-01   3.57812335e-02   4.99454423e-02   3.12127706e+00
  -1.54698463e+01   4.04872721e+00  -1.07515901e-02  -1.38699758e+00
   2.42353741e-01  -8.69095363e-03  -9.11917342e-01   1.19435253e-02
  -5.48080157e-01]
```

We predict the target values for both the `train` and `test` datasets, and calculate their **mean squared error (MSE)**:

```
pred_train = lm.predict(X_train)
pred_test = lm.predict(X_test)
print("MSE for Y_train:", np.mean((Y_train - lm.predict(X_train)) ** 2))
print("MSE with Y_test:", np.mean((Y_test - lm.predict(X_test)) ** 2))
```

The output of the preceding code is as follows:

```
MSE for Y_train: 22.86266796675359
MSE with Y_test: 19.650604104730895
```

We see that the MSE for both the `train` and `test` datasets are `22.86` and `19.65`, respectively. This means the model's performance is almost similar in both the training and testing phase and can be deployed for predicting house prices on new independent identical datasets.

Next, let's paint a residual plot to see whether the residuals follow a linear pattern:

```
plt.scatter(pred_train,pred_train - Y_train, c = 'b',s=40,alpha=0.5)
plt.scatter(pred_test,pred_test - Y_test, c = 'r',s=40,alpha=0.7)
plt.hlines(y = 0, xmin=0, xmax = 50)
plt.title('Residual Plot - training data (blue) and test data(green)')
plt.ylabel('Residuals')
```

The output of the preceding code is as follows:

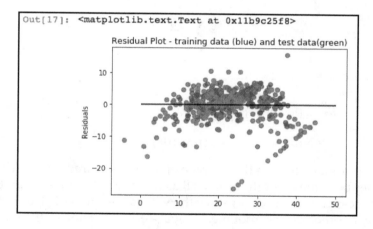

As the residuals are symmetrically distributed around the horizontal dashed line, then they exhibit a perfect linear pattern.

Developing a model is easy, but designing a useful model is difficult. Evaluating the performance of a ML model is a crucial step in an ML pipeline. Once a model is ready, we have to assess it to establish its correctness. In the following section, we will walk you through some of the widely-used evaluation metrics employed to evaluate a regression model.

Important evaluation metrics – regression algorithms

Assessing the value of a ML model is a two-phase process. First, the model has to be evaluated for its statistical accuracy, that is, whether the statistical hypotheses are correct, model performance is outstanding, and the performance holds true for other independent datasets. This is accomplished using several model evaluation metrics. Then, a model is evaluated to see if the results are as expected as per business requirement and the stakeholders genuinely get some insights or useful predictions out of it.

A regression model is evaluated based on the following metrics:

- **Mean absolute error** (**MAE**): It is the sum of absolute values of prediction error. The prediction error is defined as the difference between predicted and actual values. This metric gives an idea about the magnitude of the error. However, we cannot judge the direction of whether the model has overpredicted or underpredicted. One should always aim for a low MAE score:

$$MAE = \sum_{i=1}^{n} \frac{|y_i - y_i^\Lambda|}{n}$$

  Where, y_i = Actual values

  y_i^Λ = Predicted values

  n = Number of cases (records)

- **Mean squared error**: It is the average of sum of squared errors. This metric describes both the magnitude as well as the direction of the error. However, the unit of measurement is changed as the values are squared. This deficiency is filled by another metric: root mean square error. The lower the score, the better the model is:

$$MSE = \sum_{i=1}^{n} \frac{(y_i - y_i^\Lambda)^2}{n}$$

- **Root mean square error** (**RMSE**): This metric is calculated by the square root of the mean squared error. Taking a square root converts the unit of measurement back to the original units. A model with a low RMSE score is a good model:

$$RMSE = \sqrt{\sum_{i=1}^{n} \frac{(y_i - y_i^{\Lambda})^2}{n}}$$

- **R² score**: It is also known as **coefficient of determination**. It describes the percentage of variance explained by the model. For example, if R^2 is 0.9, then the attributes or features used in the model can represent 90% of its variation. R^2 varies from 0 to 1, and the higher this value, the better the model is. However, one needs to have a good testing strategy in place to validate that the model doesn't overfit:

$$R^2 = 1 - \sum_{i=1}^{n} \frac{(y_i - y_i^{\Lambda})^2}{(y_i - y_i^{-})^2}$$

Where, y_i = Actual values

y_i^{Λ} = Predicted values

n = Number of cases (records)

y_i^{-} = Mean of y

Overfitting occurs when a machine learning model learns the training data very well. These models have low bias and high variance in their results. In such cases, the model might lead to poor predictions on new data.

In this section, we learned about regression analysis as one of the supervised ML methods. It can be used in scenarios where the target data is continuous numerical data, such as predicting the desired salary of an employee, predicting house prices, or predicting spend values.

What if the target has discrete data? How do we predict whether a customer will churn or not? How do we predict whether a loan/credit card should be approved for a prospect? Linear regression will not work for these cases as these problems violate its underlying assumptions. Do we have any other methods? For these situations, we can use classification models.

 Classification modeling is another form of supervised machine learning methods that is used to predict targets with discrete input target values. The classification algorithms are known as **classifiers**, as they identify the set of categories that input data support and use this information to assign a class to an unidentified or unknown target label.

In the next sections, we will walk through some of the widely-used classifiers, such as logistics regression, decision trees, SVMs, and k-Nearest Neighbors. Logistics regression can be considered as a bridge between regression and classification methods. It is a classifier camouflaged with a regression in its signature. However, it is one of the most effective and explainable classification models.

Logistic regression

Let's start again with the *triple W* for logistics regression. To reiterate the tripe W method, we first ask the algorithm what it is, followed by where it can be used, and finally by what method we can implement the model.

What is logistic regression?

Logistic regression can be thought of as an extension to linear regression algorithms. It fundamentally works like linear regression, but it is meant for discrete or categorical outcomes.

Where is logistic regression used?

Logistic regression is applied in the case of discrete target variables such as binary responses. In such scenarios, some of the assumptions of linear regression, such as target attribute and features, don't follow a linear relationship, the residuals might not be normally distributed, or the error terms are heteroscedastic. In logistic regression, the target is reconstructed to the log of its odds ratio to fit the regression equation, as shown here:

$$log(\frac{P}{P-1}) = mx + b + \epsilon$$

The odds ratio reflects the probability or likelihood of occurrence of a particular event against the probability of that same event not taking place. If P is the probability of the presence of one event/class, $P - 1$ is the probability of the presence of the second event/class.

By which method can logistic regression be implemented?

A logistic regression model can be created by importing scikit-learn's `LogisticRegression` method. We load the packages as we did previously for creating a linear regression model:

```
import pandas as pd
import numpy as np
from sklearn import preprocessing
import matplotlib.pyplot as plt
from sklearn.linear_model import LogisticRegression
```

We will use the dataset of an HR department that has the list of employees who have attrited in the past along with the employees who are continuing in the job:

```
hr_data = pd.read_csv('data/hr.csv', header=0)
hr_data.head()
hr_data = hr_data.dropna()
print(hr_data.shape)
print(list(hr_data.columns))
```

The output of the preceding code is as follows:

```
(14999, 10)
['satisfaction_level', 'last_evaluation', 'number_project', 'average_montly_hours', 'time_spend_company', 'Work_accid
ent', 'left', 'promotion_last_5years', 'sales', 'salary']
```

The dataset has 14999 rows and 10 columns. The data.columns function displays names of the attributes. The salary attribute has three values—high, low, and medium, and sales has seven values—IT, RandD, marketing, product_mng, sales, support, and technical. To use this discrete input data in the model, we need to convert it into numeric format. There are various ways to do so. One of the ways is to dummy encode the values, also known as **one-hot encoding**. Using this method, dummy columns are generated for each class of a categorical attribute.

For each dummy attribute, the presence of the class is represented by 1, and its absence is represented by 0.

Discrete data can either be nominal or ordinal. When there is a natural ordering of values in the discrete data, it is termed as **ordinal**. For example, categorical values such as high, medium, and low are ordered values. For these cases, label encoding is mostly used. When we cannot derive any relationship or order from the categorical or discrete values, it is termed as **nominal**. For example, colors such as red, yellow, and green have no order. For these cases, dummy encoding is a popular method.

The get_dummies method of pandas provides an easy interface for creating dummy variables in Python. The input for the function is the dataset and names of the attributes that are to be dummy encoded. In this case, we will be dummy encoding salary and sales attributes of the HR dataset:

```
data_trnsf = pd.get_dummies(hr_data, columns =['salary', 'sales'])
data_trnsf.columns
```

The output of the preceding code is as follows:

```
Index(['satisfaction_level', 'last_evaluation', 'number_project',
       'average_montly_hours', 'time_spend_company', 'Work_accident', 'left',
       'promotion_last_5years', 'salary_high', 'salary_low', 'salary_medium',
       'sales_IT', 'sales_RandD', 'sales_accounting', 'sales_hr',
       'sales_management', 'sales_marketing', 'sales_product_mng',
       'sales_sales', 'sales_support', 'sales_technical'],
      dtype='object')
```

Now, the dataset is ready for modeling. The `sales` and `salary` attributes are successfully one-hot encoded. Next, as we are going to predict the attrition, we are going to use the `left` attribute as the target as it contains the information on whether an employee attrited or not. We can drop the `left` data from the input predictors dataset referred as to X in the code. The left attribute is denoted by Y (target):

```
X = data_trnsf.drop('left', axis=1)
X.columns
```

The output of the preceding code is as follows:

```
Index(['satisfaction_level', 'last_evaluation', 'number_project',
       'average_montly_hours', 'time_spend_company', 'Work_accident',
       'promotion_last_5years', 'salary_high', 'salary_low', 'salary_medium',
       'sales_IT', 'sales_RandD', 'sales_accounting', 'sales_hr',
       'sales_management', 'sales_marketing', 'sales_product_mng',
       'sales_sales', 'sales_support', 'sales_technical'],
      dtype='object')
```

We split the dataset into `train` and `test` sets with a ratio of 70:30. 70% of the data will be used to train the logistic regression model and the remaining 30% to evaluate the accuracy of the model:

```
from sklearn.model_selection import train_test_split
X_train, X_test, Y_train, Y_test = train_test_split(X, data_trnsf.left,
test_size=0.3, random_state=42)
print(X_train)
```

As we execute the code snippet, four datasets are created. X_train and X_test are the `train` and `test` input predictor data. Y_train and Y_test are `train` and `test` input target data. Now, we will fit the model on the train data and evaluate the accuracy of the model on the test data. First, we create an instance of the `LogisticsRegression()` classifier class. Next, we fit the classifier on the training data:

```
attrition_classifier = LogisticRegression()
attrition_classifier.fit(X_train, Y_train)
```

Once the model is successfully created, we use the `predict` method on the test input predictor dataset to predict the corresponding target values (Y_pred):

```
Y_pred = attrition_classifier.predict(X_test)
```

We need to create a `confusion_matrix` for evaluating a classifier. Most of the model evaluation metrics are based on the confusion matrix itself. There is a detailed discussion on confusion matrix and other evaluation metrics right after this section. For now, let's consider the confusion matrix as a matrix of four values that provides us with the count of values that were correctly and incorrectly predicted. Based on the values in the confusion matrix, the classifier's accuracy is calculated. The accuracy of our classifier is 0.79 or 79%, which means 79% of cases were correctly predicted:

```
from sklearn.metrics import confusion_matrix
confusion_matrix = confusion_matrix(Y_test, Y_pred)
print(confusion_matrix)

print('Accuracy of logistic regression model on test dataset:
{:.2f}'.format(attrition_classifier.score(X_test, Y_test)))
```

The output of the preceding code is as follows:

```
[[3175  253]
 [ 711  361]]
Accuracy of logistic regression classifier on test set: 0.79
```

Sometimes, the accuracy might not be a good measure to judge the performance of a model. For example, in the case of unbalanced datasets, the predictions might be biased towards the majority class. So, we need to look at other metrics such as f1-score, **area under curve** (**AUC**), precision, and recall that gives a fair judgment about the model. We can retrieve the scores for all these metrics by importing the `classification_report` from scikit-learn's `metric` method:

```
from sklearn.metrics import classification_report
print(classification_report(Y_test, Y_pred))
```

The output of the preceding code is as follows:

	precision	recall	f1-score	support
0	0.82	0.93	0.87	3428
1	0.59	0.34	0.43	1072
avg / total	0.76	0.79	0.76	4500

Receiver Operating Characteristic (ROC) is most commonly used to visualize the performance of a binary classifier. AUC measure is the area under the ROC curve, and it provides a single number that summarizes the performance of the classifier based on the ROC curve. The following code snippet can be used to draw a ROC curve using Python:

```
from sklearn.metrics import roc_curve
from sklearn.metrics import auc

# Compute false positive rate(fpr), true positive rate(tpr), thresholds and
roc auc(Area under Curve)
fpr, tpr, thresholds = roc_curve(Y_test, Y_pred)
auc = auc(fpr,tpr)

# Plot ROC curve
plt.plot(fpr, tpr, label='AUC = %0.2f' % auc)
#random prediction curve
plt.plot([0, 1], [0, 1], 'k--')
#Set the x limits
plt.xlim([0.0, 1.0])
#Set the Y limits
plt.ylim([0.0, 1.0])
#Set the X label
plt.xlabel('False Positive Rate(FPR) ')
#Set the Y label
plt.ylabel('True Positive Rate(TPR)')
#Set the plot title
plt.title('Receiver Operating Characteristic(ROC) Cure')
# Location of the AUC legend
plt.legend(loc="right")
```

The output of the preceding code is as follows:

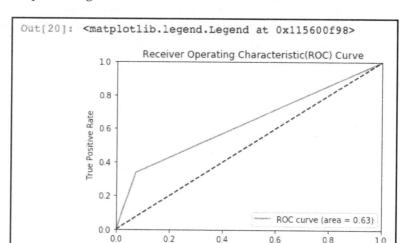

The AUC for our model is **0.63**. We are already seeing some of the metrics that are used to evaluate a classification model, and some of these are appearing strange. So, let's understand the metrics before moving onto our discussion on classification algorithms.

Important evaluation metrics – classification algorithms

Most of the metrics used to assess a classification model are based on the values that we get in the four quadrants of a confusion matrix. Let's begin this section by understanding what it is:

- **Confusion matrix**: It is the cornerstone of evaluating a classification model (that is, classifier). As the name stands, the matrix is sometimes confusing. Let's try to visualize the confusion matrix as two axes in a graph. The *x* axis label is prediction, with two values—**Positive** and **Negative**. Similarly, the *y* axis label is actually with the same two values—**Positive** and **Negative**, as shown in the following figure. This matrix is a table that contains the information about the count of actual and predicted values by a classifier:

		Prediction	
		Postive	Negative
Actuals	Positive	True Positive(TP)	False Postive(FP)
	Negative	False Negative(FN)	True Negative(TN)

- If we try to deduce information about each quadrant in the matrix:
    - Quadrant one is the number of positive class predictions that were accurately identified. So, it is termed as **True Positive** (**TP**).
    - Quadrant two, also known as **False Positive** (**FP**), is the number of inaccurate predictions for actual positive cases.
    - Quadrant three, which is known as **False Negative** (**FN**), is the number of inaccurate predictions for negative cases.
    - Quadrant four is **True Negative** (**TN**), which is the number of negative class predictions that were accurately classified.
- **Accuracy**: Accuracy measures how frequently the classifier makes an accurate prediction. It is the ratio of the number of correct predictions to the total number of predictions:

$$Accuracy = TP/(TP + FP + FN + TN)$$

- **Precision**: Precision estimates the proportions of true positives that were accurately identified. It is the ratio of true positives to all predicted positives:

$$Precision = TP/(TP + FN)$$

- **Recall**: Recall is also termed sensitivity or **true positive rate** (**TPR**). It estimates the proportions of true positives out of all observed positive values of a target:

$$Recall = TP/(TP + FP)$$

- **Misclassification rate**: It estimates how frequently the classifier has predicted inaccurately. It is the ratio of incorrect predictions to all predictions:

$$Misclassification\ Rate = (FP + FN)/(TP + FP + FN + TN)$$

- **Specificity**: Specificity is also known as **true negative rate** (**TNR**). It estimates the proportions of true negatives out of all observed negative values of a target:

$$Specificity = TN/(FP + TN)$$

- **ROC curve**: The ROC curve summarizes the performance of a classifier over all possible thresholds. The graph for ROC curve is plotted with **true positive rate** (**TPR**) in the y axis and **false positive rate** (**FPR**) in the x axis for all possible thresholds.
- **AUC**: AUC is the area under a ROC curve. If the classifier is outstanding, the true positive rate will increase, and the area under the curve will be close to 1. If the classifier is similar to random guessing, the true positive rate will increase linearly with the false positive rate (1–sensitivity). In this case, the AUC will be around 0.5. The better the AUC measure, the better the model.
- **Lift**: Lift helps to estimate the improvement in a model's predictive ability over the average or baseline model. For example, the accuracy of the baseline model for an HR attrition dataset is 40%, but the accuracy of a new model on the same dataset is 80%. Then, that model has a lift of 2 (80/40).
- **Balanced accuracy**: Sometimes, the accuracy is not a good measure alone to evaluate a model. For cases where the dataset is unbalanced, it might not be a useful evaluation metric. In such cases, balanced accuracy can be used as one of the evaluation metrics. Balanced accuracy is a measure calculated on the average accuracy obtained in either class:

$$Balanced\ Accuracy = 0.5 * ((TP/(TP + FN)) + (TN/(TN + FP))$$

 Unbalanced dataset—Where one class dominates the other class. In such cases, there is an inherent bias in prediction towards the major class. However, this is a problem with base learners such as decision trees and logistic regression. For ensemble models such as random forest it can handle unbalanced classes well.

- **F1 score**: An F1 score is also a sound measure to estimate an imbalanced classifier. The F1 score is the harmonic mean of precision and recall. Its value lies between 0 and 1:

$$F1\ Score = 2 * PR/(P + R), where P = Precision, R = Recall$$

- **Hamming loss**: This identifies the fraction of labels that are incorrectly predicted.
- **Matthews Correlation Coefficient** (**MCC**): MCC is a correlation coefficient between target and predictions. It varies between -1 and +1. -1 when there is complete disagreement between actuals and prediction, 1 when there is a perfect agreement between actuals and predictions, 0 when the prediction may as well be random concerning the actuals. As it involves values of all the four quadrants of a confusion matrix, it is considered as a balanced measure.

Sometimes, creating a model for prediction is not only a requirement. We need insights on how the model was built and the critical features that describe the model. Decision trees are go to model in such cases.

Decision trees

Decision trees are extensively-used classifiers in the ML world for their transparency on representing the rules that drive a classification/prediction. Let us ask the triple W questions to this algorithm to know more about it.

What are decision trees?

Decision trees are arranged in a hierarchical tree-like structure and are easy to explain and interpret. They are not susceptive to outliers. The process of creating a decision tree is a recursive partitioning method where it splits the training data into various groups with an objective to find homogeneous pure subgroups, that is, data with only one class.

 Outliers are values that lie far away from other data points and distort the data distribution.

Where are decision trees used?

Decision trees are well-suited for cases where there is a need to explain the reason for a particular decision. For example, financial institutions might need a complete description of rules that influence the credit score of a customer prior to issuing a loan or credit card.

By which method can decision trees be implemented?

Decision tree models can be created by importing scikit-learn's `DecisionTreeClassifier`:

```
import numpy as np
import pandas as pd
from sklearn.tree import DecisionTreeClassifier
from sklearn.metrics import accuracy_score
```

```
from sklearn import tree
```

Next, we read the HR attrition dataset and do all the data preprocessing that was done in the previous logistics regression example:

```
hr_data = pd.read_csv('data/hr.csv', header=0)
hr_data.head()
hr_data = hr_data.dropna()
print(" Data Set Shape ", hr_data.shape)
print(list(hr_data.columns))
print(" Sample Data ", hr_data.head())
```

The output of the preceding code is as follows:

```
Data Set Shape  (14999, 10)
['satisfaction_level', 'last_evaluation', 'number_project', 'average_montly_hours', 'time_spend_company', 'Work_accid
ent', 'left', 'promotion_last_5years', 'sales', 'salary']
Sample Data      satisfaction_level  last_evaluation  number_project  average_montly_hours  \
0                       0.38             0.53               2                  157
1                       0.80             0.86               5                  262
2                       0.11             0.88               7                  272
3                       0.72             0.87               5                  223
4                       0.37             0.52               2                  159

   time_spend_company  Work_accident  left  promotion_last_5years  sales  \
0                   3              0     1                      0  sales
1                   6              0     1                      0  sales
2                   4              0     1                      0  sales
3                   5              0     1                      0  sales
4                   3              0     1                      0  sales

   salary
0     low
1  medium
2  medium
3     low
4     low
```

The following code creates the dummy variables for categorical data and splits the data into train and test sets:

```
data_trnsf = pd.get_dummies(hr_data, columns =['salary', 'sales'])
data_trnsf.columns
X = data_trnsf.drop('left', axis=1)
X.columns
from sklearn.model_selection import train_test_split
X_train, X_test, Y_train, Y_test = train_test_split(X, data_trnsf.left,
test_size=0.3, random_state=42)
print(X_train)
```

Next, to create a decision tree classifier, we need to instantiate a
DecisionTreeClassifier with at least the required parameters. The following are some
of the parameters that are used to generate a decision tree model:

- criterion: Impurity metrics for forming decision trees; it can be either entropy
  or gini
- max_depth: Maximum depth of a tree
- min_samples_leaf: Minimum number of samples required to build a leaf node
- max_depth and min_sample_leafs are two of the tree pre-pruning criteria

Let's create a decision tree model using some of these parameters:

```
attrition_tree = DecisionTreeClassifier(criterion = "gini", random_state =
100,
max_depth=3, min_samples_leaf=5)
attrition_tree.fit(X_train, Y_train)
```

The output of the preceding code is as follows:

```
Out[8]: DecisionTreeClassifier(class_weight=None, criterion='gini', max_depth=3,
            max_features=None, max_leaf_nodes=None,
            min_impurity_split=1e-07, min_samples_leaf=5,
            min_samples_split=2, min_weight_fraction_leaf=0.0,
            presort=False, random_state=100, splitter='best')
```

Next, we generate a confusion matrix to evaluate the model:

```
Y_pred = attrition_tree.predict(X_test)
from sklearn.metrics import confusion_matrix
confusionmatrix = confusion_matrix(Y_test, Y_pred)
print(confusionmatrix)
```

The output of the preceding code is as follows:

```
[[3289  139]
 [  92  980]]
```

If we view the confusion matrix, we can assume that the classifier has done a reliable job in
classifying both true positives and true negatives. However, let us validate our assumption
based on the summarized evaluation metrics:

```
print('Accuracy of Decision Tree classifier on test set:
{:.2f}'.format(attrition_tree.score(X_test, Y_test)))
```

```
from sklearn.metrics import classification_report
print(classification_report(Y_test, Y_pred))
```

The output of the preceding code is as follows:

```
Accuracy of Decision Tree classifier on test set: 0.95
                precision     recall   f1-score    support

            0       0.97       0.96       0.97       3428
            1       0.88       0.91       0.89       1072

avg / total         0.95       0.95       0.95       4500
```

The accuracy, along with other metrics, are 0.95, which is a pretty good score.

The tree-based model had a better result than the logistic regression model. Now, let us understand another popular classification modeling technique based on the support vectors.

Support Vector Machines

SVM is a supervised ML algorithm used primarily for classification tasks, however, it can be used for regression problems as well.

What is SVM?

SVM is a classifier that works on the principle of separating hyperplanes. Given a training dataset, the algorithms find a hyperplane that maximizes the separation of the classes and uses these partitions for the prediction of a new dataset. The hyperplane is a subspace of one dimension less than its ambient plane. This means the line is a hyperplane for a two-dimensional dataset.

Where is SVM used?

SVM has similar use cases as that of other classifiers, but SVM is suited well for cases when the number of features/attributes are high compared to the number of data points/records.

By which method can SVM be implemented?

The process to create an SVM model is similar to other classification methods that we studied earlier. The only difference is to import the `svm` method from scikit-learn's library. We import the `HR` attrition dataset using `pandas` library and split the dataset to `train` and `test` sets:

```
import numpy as np
import pandas as pd
from sklearn import svm
from sklearn.metrics import accuracy_score

hr_data = pd.read_csv('data/hr.csv', header=0)
hr_data.head()
hr_data = hr_data.dropna()
print(" Data Set Shape ", hr_data.shape)
print(list(hr_data.columns))
print(" Sample Data ", hr_data.head())
data_trnsf = pd.get_dummies(hr_data, columns =['salary', 'sales'])
data_trnsf.columns
X = data_trnsf.drop('left', axis=1)
X.columns
from sklearn.model_selection import train_test_split

X_train, X_test, Y_train, Y_test = train_test_split(X, data_trnsf.left,
test_size=0.3, random_state=42)
print(X_train)
```

Next, we create an SVM model instance. We set the kernel to be linear, as we want a line to separate the two classes. Finding optimal hyperplanes for linearly-separable data is easy. However, when the data is not linearly separable, the data is mapped into a new space to make it linearly separable. This methodology is known as a **kernel trick**:

```
attrition_svm = svm.SVC(kernel='linear')
attrition_svm.fit(X_train, Y_train)
```

The output of the preceding code is as follows:

```
Out[9]: SVC(C=1, cache_size=200, class_weight=None, coef0=0.0,
        decision_function_shape=None, degree=3, gamma=1, kernel='linear',
        max_iter=-1, probability=False, random_state=None, shrinking=True,
        tol=0.001, verbose=False)
```

After fitting the SVM model instance to the train data, we predict the Y values for the `test` set and create a confusion matrix to evaluate the model performance:

```
Y_pred = attrition_svm.predict(X_test)
from sklearn.metrics import confusion_matrix
confusionmatrix = confusion_matrix(Y_test, Y_pred)
print(confusionmatrix)
```

The output of the preceding code is as follows:

```
[[3212  216]
 [ 811  261]]
```

Then, the values for model accuracy and other metrics are calculated:

```
print('Accuracy of SVM classifier on test set:
{:.2f}'.format(attrition_svm.score(X_test, Y_test)))
from sklearn.metrics import classification_report
print(classification_report(Y_test, Y_pred))
```

The output of the preceding code is as follows:

```
Accuracy of SVM classifier on test set: 0.77
              precision    recall  f1-score   support

           0       0.80      0.94      0.86      3428
           1       0.55      0.24      0.34      1072

avg / total       0.74      0.77      0.74      4500
```

We see that the SVM model with default parameters did not perform better than the decision tree model. So, until now decision tree holds its place right at the top in the HR attrition prediction leaderboard. Let us try another classification algorithm, **k-Nearest Neighbors (KNN)**, which is easier to understand and to use, but is much more resource intensive.

k-Nearest Neighbors

Before we build a KNN model for the HR attrition dataset, let us understand KNN's triple W.

What is k-Nearest Neighbors?

KNN is one of the most straightforward algorithms that stores all available data points and predicts new data based on distance similarity measures such as Euclidean distance. It is an algorithm that can make predictions using the training dataset directly. However, it is much more resource intensive as it doesn't have any training phase and requires all data present in memory to predict new instances.

Euclidean distance is calculated as the square root of the sum of the squared differences between two points.

$$EuclideanDistance(x_i, y_i) = \sqrt{sum((x_i - y_i)^2)}$$

Where is KNN used?

KNN can be used for building both classification and regression models. It is applied to classification tasks, both binary and multivariate. KNN can even be used for creating recommender systems or imputing missing values. It is easy to use, easy to train, and easy to interpret the results.

By which method can KNN be implemented?

Again, we follow a similar process for KNN as we did to create the previous models. We import the KNeighborsClassifier method from scikit-learn's library to use the KNN algorithm for modeling. Next, we import the HR attrition dataset using the pandas library and split the dataset into train and test sets:

```
import numpy as np
import pandas as pd
from sklearn.metrics import accuracy_score
from sklearn.neighbors import KNeighborsClassifier
hr_data = pd.read_csv('data/hr.csv', header=0)
hr_data.head()
hr_data = hr_data.dropna()
print(" Data Set Shape ", hr_data.shape)
print(list(hr_data.columns))
print(" Sample Data ", hr_data.head())
data_trnsf = pd.get_dummies(hr_data, columns =['salary', 'sales'])
data_trnsf.columns
X = data_trnsf.drop('left', axis=1)
X.columns
```

```
from sklearn.model_selection import train_test_split
X_train, X_test, Y_train, Y_test = train_test_split(X, data_trnsf.left,
test_size=0.3, random_state=42)
print(X_train)
```

To create a KNN model, we need to specify the number of nearest neighbors to be considered for distance calculation.

 In real life, when we create models, we create different models for a range of n_neighbors values with various distance measures and choose the model that returns the highest accuracy. This process is also known as **tuning the hyperparameters**.

For the following HR attrition model, we defined n_neighbors to be 6 and distance metric as Euclidean:

```
n_neighbors = 6
attrition_knn = KNeighborsClassifier(n_neighbors=n_neighbors,
metric='euclidean')
attrition_knn.fit(X_train, Y_train)
```

The output of the preceding code is as follows:

```
Out[9]:  KNeighborsClassifier(algorithm='auto', leaf_size=30, metric='euclidean',
                metric_params=None, n_jobs=1, n_neighbors=6, p=2,
                weights='uniform')
```

Then the prediction is made on the test dataset, and we review the confusion matrix along with other evaluation metrics:

```
Y_pred = attrition_knn.predict(X_test)
from sklearn.metrics import confusion_matrix
confusionmatrix = confusion_matrix(Y_test, Y_pred)
print(confusionmatrix)
```

The output of the preceding code is as follows:

```
[[3273   155]
 [ 109   963]]
```

The following code reports the accuracy score and values for other metrics:

```
print('Accuracy of KNN classifier on test set:
{:.2f}'.format(attrition_knn.score(X_test, Y_test)))
from sklearn.metrics import classification_report
print(classification_report(Y_test, Y_pred))
```

The output of the preceding code is as follows:

Accuracy of Decision Tree classifier on test set: 0.94				
	precision	recall	f1-score	support
0	0.97	0.95	0.96	3428
1	0.86	0.90	0.88	1072
avg / total	0.94	0.94	0.94	4500

The KNN result is better than the SVM model, however, it is still lower than the decision tree's score. KNN is a resource-intensive algorithm. It is wise to use a model of some different algorithm if there is just a marginal improvement using KNN. However, it is at the user's discretion on what is best depending on their environment and the problem they are trying to solve.

Ensemble methods

Ensembling models are a robust approach to enhancing the efficiency of the predictive models. It is a well-thought out strategy that is very similar to a power-packed word—TEAM !! Any task done by a team leads to significant accomplishments.

What are ensemble models?

Likewise, in the ML world, an ensemble model is a *team of models* operating together to enhance the result of their work. Technically, ensemble models comprise of several supervised learning models that are individually trained, and the results are merged in various ways to achieve the final prediction. This result has higher predictive power than the results of any of its constituting learning algorithms independently.

Mostly, there are three kinds of ensemble learning methods that are used:

- Bagging
- Boosting
- Stacking/Blending

Bagging

Bagging is also known as **bootstrap aggregation**. It is a way to decrease the variance error of a model's result. Sometimes the weak learning algorithms are very sensitive—a slightly different input leads to very offbeat outputs. Random forest reduces this variability by running multiple instances, which leads to lower variance. In this method, random samples are prepared from training datasets using the random sample with replacement models (bootstrapping process).

Models are developed on each sample using supervised learning methods. Lastly, the results are merged by averaging the predictions or selecting the best prediction utilizing the majority voting technique. Majority voting is a process in which the prediction of the ensemble is the class with the highest number of predictions in all of the classifiers. There are also various other methods, such as weighing and rank averaging, for producing the final results.

There are various bagging algorithms, such as bagged decision trees, random forest, and extra trees, that are available in scikit-learn. We will demonstrate the most popular random forest model and you can try out the rest. We can implement random forest by importing `RandomForestClassifier` from scikit-learn's `ensemble` package. As we are still working with HR attrition data, some part of the code segment remains the same for this demonstration as well:

```
import numpy as np
import pandas as pd
from sklearn.ensemble import RandomForestClassifier
from sklearn.metrics import accuracy_score
from sklearn import tree
hr_data = pd.read_csv('data/hr.csv', header=0)
hr_data.head()
hr_data = hr_data.dropna()
print(" Data Set Shape ", hr_data.shape)
print(list(hr_data.columns))
print(" Sample Data ", hr_data.head())
data_trnsf = pd.get_dummies(hr_data, columns =['salary', 'sales'])
data_trnsf.columns
X = data_trnsf.drop('left', axis=1)
```

```
X.columns
from sklearn.model_selection import train_test_split
X_train, X_test, Y_train, Y_test = train_test_split(X, data_trnsf.left,
test_size=0.3, random_state=42)
print(X_train)
```

There are no mandatory parameters to instantiate a random forest model. However, there are a few parameters that are important to understand for creating a good random forest model, described as follows:

- n_estimators: We can specify the number of trees to be created in the model. The default is 10.
- max_features: This specifies the number of variables/features to be chosen randomly as candidates at each split. The default is $\sqrt{number\_of\_features}$.

We create a random forest model using n_estimators as 100 and max_features to be 3, as shown in the following code snippet:

```
num_trees = 100
max_features = 3
attrition_forest = RandomForestClassifier(n_estimators=num_trees,
max_features=max_features)
attrition_forest.fit(X_train, Y_train)
```

The output of the preceding code is as follows:

```
Out[6]: RandomForestClassifier(bootstrap=True, class_weight=None, criterion='gini',
            max_depth=None, max_features=3, max_leaf_nodes=None,
            min_impurity_split=1e-07, min_samples_leaf=1,
            min_samples_split=2, min_weight_fraction_leaf=0.0,
            n_estimators=100, n_jobs=1, oob_score=False, random_state=None,
            verbose=0, warm_start=False)
```

Once a model is fitted successfully, we predict the Y_pred from the test or hold out dataset:

```
Y_pred = attrition_forest.predict(X_test)
from sklearn.metrics import confusion_matrix
confusionmatrix = confusion_matrix(Y_test, Y_pred)
print(confusionmatrix)
```

The results in the confusion matrix are looking very good with fewer misclassifications and accurate predictions. Let's check how the evaluation metrics come out:

```
[[3417    11]
 [  52 1020]]
```

Next, we check the accuracy of `Random Forest classifier` and `print` the classification report:

```
print('Accuracy of Random Forest classifier on test set:
{:.2f}'.format(attrition_forest.score(X_test, Y_test)))
from sklearn.metrics import classification_report
print(classification_report(Y_test, Y_pred))
```

The output of the preceding code is as follows:

```
Accuracy of Random Forest classifier on test set: 0.99
            precision    recall  f1-score   support

         0       0.99      1.00      0.99      3428
         1       0.99      0.95      0.97      1072

avg / total       0.99      0.99      0.99      4500
```

This is an excellent model, having all evaluation metrics near to perfect prediction. It is too good to believe and might be a case of overfitting. However, let us consider random forest to be the best algorithm on our HR attrition dataset for now, and move on to another widely used ensemble modeling technique—boosting.

Boosting

Boosting is an iterative process in which consecutive models are built one after the another based on the flaws of the predecessors. This helps to diminish the bias in the model and also leads to a decrease in variance as well. Boosting tries to generate new classifiers that are better equipped to predict the values for which the previous model's performance was low. Unlike bagging, the resampling of the training data is conditioned on the performance of the earlier classifiers. Boosting uses all data to train the individual classifiers, but instances that were misclassified by the previous classifiers are given more importance so that subsequent classifiers enhance the results.

Gradient Boosting Machines (GBMs), which is also known as **Stochastic Gradient Boosting (SGB)**, is an example of the boosting method. Once again, we import the required packages and load the HR attrition dataset. Also, we do the same process of converting the categorical dataset to one-hot encoded values and split the dataset into train and test set at a ratio of 70:30:

```
import numpy as np
import pandas as pd
from sklearn.ensemble import GradientBoostingClassifier
from sklearn.metrics import accuracy_score
from sklearn import tree
hr_data = pd.read_csv('data/hr.csv', header=0)
hr_data.head()
hr_data = hr_data.dropna()
print(" Data Set Shape ", hr_data.shape)
print(list(hr_data.columns))
print(" Sample Data ", hr_data.head())

data_trnsf = pd.get_dummies(hr_data, columns =['salary', 'sales'])
data_trnsf.columns
X = data_trnsf.drop('left', axis=1)
X.columns

from sklearn.model_selection import train_test_split
X_train, X_test, Y_train, Y_test = train_test_split(X, data_trnsf.left,
test_size=0.3, random_state=42)
print(X_train)
```

There are a few best parameters that are important for a GradientBoostedClassifier. However, not all are mandatory:

- n_estimators: This is similar to n_estimators of a random forest algorithm, but the trees are created sequentially, which are considered as different stages in a boosting method. Using these parameters, we specify the number of trees or boosting stages in the model. The default is 100.
- max_depth: This is the number of features to consider when looking for the best split. When the max_features is less than the number of features, it leads to the reduction of variance, but increases bias in the model.

- `max_depth`: The maximum depth of each tree that is to be grown. The default value is 3:

```
num_trees = 100
attrition_gradientboost=
GradientBoostingClassifier(n_estimators=num_trees, random_state=42)
attrition_gradientboost.fit(X_train, Y_train)
```

The output of the preceding code is as follows:

```
Out[6]:  GradientBoostingClassifier(criterion='friedman_mse', init=None,
                    learning_rate=0.1, loss='deviance', max_depth=3,
                    max_features=None, max_leaf_nodes=None,
                    min_impurity_split=1e-07, min_samples_leaf=1,
                    min_samples_split=2, min_weight_fraction_leaf=0.0,
                    n_estimators=100, presort='auto', random_state=42,
                    subsample=1.0, verbose=0, warm_start=False)
```

Once the model is successfully fitted to the dataset, we use the trained model to predict the Y values for `test` data:

```
Y_pred = attrition_gradientboost.predict(X_test)

from sklearn.metrics import confusion_matrix
confusionmatrix = confusion_matrix(Y_test, Y_pred)
print(confusionmatrix)
```

The following confusion matrix looks good with minimal misclassification errors:

```
[[3389    39]
 [  85   987]]
```

We print the accuracy and other metrics to evaluate the classifier:

```
print('Accuracy of Gradient Boosting Classifier classifier on test set:
{:.2f}'.format(attrition_gradientboost.score(X_test, Y_test)))
from sklearn.metrics import classification_report
print(classification_report(Y_test, Y_pred))
```

The output of the preceding code is as follows:

```
Accuracy of Gradient Boosting Classifier classifier on test set: 0.97
              precision     recall  f1-score    support

           0      0.98       0.99      0.98       3428
           1      0.96       0.92      0.94       1072

avg / total      0.97       0.97      0.97       4500
```

The accuracy is 97%, which is excellent, but not as good as the random forest model. There is another kind of ensemble model which we will discuss in the following section.

Stacking/blending

In this method, multiple layers of classifiers are stacked/piled up one over the other. The prediction probabilities of the first layer of classifiers are applied to train the second layer of classifiers and so on. The final result is achieved by employing a base classifier such as logistic regression. We can also use different algorithms, such as decision trees, random forest, or GBM, as a final layer classifier.

There is no out-of-the-box implementation for stacked ensembles in scikit-learn. However, we will demonstrate creating an automated function for stacked ensemble using scikit-learn's base algorithms in Chapter 4, *Automated Algorithm Selection*.

Comparing the results of classifiers

We have created around six classification models on the HR attrition dataset. The following table summarizes the evaluation scores for each model:

	Accuracy	Precision	Recall	f1-score
Logistic Regression	0.79	0.76	0.79	0.76
Decision Trees	0.95	0.95	0.95	0.95
SVM	0.77	0.74	0.77	0.74
KNN	0.94	0.94	0.94	0.94
Random Forest	0.99	0.99	0.99	0.99
Gradient Boosted Classifier	0.97	0.97	0.97	0.97

The random forest model appears to be a winner among all six models, with a record-breaking 99% accuracy. Now, we need not further improve the random forest model, but check whether it can generalize well to a new dataset and the results are not overfitting the `train` dataset. One of the methods is to do cross-validation.

Cross-validation

Cross-validation is a way to evaluate the accuracy of a model on a dataset that was not used for training, that is, a sample of data that is unknown to trained models. This ensures generalization of a model on independent datasets when deployed in a production environment. One of the methods is dividing the dataset into two sets—train and test sets. We demonstrated this method in our previous examples.

Another popular and more robust method is a k-fold cross-validation approach, where a dataset is partitioned into *k* subsamples of equal sizes. Where *k* is a non-zero positive integer. During the training phase, *k-1* samples are used to train the model and the remaining one sample is used to test the model. This process is repeated for k times with one of the k samples used exactly once to test the model. The evaluation results are then averaged or combined in some way, such as majority voting to provide a single estimate.

We will generate a 5 and 10 fold cross-validation on the random forest model created earlier to evaluate its performance. Just add the following code snippet at the end of the random forest code:

```
crossval_5_scores = cross_val_score(attrition_forest, X_train, Y_train,
cv=5)
print(crossval_5_scores)
print(np.mean(crossval_5_scores))
crossval_10_scores = cross_val_score(attrition_forest, X_train, Y_train,
cv=10)
print(crossval_10_scores)
print(np.mean(crossval_10_scores))
```

The accuracy score is 0.9871 and 0.9875 for 5 and 10 fold cross-validation respectively. This is a good score and very close to our actual random forest model score of 0.99, as shown in the following screenshot. This ensures that the model might generalize well to other independent datasets:

```
[0.98714286 0.98571429 0.98571429 0.98809524 0.9890424 ]
0.9871418135620136
[0.98857143 0.98666667 0.98666667 0.98571429 0.98285714 0.98857143
 0.98857143 0.98857143 0.98952381 0.98951382]
0.9875228108402562
```

Now that we have some idea of what supervised machine learning is all about, it's time to switch gears to unsupervised machine learning.

We introduced unsupervised learning earlier in the chapter. To reiterate the objective:

The objective of unsupervised learning is to identify patterns by deducing structures and the relations of the attributes in the input dataset.

So, what algorithms and methods can we use to identify the patterns? There are many, such as clustering and autoencoders. We will cover clustering in the following section and autoencoders in Chapter 7, *Dive into Deep Learning*.

Clustering

We will begin this section with a question. How do we start learning a new algorithm or a machine learning method? We start with triple W. So, let's being with that for the clustering method.

What is clustering?

Clustering is a technique to group similar data together, and a group has some unique characteristics that are different from other groups. Data can be clustered together using various methods. One of them is rule-based, where the groups are formed based on certain predefined conditions, such as grouping customers based on their age or industry. Another method is to use ML algorithms to cluster data together.

Where is clustering used?

Being an unsupervised learning process, it is most often used in industries to deduce logical relationships and patterns from data. Clustering finds its application across sectors and business functions. It is used for information retrieval, customer segmentation, image segmentation, clustering unstructured text like web pages, news articles, and so on.

By which method can clustering be implemented?

There are various machine learning methods to create clusters. The clustering algorithms fall into one of the following groups:

- **Hierarchical clustering**: It is also known as **agglomerative clustering**, that tries to link each data point by a distance measure to its nearest neighbor. This is a recursive process that starts with one record and iteratively pairs them together until all unite together into a single cluster. If we imagine, its structure is similar to that of an inverted tree and can be visualized through a dendrogram plot. One of the problems of using this method is the process of determining the clusters. It is resource intensive, but one can visualize the dendrogram plot and choose the number of clusters.

- **Partition-based clustering**: In this method, the data is split into partitions. The partitioning is based on the distances between the data points. The k-means algorithm is a commonly used partition clustering method. In this method, the choice of the appropriate distance function influences the shape of clusters. Euclidean, Manhattan, and cosine distances are three distance functions that are extensively used for creating k-means clusters. Euclidean distance is most sensitive to the scale of the input vectors. In such cases, one has to normalize or standardize the scale of input vectors or pick a scale-insensitive distance measure such as cosine distance.

- **Density-based technique**: Here the clusters are formed by using a specific probability distribution of the data points. The idea is to continue spreading the clusters as long as the density in the neighborhood surpasses a defined threshold. The high-density regions are labeled as clusters segregated from the low-density areas, which might be noise. Noise is a random variation or error in data that is statistically uncertain and cannot be explained.

- **Grid-based method**: In this method, first, hyper-rectangular grid cells are created by dividing the attributes of a dataset. It then drops low-density cells that are under a defined threshold parameter. The adjacent high-density cells are then fused together until the objective function is achieved or remains constant. The resulting cells are interpreted as clusters.

We are going to walk through hierarchical clustering and k-means clustering, which are two widely used methods in industries.

Hierarchical clustering

We can use scikit-learn to perform hierarchical clustering in Python. We need to import the `AgglomerativeClustering` method from `sklearn.cluster` for creating the clusters. Hierarchical clustering works on distance measures, so we need to convert categorical data to a suitable numeric format prior to building the model. We have used one-hot encoding to convert a categorical attribute to a numeric format, and there exist various other methods to accomplish this task. This topic will be covered in detail in the next chapter:

```
import pandas as pd
import numpy as np
from sklearn import preprocessing
from sklearn.cluster import AgglomerativeClustering
hr_data = pd.read_csv('data/hr.csv', header=0)
hr_data.head()
hr_data = hr_data.dropna()
print(hr_data.shape)
print(list(hr_data.columns))
data_trnsf = pd.get_dummies(hr_data, columns =['salary', 'sales'])
data_trnsf.columns
```

Next, we need to instantiate `AgglomerativeClustering` with the following parameters and fit the data to the model:

- `n_clusters`: Number of clusters to find. The default is two.
- `affinity`: It is the distance metrics used to compute the linkage. The default is euclidean; manhattan, cosine, l1, l2, and precomputed are the other distance metrics that can be used.
- `linkage`: This parameter determines the metrics to be used for merging the pair of clusters. The different linkage metrics are:
  - **Ward**: It minimizes the variance of the clusters being merged. It is the default parameter value.
  - **Average**: It uses the average of the distances of each observation of the two sets.
  - **Complete**: It uses the maximum distances between all observations of the two sets.

Now, let us build an `AgglomerativeClustering` model using some of the described parameters:

```
n_clusters = 3
clustering = AgglomerativeClustering(n_clusters=n_clusters,
affinity='euclidean', linkage='complete')
clustering.fit(data_trnsf)
cluster_labels = clustering.fit_predict(data_trnsf)
```

Once the model is ready, we need to evaluate the model. The best way to evaluate the clustering results is human inspection of the clusters formed and determining what each cluster represents and what values the data in each cluster have in common.

In conjunction with the human inspection, one can also use silhouette scores to determine the best models. Silhouette values lie in the range of -1 and +1:

- +1 indicates that the data in a cluster is close to the assigned cluster, and far away from its neighboring clusters
- -1 indicates that the data point is more close to its neighboring cluster than to the assigned cluster

When the average silhouette score of a model is -1 it is a terrible model, and a model with a +1 silhouette score is an ideal model. So, this is why the higher the average silhouette score, the better the clustering model:

```
silhouette_avg = silhouette_score(data_trnsf, cluster_labels)
print("For n_clusters =", n_clusters,"The average silhouette_score is :",
silhouette_avg)
```

The output of the preceding code is as follows:

```
For n_clusters = 3 The average silhouette_score is : 0.496869735878
```

As the average silhouette score for our model is 0.49, we can assume that the clusters are well formed.

We can compare this score with the k-means clustering results and pick the best model for creating three clusters on the HR attrition dataset.

Partitioning clustering (KMeans)

We need to import a KMeans method from the scikit-learn package and the rest of the code remains similar to the hierarchical clustering's code:

```
import pandas as pd
import numpy as np
from sklearn import preprocessing
import matplotlib.pyplot as plt
from sklearn.cluster import KMeans
from sklearn.metrics import silhouette_samples, silhouette_score
hr_data = pd.read_csv('data/hr.csv', header=0)
hr_data.head()
hr_data = hr_data.dropna()
print(hr_data.shape)
print(list(hr_data.columns))
data_trnsf = pd.get_dummies(hr_data, columns =['salary', 'sales'])
data_trnsf.columns
```

We need to specify the number of clusters (n_clusters) in the k-means function to create a model. It is an essential parameter for creating k-means clusters. Its default value is eight. Next, the data is fitted to the KMeans instance, and a model is built. We need to fit_predict the values to get the cluster labels, as was done for AgglomerativeClustering:

```
n_clusters = 3
kmeans = KMeans(n_clusters=n_clusters)
kmeans.fit(data_trnsf)
cluster_labels = kmeans.fit_predict(data_trnsf)
```

If we want to view the cluster centroid and labels, we can use cluster_centers_ and means_labels_ to do that:

```
centroid = kmeans.cluster_centers_
labels = kmeans.labels_
print (centroid)
print(labels)
silhouette_avg = silhouette_score(data_trnsf, cluster_labels)
print("For n_clusters =", n_clusters,"The average silhouette_score is :",
silhouette_avg)
```

The output of the preceding code is as follows:

```
[[  6.75324232e-01   7.28759954e-01   3.82161547e+00   2.02696701e+02
    3.41501706e+00   1.71786121e-01   6.05233220e-02   2.38907850e-02
    9.67007964e-02   4.67121729e-01   4.36177474e-01   7.73606371e-02
    5.09670080e-02   4.73265074e-02   4.73265074e-02   5.05119454e-02
    5.62002275e-02   6.07508532e-02   2.73037543e-01   1.51535836e-01
    1.84982935e-01]
 [  5.81896364e-01   6.47789091e-01   3.25945455e+00   1.46582364e+02
    3.31472727e+00   1.34545455e-01   2.93090909e-01   2.03636364e-02
    7.74545455e-02   5.00909091e-01   4.21636364e-01   7.96363636e-02
    5.18181818e-02   5.47272727e-02   5.23636364e-02   3.83636364e-02
    5.94545455e-02   6.12727273e-02   2.79454545e-01   1.48909091e-01
    1.74000000e-01]
 [  5.92360893e-01   7.78814655e-01   4.37284483e+00   2.58326607e+02
    3.76763323e+00   1.32053292e-01   3.31700627e-01   1.99843260e-02
    7.56269592e-02   4.91379310e-01   4.32993730e-01   8.79702194e-02
    5.44670846e-02   5.05485893e-02   4.76097179e-02   3.85971787e-02
    5.56426332e-02   5.83855799e-02   2.74882445e-01   1.45768025e-01
    1.86128527e-01]]
[1 2 2 ..., 1 2 1]
For n_clusters = 3 The average silhouette_score is : 0.581903917045
```

The average `silhouette_score` for k-means clustering is `0.58`, which is more than the average silhouette score obtained for hierarchical clusters.

This means that the three clusters are better formed in a k-means model than that of the hierarchical model built on the `HR` attrition dataset.

Summary

The ML and its automation journey are long. The aim of this chapter was to familiarize ourselves with machine learning concepts; most importantly, the scikit-learn and other Python packages, so that we can smoothly accelerate our learning in the next chapters, create a linear regression model and six classification models, and learn about clustering techniques and compare the models with each other.

We used a single `HR` attrition dataset for creating all classifiers. We observed that there are many similarities in these codes. The libraries imported are all similar except the one used to instantiate the machine learning class. The data preprocessing module is redundant in all code. The machine learning technique changes based on the task and data of the target attribute. Also, the evaluation methodology is equivalent to the similar type of ML methods.

Do you think that some of these areas are redundant and need automation? Yes, they can be, but it is not that easy. When we start thinking of automation, everything in and around the model needs to be wired together. Each of the code sections is a module of its own.

The next chapter is all about the data preprocessing module. It is the most crucial and time-consuming subject in a machine learning project. We will discuss various data preparation tasks that are required to create a reliable machine learning model.

Data Preprocessing 3

Anyone who is interested in **machine learning** (**ML**) would have certainly heard that 80% of a data scientist or machine learning engineer's time is spent on preparing the data, and the remaining 20% is spent on building and evaluating the model. The considerable time spent preparing the data is considered as an investment to construct a good model. A simple model this is made using an excellent dataset outpaces a complex model developed using a lousy dataset. In real life, finding a reliable dataset is very difficult. We have to create and nurture good data. You must be wondering, how do you create good data? This is something that we will discover in this chapter. We will study everything that is needed to create an excellent and viable dataset. In theory, good is relative to what task we have at hand and how we perceive and consume the data. In this chapter, we will walk you through the following topics:

- Data transformation
- Feature selection
- Dimensionality reduction
- Feature generation

For each of the topics, we will discuss the variety of things that can be done over different types of data we encounter in a dataset. We will also consider a few automated open source feature preparation tools that come in handy for preparing data in Python.

Let's begin with the first topic of data transformation.

Technical requirements

All the code examples can be found in the `Chapter 03` folder in GitHub.

Data transformation

Let's assume we are working on an ML model whose task is to predict employee attrition. Based on our business understanding, we might include some relevant variables that are necessary to create a good model. On the other hand, we might choose to discard some features, such as `EmployeeID`, which carry no relevant information.

 Identifying the `ID` columns is known as **identifier detection**. `Identifier` columns don't add any information to a model in pattern detection and prediction. So, `identifier` column detection functionality can be a part of the `AutoML` package and we use it based on the algorithm or a task dependency.

Once we have decided on the fields to use, we may explore the data to transform certain features that aid in the learning process. The transformation adds some experience to the data, which benefits ML models. For example, an employee start date of 11-02-2018 doesn't provide any information. However, if we transform this feature to four attributes—date, day, month, and year, it adds value to the model building exercise.

The feature transformations also depend much on the type of ML algorithm used. Broadly, we can classify the supervised models into two categories—tree-based models and non-tree-based models.

 Tree-based models handle the abnormality in most features by themselves. Non-tree-based models, such as nearest neighbors and linear regression, improve their predictive power when we do feature transformations.

Enough of the theoretical explanations. Now, let's straight away jump into some of the feature transformations that can be performed over the various datatypes that we encounter frequently. We will start with numerical features first.

Numerical data transformation

The following are some of the most widely-used methods to transform numerical data:

- Scaling
- Missing values
- Outliers

The techniques shown here can be embedded in functions that can be directly applied to transform numerical data in an AutoML pipeline.

Scaling

Standardization and **normalization** are the two terms for **scaling** techniques used in the industry. Both these techniques ensure that the numerical features used in the model are weighted equally in their representation. Most of the time people use standardization and normalization interchangeably. Though both of them are scaling techniques, there is a thin line of difference between the two.

 Standardization assumes the data to be normally distributed. It rescales the data to mean as zero and standard deviation as one. Normalization is a scaling technique that assumes no prior distribution of the data. In this technique, the numerical data is rescaled to a fixed range either: 0 to 1, -1 to +1, and so on.

The following are a few widely used techniques for standardizing or normalizing data:

- **Z- score standardization**: Here, the data is rescaled with a mean of zero and standard deviation of one if the data follows a Gaussian distribution. One of the prior requirements is having the numerical data normally distributed. Mathematically, it is denoted as $Z = X - \bar{X}/\sigma$, where $\bar{x}$ is the mean of the values and σ is the standard deviation of the values.

Scikit-learn provides various methods to standardize and normalize the data. Let's first load the HR attrition dataset using the following code snippet:

```
%matplotlib inline
import numpy as np
import pandas as pd
hr_data = pd.read_csv('data/hr.csv', header=0)
print (hr_data.head())
```

The output of the preceding code displays the various attributes that the dataset has along with a few data points:

```
   satisfaction_level  last_evaluation  number_project  average_montly_hours  \
0                0.38             0.53               2                   157
1                0.80             0.86               5                   262
2                0.11             0.88               7                   272
3                0.72             0.87               5                   223
4                0.37             0.52               2                   159

   time_spend_company  Work_accident  left  promotion_last_5years  sales  \
0                   3              0     1                      0  sales
1                   6              0     1                      0  sales
2                   4              0     1                      0  sales
3                   5              0     1                      0  sales
4                   3              0     1                      0  sales

   salary
0      low
1   medium
2   medium
3      low
4      low
```

Let's analyze the distribution of the dataset using the following code:

```
hr_data[hr_data.dtypes[(hr_data.dtypes=="float64")|(hr_data.dtypes=="int64"
)].index.values].hist(figsize=[11,11])
```

The output of the previous code is a few histograms of various numerical attributes:

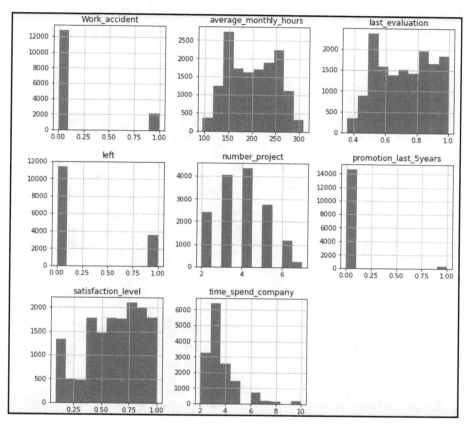

As an example, let's use `StandardScaler` from the `sklearn.preprocessing` module to standardize the values of the `satisfaction_level` column. Once we import the method, we first need to create an instance of the `StandardScaler` class. Next, we need to fit and transform the column that we need to standardize using the `fit_transform` method. In the following example, we use the `satisfaction_level` attribute to be standardized:

```
from sklearn.preprocessing import StandardScaler
scaler = StandardScaler()
hr_data_scaler=scaler.fit_transform(hr_data[['satisfaction_level']])
hr_data_scaler_df = pd.DataFrame(hr_data_scaler)
hr_data_scaler_df.max()
hr_data_scaler_df[hr_data_scaler_df.dtypes[(hr_data_scaler_df.dtypes=="floa
t64")|(hr_data_scaler_df.dtypes=="int64")].index.values].hist(figsize=[11,1
1])
```

Once we execute the preceding code, we can again view `satisfication_level` instances histogram and observe that the values are standardized between **-2** to **1.5**:

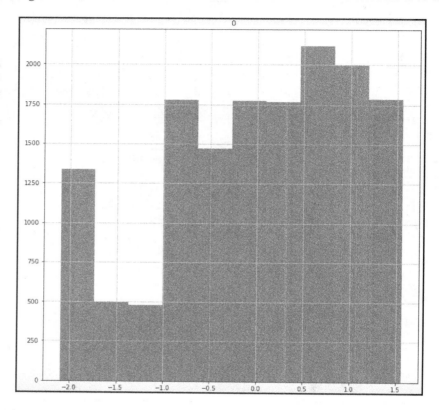

- **Min-max normalization**: In this technique the minimum value of a variable is subtracted from its actual value over the difference of its maximum and minimum values. Mathematically, it is represented by the following:

$$z = \frac{x - min(x)}{max(x) - min(x)}$$

The `MinMaxScaler` method is available in scikit-learn's `preprocessing` module. In this example, we normalize four attributes of the `HR` attrition dataset—`average_monthly_hours`, `last_evaluation`, `number_project`, and `satisfaction_level`. We follow the similar process that we followed for `StandardScaler`. We need first to import `MinMaxScaler` from the `sklearn.preprocessing` module and create an instance of the `MinMaxScaler` class.

Next, we need to fit and transform the columns using the `fit_transform` method:

```
from sklearn.preprocessing import MinMaxScaler
minmax=MinMaxScaler()
hr_data_minmax=minmax.fit_transform(hr_data[[ 'average_montly_hours',
  'last_evaluation', 'number_project', 'satisfaction_level']])
hr_data_minmax_df = pd.DataFrame(hr_data_minmax)
hr_data_minmax_df.min()
hr_data_minmax_df.max()
hr_data_minmax_df[hr_data_minmax_df.dtypes[(hr_data_minmax_df.dtypes=="floa
t64")|(hr_data_minmax_df.dtypes=="int64")].index.values].hist(figsize=[11,1
1])
```

The following histograms depict that the four attributes that were transformed are having the values distributed between **0** and **1**:

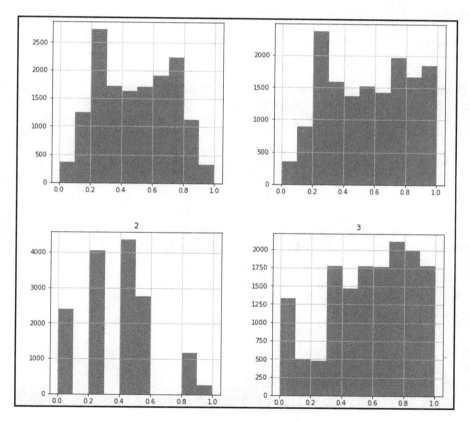

Missing values

We often come across datasets where not all of the values are available for specific variables/attributes. This can happen for several reasons, such as ignored questions in a survey, typing errors, a device malfunctioning, and so on. Encountering these missing values is expected in a data mining project, and dealing with these values is essential.

Missing value imputation occupies most of a data scientist's time. There are various ways through which we can impute missing values. The deciding factor is what to use when attributing these kind of unavailable values. The process on deciding what and when to use for imputing missing values is a talent and comes from experience in working with data. Sometimes it is better to remove these values directly and, for some assignments, it is better to use advanced mining techniques to impute the values.

So, the two most significant questions arise:

- When do you use which imputation method?
- What is the best way to impute a value?

We think it comes from the experience of handling missing values; the best way to start is by doing a comparative study by applying different imputation methods on the data and then selecting the appropriate technique to assign the null values with the least-biased estimate.

Generally, when we encounter a missing value, we try to examine why a value is missing in the first place. Is it because of some issues while collecting the data, or is the culprit the data source itself? It is better to fix the problem from the root, rather than straight away imputing the value. This is an ideal case, and, most of the time, it is not possible. For example, if we are working on a survey dataset and a few respondents have chosen not to reveal specific information, in such cases imputing the values might be inevitable.

So, before we start imputing the values, we can use the following guidelines:

- Investigate the missing data
- Analyze the missing data
- Decide the best strategy that yields least-biased estimates

We can remember this as an **IAD** rule (that is investigate, analyze, and decide) for missing value imputation. The following are some of the available ways that we can deal with the missing values:

1. **Remove or delete the data**: When very few data points are missing, we can ignore the data and analyze those cases separately. This method is known as **list wise deletion**. However, this is not advisable when there are too many missing values as we might lose some of the valuable information in the data. Pairwise deletion is another technique, where we can delete only the missing values. This indicates that we analyze all cases where only data of interest is present. That is a safe strategy, but, using this method, we might get different results from each sample every time even if there is a small change in the data.

   We will again use the HR attrition dataset to demonstrate the missing value treatment. Let's first load the dataset and view the number of nulls in the dataset:

   ```
   import numpy as np
   import pandas as pd
   hr_data = pd.read_csv('data/hr.csv', header=0)
   print (hr_data.head())
   print('Nulls in the data set' ,hr_data.isnull().sum())
   ```

As we can see from the following output, the dataset is relatively clean with just `promotion_last_5years` having some missing values. So, we will synthetically ingest a few missing values into some columns:

```
   satisfaction_level  last_evaluation  number_project  average_montly_hours  \
0                0.38             0.53               2                   157
1                0.80             0.86               5                   262
2                0.11             0.88               7                   272
3                0.72             0.87               5                   223
4                0.37             0.52               2                   159

   time_spend_company  Work_accident  left  promotion_last_5years  sales  \
0                   3              0     1                      0  sales
1                   6              0     1                      0  sales
2                   4              0     1                      0  sales
3                   5              0     1                      0  sales
4                   3              0     1                      0  sales

   salary
0     low
1  medium
2  medium
3     low
4     low
Nulls in the data set satisfaction_level        0
last_evaluation          0
number_project           0
average_montly_hours     0
time_spend_company       0
Work_accident            0
left                     0
promotion_last_5years    0
sales                    0
salary                   0
dtype: int64
```

We use the following code snippet to replace a few values in columns `promotion_last_5years`, `average_montly_hours`, and `number_project` with null values:

```
#As there are no null introduce some nulls by replacing 0 in
promotion_last_5years with NaN
hr_data[['promotion_last_5years']] = hr_data[[
'promotion_last_5years']].replace(0, np.NaN)
#As there are no null introduce some nulls by replacing 262 in
promotion_last_5years with NaN
hr_data[['average_montly_hours']] = hr_data[[
'average_montly_hours']].replace(262, np.NaN)
#Replace 2 in number_project with NaN
hr_data[['number_project']] = hr_data[[
'number_project']].replace(2, np.NaN)
print('Nulls in the data set', hr_data.isnull().sum())
```

After this exercise, there are some null values inserted for those three columns, as we can view from the following results:

```
Nulls in the data set satisfaction_level            0
last_evaluation              0
number_project            2388
average_montly_hours        86
time_spend_company           0
Work_accident                0
left                         0
promotion_last_5years    14680
sales                        0
salary                       0
dtype: int64
```

Before we remove the rows, let's first create a copy of the `hr_data`, so that we don't replace the original dataset, which is going to be used to demonstrate the other missing value imputation methods. Next, we drop the rows with missing values using the `dropna` method:

```
#Remove rows
hr_data_1 = hr_data.copy()
print('Shape of the data set before removing nulls ',
hr_data_1.shape)
# drop rows with missing values
hr_data_1.dropna(inplace=True)
# summarize the number of rows and columns in the dataset
print('Shape of the data set after removing nulls
',hr_data_1.shape)
```

We can observe that the number of rows after this exercise is reduced to 278 from 14999. Deleting rows has to be used carefully. As `promotion_last_5years` had around 14,680 missing values, 14,680 records were removed completely:

```
Shape of the data set before removing nulls  (14999, 10)
Shape of the data set after removing nulls   (278, 10)
```

2. **Use a global constant to fill in the missing value**: We can use a global constant, such as NA or -999, to separate the missing value from the rest of the dataset. Also, there are empty values which don't have any values, but they form an inherent part of the dataset. Those values are deliberately kept as blanks. When the empty values cannot be separated from the missing values, using a global constant is a safe strategy.

We can use the `fillna` method to replace missing values with a constant value such as -999. The following snippet demonstrates the use of this method:

```
#Mark global constant for missing values
hr_data_3 = hr_data.copy()
# fill missing values with -999
hr_data_3.fillna(-999, inplace=True)
# count the number of NaN values in each column
print(hr_data_3.isnull().sum())
print(hr_data_3.head())
```

We can view from the following results that all missing values are replaced with -999 values:

```
satisfaction_level       0
last_evaluation          0
number_project           0
average_montly_hours     0
time_spend_company       0
Work_accident            0
left                     0
promotion_last_5years    0
sales                    0
salary                   0
dtype: int64
   satisfaction_level  last_evaluation  number_project  average_montly_hours  \
0                0.38             0.53          -999.0                 157.0
1                0.80             0.86             5.0                -999.0
2                0.11             0.88             7.0                 272.0
3                0.72             0.87             5.0                 223.0
4                0.37             0.52          -999.0                 159.0

   time_spend_company  Work_accident  left  promotion_last_5years  sales  \
0                   3              0     1                 -999.0  sales
1                   6              0     1                 -999.0  sales
2                   4              0     1                 -999.0  sales
3                   5              0     1                 -999.0  sales
4                   3              0     1                 -999.0  sales

   salary
0     low
1  medium
2  medium
3     low
4     low
```

3. **Replace missing values with the attribute mean/median**: This is the most liked method by data scientists and machine learning engineers. We can replace missing values with either the mean or median for numerical values and mode for categorical values. The disadvantage of this method is that it might decrease the variability in the attribute, which would, in turn, weaken the correlation estimates. If we are dealing with a supervised classification model, we can also replace the missing values with group mean or median for numerical values and grouped mode for categorical values. In these grouped mean/median methods, the attribute values are grouped by target values, and the missing values in that group are replaced with the group's mean/ median.

We can use the same `fillna` method with the mean function as a parameter to replace missing values with mean values. The following code demonstrates its usage:

```
#Replace mean for missing values
hr_data_2 = hr_data.copy()
# fill missing values with mean column values
hr_data_2.fillna(hr_data_2.mean(), inplace=True)
# count the number of NaN values in each column
print(hr_data_2.isnull().sum())
print(hr_data_2.head())
```

We can see from the following output that the missing values are replaced with the mean of each attribute:

```
satisfaction_level      0
last_evaluation         0
number_project          0
average_montly_hours    0
time_spend_company      0
Work_accident           0
left                    0
promotion_last_5years   0
sales                   0
salary                  0
dtype: int64
   satisfaction_level  last_evaluation  number_project  average_montly_hours  \
0                0.38             0.53        4.144477            157.000000
1                0.80             0.86        5.000000            200.698853
2                0.11             0.88        7.000000            272.000000
3                0.72             0.87        5.000000            223.000000
4                0.37             0.52        4.144477            159.000000

   time_spend_company  Work_accident  left  promotion_last_5years  sales  \
0                   3              0     1                    1.0  sales
1                   6              0     1                    1.0  sales
2                   4              0     1                    1.0  sales
3                   5              0     1                    1.0  sales
4                   3              0     1                    1.0  sales

   salary
0     low
1  medium
2  medium
3     low
4     low
```

4. **Using an indicator variable**: We can also generate a binary variable indicating whether there are missing values or not in a record. We can stretch this to multiple attributes where we can create binary indicator variables for each attribute. We can also impute missing values and build the binary indicator variables that will denote whether it is a real or imputed variable. Results are not biased if a value is missing because of a genuine skip.

As we did to demonstrate other imputation methods, let's first copy the original data and make new columns that indicate the attributes and values that are imputed. The following code first creates new columns, appending _was_missing, to the original column names for those attributes that had missing values.

Next, the missing values are replaced with a global constant -999. Though we used the global constant imputation method, you can use any of the imputation methods to impute the missing values:

```
# make copy to avoid changing original data (when Imputing)
hr_data_4 = hr_data.copy()
# make new columns indicating what is imputed
cols_with_missing = (col for col in hr_data_4.columns
 if hr_data_4[col].isnull().any())
for col in cols_with_missing:
 hr_data_4[col + '_was_missing'] = hr_data_4[col].isnull()
hr_data_4.fillna(-999, inplace=True)
hr_data_4.head()
```

We can see from the following result that new columns are created, indicating the presence and absence of missing values in the attributes:

Out[28]:

Work_accident	left	promotion_last_5years	sales	salary	number_project_was_missing	average_montly_hours_was_missing	promotion_last_5years_was_missing
0	1	-999.0	sales	low	True	False	True
0	1	-999.0	sales	medium	False	True	True
0	1	-999.0	sales	medium	False	False	True
0	1	-999.0	sales	low	False	False	True
0	1	-999.0	sales	low	True	False	True

5. **Use a data mining algorithm to predict the most probable value**: We can apply ML algorithms, such as KNN, linear regression, random forest or decision trees techniques, to predict the most likely value of the missing attribute. One of the disadvantages of this method is that it might overfit the data if there is a plan to use the same algorithm for the same dataset for another task such as prediction or classification.

In Python, `fancyimpute` is a library that provides the advanced data mining options to impute missing values. This is something that we use most often and so we thought to demonstrate this package. There might be some other libraries in Python that can also do a similar task. First, we need to install the `fancyimpute` library using the following command. This has to be executed from the Command Prompt:

```
pip install fancyimpute
```

Once installed, we can return to the Jupyter notebook and import the KNN method from the `fancyimpute` library. The KNN imputation method is only going to work for numeric values. So, we first select only numeric columns from the `hr_data` set. Next, a KNN model with *k* equals to 3 is created and the missing values are replaced for numeric attributes:

```
from fancyimpute import KNN

hr_data_5 = hr_data.copy()
hr_numeric = hr_data_5.select_dtypes(include=[np.float])
hr_numeric = pd.DataFrame(KNN(3).complete(hr_numeric))
hr_numeric.columns = hr_numeric.columns
hr_numeric.index = hr_numeric.index
hr_numeric.head()
```

The `fancyimpute` library uses TensorFlow backend and it takes some time to execute. Once the execution is complete, we can scroll down to see the imputation results, as shown in the following result screenshot:

```
Imputing row 14201/14999 with 1 missing, elapsed time: 49.231
Imputing row 14301/14999 with 1 missing, elapsed time: 49.286
Imputing row 14401/14999 with 2 missing, elapsed time: 49.357
Imputing row 14501/14999 with 2 missing, elapsed time: 49.448
Imputing row 14601/14999 with 2 missing, elapsed time: 49.505
Imputing row 14701/14999 with 1 missing, elapsed time: 49.560
Imputing row 14801/14999 with 2 missing, elapsed time: 49.638
Imputing row 14901/14999 with 2 missing, elapsed time: 49.691
```

Out[14]:

	satisfaction_level	last_evaluation	number_project	average_montly_hours	promotion_last_5years
0	0.38	0.53	3.000000	157.000000	1.0
1	0.80	0.86	5.000000	215.666667	1.0
2	0.11	0.88	7.000000	272.000000	1.0
3	0.72	0.87	5.000000	223.000000	1.0
4	0.37	0.52	3.494849	159.000000	1.0

Outliers

Outliers are extreme values that don't conform to the overall data pattern. They usually lie far away from the other observations and distort the overall distribution of the data. Including them in the model building process might lead to wrong results. It is very much essential to treat them appropriately. Outliers can be of two types—univariate and multivariate.

Detecting and treating univariate outliers

As the names imply, univariate outliers are based on a single attribute in a dataset. Univariate outliers are discovered using box plots and by seeing the distribution of the values of an attribute. However, when we build AutoML pipelines, we don't have the privilege to visualize the data distribution. Instead, the AutoML system should be able to detect the outliers and treat them by itself.

So, we can deploy any of the following three methods for automated univariate outlier detection and treatment:

- Interquartile range and filtering
- Winsorizing
- Trimming

Let's create a dummy outlier dataset to demonstrate the outlier detection and treatment method:

```
%matplotlib inline
import numpy as np
import matplotlib.pyplot as plt
number_of_samples = 200
outlier_perc = 0.1
number_of_outliers = number_of_samples - int ( (1-outlier_perc) *
number_of_samples )
# Normal Data
normal_data = np.random.randn(int ( (1-outlier_perc) * number_of_samples
),1)
# Inject Outlier data
outliers = np.random.uniform(low=-9,high=9,size=(number_of_outliers,1))
# Final data set
final_data = np.r_[normal_data,outliers]
```

Let's plot the newly created dataset using the following code:

```
#Check data
plt.cla()
plt.figure(1)
plt.title("Dummy Data set")
plt.scatter(range(len(final_data)),final_data,c='b')
```

We can see from the following plot that there are a few outliers at the end of the dataset:

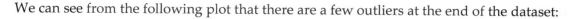

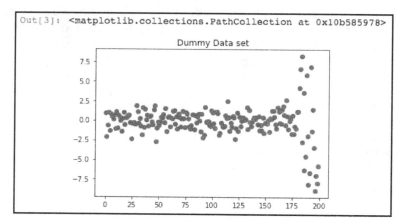

We can also generate a box plot to observe the outliers using the following code. The box plot, also known as **box and whisker**, is a way of representing the distribution of data based on the five-number summary: minimum value, first quartile, median, third quartile, and maximum value. Anything that lies below the minimum and above the maximum mark is acknowledged as an outlier:

```
## Detect Outlier###
plt.boxplot(final_data)
```

From the resulting box plot, we can observe that there are some values present beyond the maximum and minimum mark. So, we can assume that we were successfully able to create some outliers:

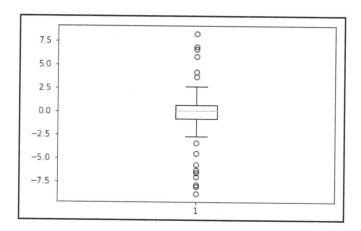

One way to remove outliers is to filter the values that lie above the maximum and below the minimum marks. To accomplish this task, first we need to calculate the **inter-quartile range (IQR)**.

Inter-quartile range

The inter-quartile range is a measure of variability or spread in the dataset. It is calculated by dividing a dataset into quartiles. Quartiles divide the dataset into four halves based on the five number summary that we studied earlier—minimum, first quartile, second quartile, third quartile, and maximum. The second quartile is the median value of the rank-ordered dataset; the first quartile is the middle value of the first half of the rank-ordered dataset, and the third quartile is the middle value of the second half of the rank-ordered dataset.

The inter-quartile range is the difference between the third quartile (quartile75 or Q3) and the first quartile (quartile25 or Q1).

We calculate the IQR in Python using the following code:

```
## IQR Method Outlier Detection and Removal(filter) ##
quartile75, quartile25 = np.percentile(final_data, [75 ,25])
## Inter Quartile Range ##
IQR = quartile75 - quartile25
print("IQR",IQR)
```

We can view from the following code that the IQR for the dataset is 1.49:

```
IQR 1.4941959696670106
```

Filtering values

We can filter the values that lie above the maximum value and below the minimum value. The minimum value can be calculated by using the formula: quartile25 - (IQR * 1.5) and maximum value as quartile75 + (IQR*1.5).

 The method to calculate maximum and minimum values is based on Turkey Fences, which was developed by John Turkey. The value 1.5 indicates about 1% of measurements as outliers and is synonymous with the 3σ principle, which is practiced as a bound in many statistical tests. We can use any value other than 1.5, which is at our discretion. However, the bound may increase or decrease the number of outliers in the dataset.

We utilize the following Python code to calculate the `Max` and `Min` values of a dataset:

```
## Calculate Min and Max values ##
min_value = quartile25 - (IQR*1.5)
max_value = quartile75 + (IQR*1.5)
print("Max", max_value)
print("Min", min_value)
```

We notice the following output after executing the preceding code. The maximum and minimum values are 2.94 and −3.03, respectively:

```
Max 2.942189924241621
Min -3.034593954426421
```

Next, we filter the values that are below the `min_value` and above the `max_value` using the following code:

```
filtered_values = final_data.copy()
filtered_values[ filtered_values< min_value] = np.nan
filtered_values[ filtered_values > max_value] = np.nan
#Check filtered data
plt.cla()
plt.figure(1)
plt.title("IQR Filtered Dummy Data set")
plt.scatter(range(len(filtered_values)),filtered_values,c='b')
```

After the code execution is finished successfully, we can see that the outliers are eliminated, and the dataset appears far better than the previous dataset:

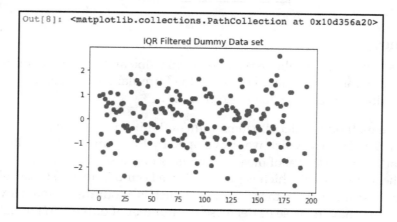

Winsorizing

Winsorizing is the method to replace extreme values with smaller absolute values. It orders the non-null values in numeric columns, computes the tail values, and then substitutes the tail values by the defined parameter.

We can use the `winsorize` method from the SciPy package to deal with outliers. SciPy is a Python library that is a collection of open source Python contributions on the scientific and technical computing space. It has an extensive collection of statistical computation modules, linear algebra, optimization, signal and image processing modules, and many more modules.

Once we import the `winsorize` method, we are required to pass the `data` and the `limit` parameters to the function. The computations and substitution of tail values are made by this method, and resulting outlier free data is generated:

```
##### Winsorization ####
from scipy.stats.mstats import winsorize
import statsmodels.api as sm
limit = 0.15
winsorized_data = winsorize(final_data, limits=limit)
#Check winsorized data
plt.cla()
plt.figure(1)
plt.title("Winsorized Dummy Data set")
plt.scatter(range(len(winsorized_data)), winsorized_data, c='b')
```

We can observe from the following plot that the extreme values are winsorized and the data appears outlier free:

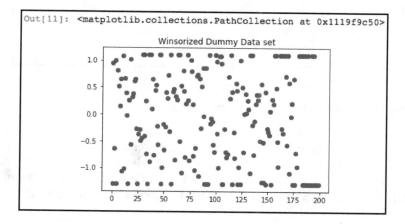

Trimming

Trimming is the same as winsorizing, except the tail values are just cropped out.

The `trimboth` method in the `stats` library slices off the dataset from both ends of the data. The `final_data` and the limit of `0.1` are passed as parameters to the function to trim 10% of data from both ends:

```
### Trimming Outliers ###
from scipy import stats
trimmed_data = stats.trimboth(final_data, 0.1)
#Check trimmed data
plt.cla()
plt.figure(1)
plt.title("Trimmed Dummy Data set")
plt.scatter(range(len(trimmed_data)),trimmed_data,c='b')
```

We can observe from the following resultant plot that the extreme values are clipped and do not exist in the dataset anymore:

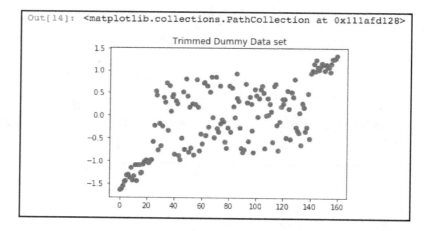

Detecting and treating multivariate outliers

A multivariate outlier is a blend of extreme scores on at least two variables. Univariate outlier detection methods are suited well to dealing with single-dimension data, but when we get past single dimension, it becomes challenging to detect outliers using those methods. Multivariate outlier detection methods are also a form of anomaly detection methods. Techniques such as one class SVM, **Local Outlier Factor** (**LOF**), and `IsolationForest` are useful ways to detect multivariate outliers.

We describe multivariate outlier detection on the HR attrition dataset using the following IsolationForest code. We need to import the IsolationForest from the sklearn.ensemble package. Next, we load the data, transform the categorical variables to one-hot encoded variables, and invoke the IsolationForest method with the number of estimators:

```
##Isolation forest
import numpy as np
import pandas as pd
from sklearn.ensemble import IsolationForest
hr_data = pd.read_csv('data/hr.csv', header=0)
print('Total number of records ',hr_data.shape)
hr_data = hr_data.dropna()
data_trnsf = pd.get_dummies(hr_data, columns =['salary', 'sales'])
data_trnsf.columns
clf = IsolationForest(n_estimators=100)
```

Then, we fit the IsolationForest instance (clf) to the data and predict the outliers using the predict method. The outliers are denoted by –1 and non-outliers (also known as **novel data**) by 1:

```
clf.fit(data_trnsf)
y_pred_train = clf.predict(data_trnsf)
data_trnsf['outlier'] = y_pred_train
print('Number of outliers ',data_trnsf.loc[data_trnsf['outlier'] ==
-1].shape)
print('Number of non outliers ',data_trnsf.loc[data_trnsf['outlier'] ==
1].shape)
```

We can see from the following output that the model was able to identify around 1500 outliers from the dataset of 14999 records:

```
Total number of records  (14999, 10)
Number of outliers  (1500, 22)
Number of non outliers  (13499, 22)
```

Binning

Binning is a process of grouping the continuous numerical values into smaller numbers of buckets or bins. It is an important technique that discretizes continuous data values. Many algorithms such as Naive Bayes and Apriori work well with discrete datasets, and so it is necessary to convert continuous data to discrete values.

There are various types of binning methodologies:

- **Equiwidth binning**: The equiwidth bins are determined by partitioning the data into k intervals of equal size:

$$w = (maxval - minval)/k$$

Where w is width of the bins, *maxval* is the maximum value in the data, *minval* is the minimum value in the data, and k is the desired number of bins

The interval boundaries are formed as follows:

$$minval + w, minval + 2w .... minval + (k-1)w$$

- **Equifrequency binning**: The equifrequency bins are determined by dividing the data into k groups, where each group includes the same number of values.

In both of the methods, the value of k is determined based on our requirements and also by trial and error processes.

Apart from these two methods, we can also explicitly mention the cut points to create bins. This is extremely helpful when we know the data and want it binned in a certain format. The following code is a function that performs binning based on the predefined cut points:

```
#Bin Values:
def bins(column, cutpoints, labels=None):
 #Define min and max values:
 min_val = column.min()
 max_val = column.max()
 print('Minimum value ',min_val)
 print(' Maximum Value ',max_val)
 break_points = [min_val] + cut_points + [max_val]
 if not labels:
   labels = range(len(cut_points)+1)
 #Create bins using the cut function in pandas
 column_bin =
pd.cut(column,bins=break_points,labels=labels,include_lowest=True)
 return column_bin
```

The following code bins the satisfaction level of employees into three categories—low, medium, and high. Anything beneath 0.3 is considered as low satisfaction, a higher than 0.6 score is considered a highly-satisfied employee score, and between these two values is considered as medium:

```
import pandas as pd
hr_data = pd.read_csv('data/hr.csv', header=0)
hr_data.head()
hr_data = hr_data.dropna()
print(hr_data.shape)
print(list(hr_data.columns))
#Binning satisfaction level:
cut_points = [0.3,0.6]
labels = ["low","medium","high"]
hr_data["satisfaction_level"] = bins(hr_data["satisfaction_level"],
cut_points, labels)
print('\n####The number of values in each bin
are:###\n\n',pd.value_counts(hr_data["satisfaction_level"], sort=False))
```

Once we execute the preceding code, we can observe from the following results that the three bins were created for the satisfaction_level attribute, with 1941 values in the low bin, 4788 in the medium bin, and 8270 in the high bin:

```
(14999, 10)
['satisfaction_level', 'last_evaluation', 'number_project', 'average_montly_hours', 'time_spend_company', 'Work_accid
ent', 'left', 'promotion_last_5years', 'sales', 'salary']
0.09
1.0

####The number of values in each bin are:###

low        1941
medium     4788
high       8270
Name: satisfaction_level, dtype: int64
```

Log and power transformations

The log and power transformation often helps the non-tree-based models by making highly-skewed distributions less skewed. This preprocessing technique helps meet the assumptions of linear regression models and assumptions of inferential statistics. Some examples of this type of transformation includes—log transformation, square root transformation, and log-log transformation.

The following is a demonstration of square root transformation using a dummy dataset:

```
import numpy as np
values = np.array([-4, 6, 68, 46, 89, -25])
# Square root transformation #
sqrt_trnsf_values = np.sqrt(np.abs(values)) * np.sign(values)
print(sqrt_trnsf_values)
```

The following is the output of the preceding square root transformation:

```
[-2.          2.44948974  8.24621125  6.78232998  9.43398113 -5.          ]
```

Next, let us try out a log transformation using another dummy dataset:

```
values = np.array([10, 60, 80, 200])
#log transformation #
log_trnsf_values = np.log(1+values)
print(log_trnsf_values)
```

The log transformation on the dummy dataset yields the following result:

```
[2.39789527 4.11087386 4.39444915 5.30330491]
```

Now that we have a fair idea about different preprocessing methods for numerical data, let's see what there is in store for the categorical data.

Categorical data transformation

Categorical data in nature is non-parametric. This means that it doesn't follow any data distributions. However, for using those variables in a parametric model they need to be transformed using various encoding methods, missing values are to be replaced, and we can reduce the number of categories using binning techniques.

Encoding

In many practical ML activities, a dataset will contain categorical variables. It is far more appropriate in an enterprise context, where most of the attributes are categorical. These variables have distinct discrete values. For example, the size of an organization can be Small, Medium, or Large, or geographic regions can be such as Americas, Asia Pacific, and Europe. Many ML algorithms, especially tree-based models, can handle this type of data directly.

However, many algorithms do not accept the data directly. Therefore, it is needed to encode these attributes into numerical values for further processing. There are various methods to encode the categorical data. Some extensively used methods are described in the following section:

- **Label encoding**: As the name implies, label encoding converts categorical labels into numerical labels. Label encoding is better suited for the ordinal categorical data. The labels are always in between 0 and n-1, where n is the number of classes.
- **One-hot encoding**: This is also known as dummy coding. In this method, dummy columns are generated for each class of a categorical attribute/predictor. For each dummy predictor, the presence of a value is represented by 1, and its absence is represented by 0.
- **Frequency-based encoding**: In this method, first the frequency is calculated for each class. Then the relative frequency for each class out of the total classes is calculated. This relative frequency is assigned as the encoded values for the attribute's levels.
- **Target mean encoding**: In this method, each class of the categorical predictors is encoded as a function of the mean of the target. This method can only be used in a supervised learning problem where there is a target feature.
- **Binary encoding**: The classes are first transformed to the numerical values. Then these numerical values are changed to their similar binary strings. This is later split into separate columns. Each binary digit becomes an independent column.
- **Hash encoding**: This method is also commonly known as feature hashing. Most of us would be aware of a hash function that is used to map data to a number. This method may assign different classes to the same bucket, but is useful when there are hundreds of categories or classes present for an input feature.

Most of these techniques, along with many others, are also implemented in Python and are available in the package `category_encoders`. You can install the `category_encoders` library using the following command:

```
pip install category_encoders
```

Next, we import the `category_encoders` library as `ce` (a short code that supports using it easily in code). We load the HR attrition dataset and one-hot encode the `salary` attribute:

```
import pandas as pd
import category_encoders as ce
hr_data = pd.read_csv('data/hr.csv', header=0)
hr_data.head()
hr_data = hr_data.dropna()
```

```
print(hr_data.shape)
print(list(hr_data.columns))
onehot_encoder = ce.OneHotEncoder(cols=['salary'])
onehot_df = onehot_encoder.fit_transform(hr_data)
onehot_df.head()
```

We can observe how easy it was to transform the categorical attribute to its corresponding one-hot encoded attributes using the `category_encoders` library:

Out[29]:

	salary_0	salary_1	salary_2	salary_-1
0	1	0	0	0
1	0	1	0	0
2	0	1	0	0
3	1	0	0	0
4	1	0	0	0

Similarly, we use `OrdinalEncoder` to label encode the `salary` data:

```
ordinal_encoder = ce.OrdinalEncoder(cols=['salary'])
ordinal_df = ordinal_encoder.fit_transform(hr_data)
ordinal_df.head(10)
ordinal_df['salary'].value_counts()
```

The preceding code maps the low, medium, and high salary brackets to three numerical values, 0, 1, and 2:

```
Out[30]:  0      7316
          1      6446
          2      1237
          Name: salary, dtype: int64
```

Similarly, you can try out the other categorical encoding methods from `CategoryEncoders`, using the following code snippets, and observe the results:

```
binary_encoder = ce.BinaryEncoder(cols=['salary'])
df_binary = binary_encoder.fit_transform(hr_data)
df_binary.head()

poly_encoder = ce.PolynomialEncoder(cols=['salary'])
df_poly = poly_encoder.fit_transform(hr_data)
df_poly.head()
```

```
helmert_encoder = ce.HelmertEncoder(cols=['salary'])
helmert_df = helmert_encoder.fit_transform(hr_data)
helmert_df.head()
```

The next topic for discussion is the method to deal with missing values for categorical attributes.

Missing values for categorical data transformation

The techniques to assess the missing values remain the same for categorical variables as well. However, some of the imputation techniques are different, and some methods are similar to the numerical missing value treatment methods that were discussed. We will demonstrate the Python code for the techniques that are specific to only categorical missing value treatment:

- **Remove or delete the data**: The process to decide whether to remove the data points that are missing for categorical variables remains the same as we discussed for numerical missing value treatment.
- **Replace missing values with the mode**: As categorical data is non-parametric, unlike numerical data they don't have a mean or median. So, the easiest way to replace missing categorical values is using the mode. The mode is the highest occurring class of a categorical variable. For example, let's assume we have a predictor of three classes: red, green, and blue. Red occurs highest in the dataset with a frequency of 30, followed by green with 20, and blue with 10. Then, missing values can be replaced using red as this has the highest occurrence of the predictor.

We will again utilize the HR attrition dataset to explain the missing value treatment for the categorical attributes. Let's first load the dataset and observe the number of nulls in the dataset:

```
import numpy as np
import pandas as pd
hr_data = pd.read_csv('data/hr.csv', header=0)
print('Nulls in the data set' ,hr_data.isnull().sum())
```

We learn from the following output that the dataset has no missing data from the categorical attributes `sales` and `salary`. So, we will synthetically ingest a few missing values to those features:

```
Nulls in the data set satisfaction_level        0
last_evaluation                 0
number_project                  0
average_montly_hours            0
time_spend_company              0
Work_accident                   0
left                            0
promotion_last_5years           0
sales                           0
salary                          0
dtype: int64
```

We use the following code snippet to replace null for the `sales` value in the `sales` attribute and low with nulls for the `salary` attribute:

```
#As there are no null introduce some nulls by replacing sales in sales
column with NaN
hr_data[['sales']] = hr_data[[ 'sales']].replace('sales', np.NaN)
#As there are no null introduce some nulls by replacing low in salary
column with NaN
hr_data[['salary']] = hr_data[[ 'salary']].replace('low', np.NaN)
print('New nulls in the data set' ,hr_data.isnull().sum())
```

Once we have executed the code, we can find some nulls in the `salary` and `sales` attribute, as shown in the following output:

```
New nulls in the data set satisfaction_level        0
last_evaluation                 0
number_project                  0
average_montly_hours            0
time_spend_company              0
Work_accident                   0
left                            0
promotion_last_5years           0
sales                        4140
salary                       7316
dtype: int64
```

Now, we can replace these nulls with the mode of each column. As we did for numerical missing value imputation, even here we first create a copy of the `hr_data` so that we don't replace the original dataset. Next, we fill the rows with the mode values using the `fillna` method, as described in the following code snippet:

```
#Replace mode for missing values
hr_data_1 = hr_data.copy()
# fill missing values with mode column values
for column in hr_data_1.columns:
  hr_data_1[column].fillna(hr_data_1[column].mode()[0], inplace=True)
# count the number of NaN values in each column
print(hr_data_1.isnull().sum())
print(hr_data_1.head())
```

We can see from the following output that the missing values in the `sales` column are replaced with `technical` and `medium` in the `salary` column:

```
satisfaction_level        0
last_evaluation           0
number_project            0
average_montly_hours      0
time_spend_company        0
Work_accident             0
left                      0
promotion_last_5years     0
sales                     0
salary                    0
dtype: int64
   satisfaction_level  last_evaluation  number_project  average_montly_hours  \
0                0.38             0.53               2                   157
1                0.80             0.86               5                   262
2                0.11             0.88               7                   272
3                0.72             0.87               5                   223
4                0.37             0.52               2                   159

   time_spend_company  Work_accident  left  promotion_last_5years     sales  \
0                   3              0     1                      0  technical
1                   6              0     1                      0  technical
2                   4              0     1                      0  technical
3                   5              0     1                      0  technical
4                   3              0     1                      0  technical

   salary
0  medium
1  medium
2  medium
3  medium
4  medium
```

- **Use a global constant to fill in the missing value**: Similar to that of numerical missing value treatment, we can use a global constant such as AAAA or NA to differentiate the missing values from the rest of the dataset:

```
#Mark global constant for missing values
hr_data_2 = hr_data.copy()
# fill missing values with global constant values
hr_data_2.fillna('AAA', inplace=True)
# count the number of NaN values in each column
print(hr_data_2.isnull().sum())
print(hr_data_2.head())
```

The output of the preceding code yields the following results with missing values replaced with AAA:

```
satisfaction_level        0
last_evaluation           0
number_project            0
average_montly_hours      0
time_spend_company        0
Work_accident             0
left                      0
promotion_last_5years     0
sales                     0
salary                    0
dtype: int64
   satisfaction_level  last_evaluation  number_project  average_montly_hours  \
0                0.38             0.53               2                   157
1                0.80             0.86               5                   262
2                0.11             0.88               7                   272
3                0.72             0.87               5                   223
4                0.37             0.52               2                   159

   time_spend_company  Work_accident  left  promotion_last_5years     sales  \
0                   3              0     1                      0  technical
1                   6              0     1                      0  technical
2                   4              0     1                      0  technical
3                   5              0     1                      0  technical
4                   3              0     1                      0  technical

      salary
0     medium
1     medium
2     medium
3     medium
4     medium
```

- **Using an indicator variable**: Similar to that which we discussed for numerical variables, we can have an indicator variable for identifying the values that were imputed for missing categorical data as well.
- **Use a data mining algorithm to predict the most probable value**: As we did for numerical attributes, we can also use data mining algorithms, such as decision trees, random forest, or KNN methods, to predict the most likely value of a missing value. The same `fancyimpute` library can be used for this task as well.

We have discussed the ways to deal with data preprocessing for structured data. In this digital age, we are capturing a lot of unstructured data, from various sources. In the following section, let's understand the methods to preprocess text data to make it ready for models to consume.

Text preprocessing

It is necessary to reduce the size of the feature space of text data by removing unnecessary text that adds noise to the text during analysis. There are a series of steps that are usually performed to preprocess the text data. However, not all steps are required for each task and they are used whenever necessary. For example, if every word in a text data item is already in lower case, there is no need to modify the case of the text to make it uniform.

There are three main elements of a text preprocessing task:

- Tokenization
- Normalization
- Substitution

We will be using the `nltk` library for demonstrating the different text preprocessing methods. Install the `nltk` library by issuing the following command in the Command Prompt:

```
pip install nltk
```

Once installation is complete, run the following code snippet in the Python environment:

```
##Run this cell only once##
import nltk
nltk.download()
```

You will get a NLTK Downloader popup. Select **all** from the **Identifier** section and wait for installation to be completed.

In this section, we will study some of the preprocessing steps that are employed to preprocess text to produce a normalized form:

1. Tokenization—this is a method to split the text into smaller chunks, such as sentences or words. Also, some text mining tasks such as preparation of Word2Vec model prefer the text to be in a paragraph or sentence style. So, we can use NLTK's `sent_tokenizer` to convert text to sentences. First, we read the text file from the `data` folder using the following code snippet:

```
import pandas as pd
import category_encoders as ce
text_file = open('data/example_text.txt', 'rt')
text = text_file.read()
text_file.close()
```

2. Next, to tokenize the text to sentences, we import the `sent_tokenize` method from the `nltk` library and pass the text as a parameter:

```
## Sentence tokenization ##
from nltk import sent_tokenize
sentence = sent_tokenize(text)
print(sentence[0])
```

The preceding code yields the following output:

```
Data Science sits at the core of any analytical exercise conducted on a Big Data or Internet of Things (IoT ) environ
ment.
```

3. Similarly, some modeling methods, such as a bag-of-words model, need the text to be in an individual word format. For this case, we can use NLTK's `word_tokenizer` method to transform text into words, as shown in the following code snippet:

```
## Word tokenization ##
from nltk import word_tokenize
words = word_tokenize(text)
print(words[:50])
```

4. The following output displays 50 tokenized words from the text. We can see some non-alphabetical characters such as punctuation marks being tokenized. This adds no value to an analytical exercise, so, we need to remove these variables:

```
['Data', 'Science', 'sits', 'at', 'the', 'core', 'of', 'any', 'analytical', 'exercise', 'conducted', 'on', 'a', 'Bi
g', 'Data', 'or', 'Internet', 'of', 'Things', '(', 'IoT', ')', 'environment', '.', 'Data', 'science', 'involves',
'a', 'wide', 'array', 'of', 'technologies', ',', 'business', ',', 'and', 'machine', 'learning', 'algorithms', '.', 'T
he', 'purpose', 'of', 'data', 'science', 'is', 'just', 'not', 'doing', 'machine']
```

5. Non-alphabetical characters such as punctuation don't add any value while preparing a bag-of-words model, so various punctuation and symbols such as .,",+, and ~ can be removed.

   There are various methods using which we can remove the non-alphabetical characters. Now we will illustrate one of the methods in Python:

```
# Remove punctuations and keep only alphabets
words_cleaned = [word for word in words if word.isalpha()]
print(words_cleaned[:50])
```

6. We can see from the following tokens that the undesired symbols such as (are removed from the list of tokens. However, there are some common words such as at and of that add no value to the analysis and can be removed using the stop word removal method:

```
['Data', 'Science', 'sits', 'at', 'the', 'core', 'of', 'any', 'analytical', 'exercise', 'conducted', 'on', 'a', 'Bi
g', 'Data', 'or', 'Internet', 'of', 'Things', 'IoT', 'environment', 'Data', 'science', 'involves', 'a', 'wide', 'arra
y', 'of', 'technologies', 'business', 'and', 'machine', 'learning', 'algorithms', 'The', 'purpose', 'of', 'data', 'sc
ience', 'is', 'just', 'not', 'doing', 'machine', 'learning', 'or', 'statistical', 'analysis', 'but', 'also']
```

7. Stop words are short function words that are used commonly while writing a text document. They might be fillers or prepositions. NLTK provides a standard English stop word collection that can be used to filter the stop words in our text. Also, sometimes, stop words specific to certain domains can be used to eliminate informal words. We can always create a list of words from our text that we feel are not relevant to our analysis.

   For removing the stop words, first we import the stopwords method from the ntlk.corpus library. Then we invoke the english stop word dictionary from the stopwords.words method and remove any common words that are found in the list of tokens:

```
# remove the stop words
from nltk.corpus import stopwords
```

```
stop_words = set(stopwords.words('english'))
words_1 = [word for word in words_cleaned if not word in
stop_words]
print(words_1[:50])
```

8. We can see from the following output that the previously appearing words such as `at` and `the` are removed from the list of tokens. However, a few similar words such as `Data` and `data` are appearing as separate words in the list of tokens. We need to convert these words into a similar case now:

```
['Data', 'Science', 'sits', 'core', 'analytical', 'exercise', 'conducted', 'Big', 'Data', 'Internet', 'Things', 'Io
T', 'environment', 'Data', 'science', 'involves', 'wide', 'array', 'technologies', 'business', 'machine', 'learning',
'algorithms', 'The', 'purpose', 'data', 'science', 'machine', 'learning', 'statistical', 'analysis', 'also', 'deriv
e', 'insights', 'data', 'user', 'statistics', 'knowledge', 'understand', 'In', 'fast', 'paced', 'environment', 'Big',
'Data', 'IoT', 'type', 'data', 'might', 'vary']
```

9. Case folding is a method to convert all words into a similar case to make the words case insensitive. It usually involves converting all uppercase letters to lowercase letters.

We can use the `lower` function to convert all uppercase letters to lower case, as shown in the following code snippet:

```
# Case folding
words_lower = [words_1.lower() for words_1 in words_1]
print(words_lower[:50])
```

We can see from the following output that words such as `Data` no longer appear in the list and are converted to all lowercase letters:

```
['data', 'science', 'sits', 'core', 'analytical', 'exercise', 'conducted', 'big', 'data', 'internet', 'things', 'io
t', 'environment', 'data', 'science', 'involves', 'wide', 'array', 'technologies', 'business', 'machine', 'learning',
'algorithms', 'the', 'purpose', 'data', 'science', 'machine', 'learning', 'statistical', 'analysis', 'also', 'deriv
e', 'insights', 'data', 'user', 'statistics', 'knowledge', 'understand', 'in', 'fast', 'paced', 'environment', 'big',
'data', 'iot', 'type', 'data', 'might', 'vary']
```

Stemming is the process of reducing the words to their base or root form. For example, *worked* and *working* is stemmed to *work*. This transform is useful as it brings all the similar words to a base form that aids in better sentiment analysis, document classification, and much more.

We import `PorterStemmer` from the `nltk.stem.porter` library and instance the `PorterStemmer` class. Next, the `words_lower` token list is passed onto the `porter.stem` class to reduce each word to its root form:

```
#Stemming
from nltk.stem.porter import PorterStemmer
porter = PorterStemmer()
stemmed_words = [porter.stem(word) for word in words_lower]
print(stemmed_words[:50])
```

The preceding code produces the following stemmed list of tokens:

```
['data', 'scienc', 'sit', 'core', 'analyt', 'exercis', 'conduct', 'big', 'data', 'internet', 'thing', 'iot', 'enviro
n', 'data', 'scienc', 'involv', 'wide', 'array', 'technolog', 'busi', 'machin', 'learn', 'algorithm', 'the', 'purpo
s', 'data', 'scienc', 'machin', 'learn', 'statist', 'analysi', 'also', 'deriv', 'insight', 'data', 'user', 'statist',
'knowledg', 'understand', 'in', 'fast', 'pace', 'environ', 'big', 'data', 'iot', 'type', 'data', 'might', 'vari']
```

Not all features or attributes are important for an ML model. In the following sections, we will learn some of the methods to reduce the number of features while working on an ML pipeline.

Feature selection

An ML model uses some critical features to learn patterns in data. All other features add noise to the model, which may lead to a drop in the model's accuracy and overfit the model to the data as well. So, selecting the right features is essential. Also, working a reduced set of important features reduces the model training time.

The following are some of the ways to select the right features prior creating a model:

- We can identify the correlated variables and remove any one of the highly-correlated values
- Remove the features with low variance
- Measure information gain for the available set of features and choose the top N features accordingly

Also, after creating a baseline model, we can use some of the below methods to select the right features:

- Use linear regression and select variables based on p values
- Use stepwise selection for linear regression and select the important variables
- Use random forest and select the top N important variables

In the following sections, we will see some of the ways available in scikit-learn to reduce the number of features available in a dataset.

Excluding features with low variance

Features without much variance or variability in the data do not provide any information to an ML model for learning the patterns. For example, a feature with only 5 as a value for every record in a dataset is a constant and is an unimportant feature to be used. Removing this feature is essential.

We can use the `VarianceThreshold` method from scikit-learn's `featureselection` package to remove all features whose variance doesn't meet certain criteria or threshold. The sklearn.feature_selection module implements feature selection algorithms. It currently includes univariate filter selection methods and the recursive feature elimination algorithm. The following is an example to illustrate this method:

```
%matplotlib inline
import pandas as pd
import numpy as np
from sklearn.feature_selection import SelectKBest
from sklearn.feature_selection import chi2
hr_data = pd.read_csv('data/hr.csv', header=0)
hr_data.head()
hr_data = hr_data.dropna()
data_trnsf = pd.get_dummies(hr_data, columns =['salary', 'sales'])
data_trnsf.columns
```

The output of the preceding code is as follows:

```
Out[10]: Index(['satisfaction_level', 'last_evaluation', 'number_project',
                'average_montly_hours', 'time_spend_company', 'Work_accident', 'left',
                'promotion_last_5years', 'salary_high', 'salary_low', 'salary_medium',
                'sales_IT', 'sales_RandD', 'sales_accounting', 'sales_hr',
                'sales_management', 'sales_marketing', 'sales_product_mng',
                'sales_sales', 'sales_support', 'sales_technical'],
               dtype='object')
```

Next, we assign `left` as a target variable and other attributes as the independent attributes, as shown in the following code:

```
X = data_trnsf.drop('left', axis=1)
X.columns
Y = data_trnsf.left# feature extraction
```

Now that we are ready with the data, we select features based on the `VarianceThreshold` method. First, we import the `VarianceThreshold` method from scikit-learn's `feature_selection` module. Then we set the threshold as `0.2` in the `VarianceThreshold` method. This means that if there is less than 20% variance in data for an attribute, it can be discarded and will not be selected as a feature. We execute the following code snippet to observe the reduced set of features:

```
#Variance Threshold
from sklearn.feature_selection import VarianceThreshold
# Set threshold to 0.2
select_features = VarianceThreshold(threshold = 0.2)
select_features.fit_transform(X)
# Subset features
X_subset = select_features.transform(X)
print('Number of features:', X.shape[1])
print('Reduced number of features:',X_subset.shape[1])
```

From the following output, we can determine that five out of 20 attributes passed the variance threshold test and showed variability, which was more than 20% variance:

```
Number of features: 20
Reduced number of features: 5
```

In the next section, we will study the univariate feature selection method, which is based on certain statistical tests to determine the important features.

Univariate feature selection

In this method, a statistical test is applied to each feature individually. We retain only the best features according to the test outcome scores.

The following example illustrates the chi-squared statistical test to select the best features from the HR attrition dataset:

```
#Chi2 Selector

from sklearn.feature_selection import SelectKBest
from sklearn.feature_selection import chi2

chi2_model = SelectKBest(score_func=chi2, k=4)
X_best_feat = chi2_model.fit_transform(X, Y)
# selected features
```

```
print('Number of features:', X.shape[1])
print('Reduced number of features:',X_best_feat.shape[1])
```

We can see from the following output that 4 best features were selected. We can change the number of best features to be considered by changing the k value:

```
Number of features: 20
Reduced number of features: 4
```

The following section demonstrates the recursive feature elimination method.

Recursive feature elimination

Recursive feature elimination is based on the idea of recursively constructing a model by removing the features, building the model with the remaining features, and computing the model's accuracy. This process is repeated until all features in the dataset are exhausted. It is a greedy optimization method to find the best performing subset of features and then rank them according to when they were eliminated.

In the following example code, the HR attrition dataset is used to illustrate the use of **recursive feature elimination** (**RFE**). The stability of the RFE method is heavily dependent on the type of algorithm used. For our demonstration, we have used the LogisticRegression method:

```
#Recursive Feature Elimination
from sklearn.feature_selection import RFE
from sklearn.linear_model import LogisticRegression

# create a base classifier used to evaluate a subset of attributes
logistic_model = LogisticRegression()

# create the RFE model and select 4 attributes
rfe = RFE(logistic_model, 4)
rfe = rfe.fit(X, Y)

# Ranking of the attributes
print(sorted(zip(map(lambda x: round(x, 4), rfe.ranking_),X)))
```

The following output displays the features sorted by their ranks:

```
[ 1  7  9 17  6  1  1  1  3  8 15  2 12  5  4 13 16 14 11 10]
[(1, 'Work_accident'), (1, 'promotion_last_5years'), (1, 'salary_high'), (1, 'satisfaction_level'), (2, 'sales_Rand
D'), (3, 'salary_low'), (4, 'sales_management'), (5, 'sales_hr'), (6, 'time_spend_company'), (7, 'last_evaluation'),
(8, 'salary_medium'), (9, 'number_project'), (10, 'sales_technical'), (11, 'sales_support'), (12, 'sales_accountin
g'), (13, 'sales_marketing'), (14, 'sales_sales'), (15, 'sales_IT'), (16, 'sales_product_mng'), (17, 'average_montly_
hours')]
```

Random forests are often used in ML pipeline for feature selection. So, it is crucial that we get to know this technique.

Feature selection using random forest

The tree-based feature selection strategies used by random forests naturally rank by how well they improve the purity of the node. First, we need to construct a random forest model. We have already discussed the process to create a random forest model in Chapter 2, *Introduction to Machine Learning using Python*:

```
# Feature Importance
from sklearn.ensemble import RandomForestClassifier
# fit a RandomForest model to the data
model = RandomForestClassifier()
model.fit(X, Y)
# display the relative importance of each attribute
print(model.feature_importances_)
print(sorted(zip(map(lambda x: round(x, 4),
model.feature_importances_),X)))
```

Once the model is constructed successfully, the model's `feature_importance_` attribute is used to visualize the imported features sorted by their rank, as shown in the following results:

```
[(0.001, 'sales_product_mng'), (0.0012, 'sales_marketing'), (0.0014, 'promotion_last_5years'), (0.0015, 'sales_Rand
D'), (0.0015, 'sales_accounting'), (0.0017, 'sales_management'), (0.0019, 'sales_hr'), (0.002, 'sales_IT'), (0.0025,
'sales_support'), (0.0037, 'sales_technical'), (0.0038, 'salary_medium'), (0.0039, 'sales_sales'), (0.0071, 'salary_l
ow'), (0.0073, 'salary_high'), (0.0121, 'Work_accident'), (0.1179, 'last_evaluation'), (0.1187, 'average_montly_hour
s'), (0.1543, 'number_project'), (0.2152, 'time_spend_company'), (0.3413, 'satisfaction_level')]
```

We discussed in this section the different methods to select a subset of features using different feature selection methods. Next, we are going to see the feature selection methods by using dimensionality reduction methods.

Feature selection using dimensionality reduction

Dimensionality reduction methods reduce dimensionality by making new synthetic features from a combination of the original features. They are potent techniques and they preserve the variability of the data. One downside of these techniques is the difficulty in interpreting the attributes as they are prepared by combining elements of various attributes.

Principal Component Analysis

Principal Component Analysis (**PCA**) transforms the data in the high-dimensional space to a space of fewer dimensions. Let's consider visualization of a 100-dimensional dataset. It is barely possible to efficiently show the shape of such high-dimensional data distribution. PCA provides an efficient way to reduce the dimensionality by forming various principal components that explain the variability of the data in a reduced dimensional space.

Mathematically, given a set of variables, $X_1, X_2,...., X_p$, where there are p original variables. In PCA we are looking for a set of new variables, $Z_1, Z_2,....,Z_p$, that are weighted averages of the original variables (after subtracting their mean):

$$Z_p = a_{i,1}(X_1 - X_1^-) + a_{i,2}(X_2 - X_2^-)+...+a_{i,p}(X_p - X_p^-)$$

$$i = 1,...,p$$

Where each pair of Z's has correlation =0

The resulting Z's are ordered by their variance, with Z_1 having the largest variance and Z_p having the smallest variance.

Always, the first component extracted in a PCA accounts for a maximum amount of total variance in the observed variables. The second component extracted will account for a maximal amount of variance in the dataset that was not accounted for by the first component and it is also uncorrelated with the first component. If we compute the correlation between the first component and second component the correlation would be zero.

We use the HR attrition data to demonstrate the use of PCA. First, we load the numpy and pandas library to the environment and load the HR dataset:

```
import numpy as np
import pandas as pd
hr_data = pd.read_csv('data/hr.csv', header=0)
```

```
print (hr_data.head())
```

The following is the output of the preceding code, which displays the first five rows of each attribute in the dataset:

```
   satisfaction_level  last_evaluation  number_project  average_montly_hours  \
0                0.38             0.53               2                   157
1                0.80             0.86               5                   262
2                0.11             0.88               7                   272
3                0.72             0.87               5                   223
4                0.37             0.52               2                   159

   time_spend_company  Work_accident  left  promotion_last_5years  sales  \
0                   3              0     1                      0  sales
1                   6              0     1                      0  sales
2                   4              0     1                      0  sales
3                   5              0     1                      0  sales
4                   3              0     1                      0  sales

   salary
0     low
1  medium
2  medium
3     low
4     low
```

PCA is well suited for numeric attributes and works well when the attributes are standardized. So, we import `StandardScaler` from the `sklearn.preprocessing` library. We include only the numeric attributes for the data preprocessing. Using the `StandardScaler` method, the numeric attributes of the HR dataset are standardized:

```
from sklearn.preprocessing import StandardScaler
hr_numeric = hr_data.select_dtypes(include=[np.float])
hr_numeric_scaled = StandardScaler().fit_transform(hr_numeric)
```

Next, we import the `PCA` method from `sklearn.decomposition` and pass `n_components` as 2. The `n_components` parameter defines the number of principal components to be built. Then, the variance explained by these two principal components is determined:

```
from sklearn.decomposition import PCA
pca = PCA(n_components=2)
principalComponents = pca.fit_transform(hr_numeric_scaled)
principalDf = pd.DataFrame(data = principalComponents, columns = ['principal
component 1', 'principal component 2'])
print(pca.explained_variance_ratio_)
```

We can see that the two principal components explain the variability of the HR dataset's numerical attributes:

```
[0.55251061 0.44748939]
```

Sometimes, the raw data that we use doesn't have enough information that can create a good model. In such cases, we need to create features. In the following section, we will describe a few different methods to create features.

Feature generation

Creating new features out of the existing features is an art and it can be done in many different ways.

The objective of feature creation is to provide ML algorithms with such predictors that makes it easy for them to understand the patterns and derive better relationship from the data.

For example, in HR attrition problems, the duration of stay of an employee in an organization is an important attribute. However, sometimes we don't have the duration of stay as a feature in the dataset, but we have the employee start date. In such cases, we can create the data for the duration of stay feature by subtracting the employee start date from the current date.

In the following sections, we will see some of the different ways to generate new features out of the data. However, this is not an extensive list, but a few different methods that can be employed to create new features. One needs to think through the problem statement, explore the data, and be creative to discover new ways to build features:

- **Numerical feature generation**: Generating new features out of numerical data is somewhat easier than other data types. Even if we don't understand the meaning of various numerical features, we can do various kinds of operations, such as adding two or more numbers, computing the relative differences, and multiplying and dividing the numbers. After this task, we identify what are the important features out of all generated features and discard the others. Though it is a resource intensive task, it helps to discover new features when we are unaware of direct methods to derive new features.

The process of adding and computing differences between a pair of numerical features is known as **pairwise feature creation**.

There is another method known as `PolynomialFeatures` creation, where we automatically perform all polynomial combinations of the features. It helps to map complex relationships between the features that can suggest some unique states.

We can generate polynomial features using scikit-learn's `PolynomialFeatures` method. Let's first create dummy data, as shown in the following code snippet:

```
#Import PolynomialFeatures
from sklearn.preprocessing import PolynomialFeatures
#Create matrix and vectors
var1 = [[0.45, 0.72], [0.12, 0.24]]
```

Next, generate polynomial features by first invoking the `PolynomialFeatures` with a parameter degree. The function will generate features with degrees less than or equal to the specified degree:

```
# Generate Polynomial Features
ploy_features = PolynomialFeatures(degree=2)
var1_ = ploy_features.fit_transform(var1)
print(var1_)
```

After the code execution is completed, it generates new features, as shown in the following screenshot:

```
[[1.      0.45    0.72    0.2025 0.324   0.5184]
 [1.      0.12    0.24    0.0144 0.0288 0.0576]]
```

- **Categorical feature creation**: There are limited ways to create new features out of the categorical data. However, we can compute the frequency of each categorical attribute or combine different variables to build new features.
- **Temporal feature creation**: If we encounter a date/time feature, we can derive various new features, such as the following:
    - Day of the week
    - Day of the month
    - Day of the quarter
    - Day of the year
    - Hour of the day

- Second of the day
- Week of the day
- Week of the year
- Month of the year

Creating these features out of a single data/time feature will assist the ML algorithm to better learn the temporal patterns in data.

Summary

In this chapter, we learned about various data transformations and preprocessing methods that are very much relevant in a machine learning pipeline. Preparing the attributes, cleaning the data, and making sure that the data is error free ensures that ML models learn the data correctly. Making the data noise free and generating good features assists a ML model in discovering the patterns in data efficiently.

The next chapter will focus on the techniques to AutoML algorithms. We will discuss various algorithm-specific feature transformations, automating supervised and unsupervised learning, and much more.

4
Automated Algorithm Selection

This chapter offers a glimpse into the vast landscape of **machine learning** (**ML**) algorithms. A bird's-eye view will show you the kind of learning problems that you can tackle with ML, which you have already learned. Let's briefly review them.

If examples/observations in your dataset have associated labels, then these labels can provide guidance to algorithms during model training. Having this guidance or supervision, you will use supervised or semi-supervised learning algorithms. If you don't have labels, you will use unsupervised learning algorithms.

There are other cases that require different approaches, such as reinforcement learning, but, in this chapter, the main focus will be on supervised and unsupervised algorithms.

The next frontier in ML pipelines is automation. When you first think about automating ML pipelines, the core elements are feature transformation, model selection, and hyperparameter optimization. However, there are some other points that you need to consider for your specific problem and you will examine the following points throughout this chapter:

- Computational complexity
- Differences in training and scoring time
- Linearity versus non-linearity
- Algorithm-specific feature transformations

Understanding these will help you to understand which algorithms may suit your needs for a given problem. By the end of this chapter:

- You will have learned the basics of automated supervised learning and unsupervised learning
- You will have learned the main aspects to consider when working with ML pipelines
- You will have practiced your skills on various use cases and built supervised and unsupervised ML pipelines

Technical requirements

Check the `requirements.txt` file for libraries to be installed to run code examples in GitHub for this chapter.

All the code examples can be found in the `Chapter 04` folder in GitHub.

Computational complexity

Computational efficiency and complexity are important aspects of choosing ML algorithms, since they will dictate the resources needed for model training and scoring in terms of time and memory requirements.

For example, a compute-intensive algorithm will require a longer time to train and optimize its hyperparameters. You will usually distribute the workload among available CPUs or GPUs to reduce the amount of time spent to acceptable levels.

In this section, some algorithms will be examined in terms of these constraints but, before getting into deeper details of ML algorithms, you need to know the basics of the complexity of an algorithm.

 The complexity of an algorithm will be based on its input size. For ML algorithms, this could be the number of elements and features. You will usually count the number of operations needed to complete the task in the worst-case scenario and that will be your algorithm's complexity.

Big O notation

You have probably heard of big O notation. It has different classes for indicating complexity such as linear—$O(n)$, logarithmic—$O(\log n)$, quadratic—$O(n2)$, cubic—$O(n3)$, and similar classes. The reason you use big O is because the runtime of algorithms is highly dependent on the hardware and you need a systematic way of measuring the performance of an algorithm based on the size of its input. Big O looks at the steps of an algorithm and figures out the worst-case scenario as mentioned.

For example, if n is the number of elements that you would like to append to a list, its complexity is O(n), because the number of appended operations depends on the n. The following code block will help you to plot how different complexities grow as a function of their input size:

```python
# Importing necessary libraries
import pandas as pd
import numpy as np
import matplotlib.pyplot as plt
import seaborn as sns

# Setting the style of the plot
plt.style.use('seaborn-whitegrid')

# Creating an array of input sizes
n = 10
x = np.arange(1, n)

# Creating a pandas data frame for popular complexity classes
df = pd.DataFrame({'x': x,
                   'O(1)': 0,
                   'O(n)': x,
                   'O(log_n)': np.log(x),
                   'O(n_log_n)': n * np.log(x),
                   'O(n2)': np.power(x, 2), # Quadratic
                   'O(n3)': np.power(x, 3) }) # Cubic

# Creating labels
labels = ['$O(1) - Constant$',
          '$O(\log{}n) - Logarithmic$',
          '$O(n) - Linear$',
          '$O(n^2) - Quadratic$',
          '$O(n^3) - Cubic$',
          '$O(n\log{}n) - N log n$']

# Plotting every column in dataframe except 'x'
for i, col in enumerate(df.columns.drop('x')):
    print(labels[i], col)
    plt.plot(df[col], label=labels[i])

# Adding a legend
plt.legend()

# Limiting the y-axis
plt.ylim(0,50)

plt.show()
```

We get the following plot as the output of the preceding code:

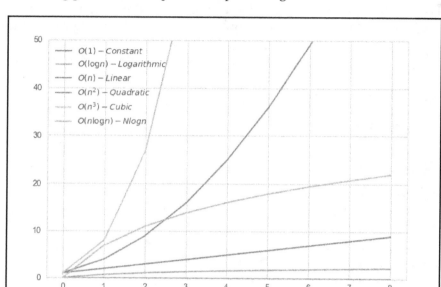

Different complexities grow as a function of their input size

One thing to note here is that there are some crossover points between different levels of complexities. This shows the role of data size. It's easy to understand the complexity of simple examples, but what about the complexity of ML algorithms? If the introduction so far has already piqued your interest, continue reading the next section.

Differences in training and scoring time

Time spent for training and scoring can make or break a ML project. If an algorithm takes too long to train on currently available hardware, updating the model with new data and hyperparameter optimization will be painful, which may force you to cross that algorithm out from your candidate list. If an algorithm takes too long to score, then this is probably a problem in the production environment since your application may require fast inference times such as milliseconds or microseconds to get predictions. That's why it's important to learn the inner workings of ML algorithms, at least the common ones at first, to sense-check algorithms suitability.

For example, supervised learning algorithms learn the relationship between sets of examples and their associated labels the during training process, where each example consists of a set of features. A training job will output an ML model upon successful completion, which can be used to make new predictions. When a model is fed with new examples without a label, relationships that are mapped between features and the labels during training are used to predict the label. Time spent for predicting is usually small, since the learned weights of the model will be applied to new data.

However, some supervised algorithms skip this training phase and they score based on all the available examples in the training dataset. Such algorithms are called **instance-based** or **lazy learners**. For instance-based algorithms, training simply means storing all feature vectors and their associated labels in memory, which is whole training dataset. This practically means that as you increase the size of your dataset, your model will require more compute and memory resources.

Simple measure of training and scoring time

Let's see a quick example of the **k-nearest neighbor (k-NN)** algorithm, which works both for classification and regression problems. When an algorithm scores a new feature vector, it checks the k nearest neighbors and outputs a result. If it's a classification problem, a prediction is made using a majority vote; if it's a regression problem, then the average of the values is used as a prediction.

Let's understand this better by working on an example classification problem. First, you will create a sample dataset and you will examine the k-NN algorithm in terms of time spent for training and scoring.

Just to make things easier, the following function will be used to measure the time spent on a given line:

```
from contextlib import contextmanager
from time import time

@contextmanager
def timer():
    s = time()
    yield
    e = time() - s
    print("{0}: {1} ms".format('Elapsed time', e))
```

You can use this function in the following way:

```
import numpy as np

with timer():
    X = np.random.rand(1000)
```

It outputs the time spent executing that line:

```
Elapsed time: 0.0001399517059326172 ms
```

Now, you can work with KNeighborsClassifier of the scikit-learn library and measure the time spent for training and scoring:

```
from sklearn.neighbors import KNeighborsClassifier

# Defining properties of dataset
nT = 100000000 # Total number of values in our dataset
nF = 10 # Number of features
nE = int(nT / nF) # Number of examples

# Creating n x m matrix where n=100 and m=10
X = np.random.rand(nT).reshape(nE, nF)

# This will be a binary classification with labels 0 and 1
y = np.random.randint(2, size=nE)

# Data that we are going to score
scoring_data = np.random.rand(nF).reshape(1,-1)

# Create KNN classifier
knn = KNeighborsClassifier(11, algorithm='brute')

# Measure training time
with timer():
    knn.fit(X, y)

# Measure scoring time
with timer():
    knn.predict(scoring_data)
```

Let's see the output:

```
Elapsed time: 1.0800271034240723 ms
Elapsed time: 0.43231201171875 ms
```

Just to have an idea about how this compares to other algorithms, you can try one more classifier, such as logistic regression:

```
from sklearn.linear_model import LogisticRegression
log_res = LogisticRegression(C=1e5)

with timer():
    log_res.fit(X, y)

with timer():
    prediction = log_res.predict(scoring_data)
```

The output for logistic regression is as follows:

```
Elapsed time: 12.989803075790405 ms
Elapsed time: 0.00024318695068359375 ms
```

It looks quite different! Logistic regression is slower in training and much faster in scoring. Why is that?

You will learn the answer to that question but, before getting into the details of the preceding results, let's talk a little about code profiling in Python.

Code profiling in Python

Some applications will require your machine learning models to be performant in terms of training and scoring time. For example, a recommender engine might require you to generate recommendations in less than a second and if you have more than a second latency, profiling is one way to understand intensive operations. Code profiling will help you a lot to understand how different parts of your program are executed. Profiling stats will give metrics, such as the number of calls, the total time spent to execute a function call including/excluding calls to its sub-functions, and incremental and total memory usage.

The cProfile module in Python will help you to see time statistics for every function. Here's a small example:

```
# cProfile
import cProfile

cProfile.run('np.std(np.random.rand(1000000))')
```

In the previous line, standard deviation is calculated for 1,000,000 random samples that are drawn from uniform distribution. The output will show time statistics for all the function calls to execute a given line:

```
 23 function calls in 0.025 seconds
    Ordered by: standard name
    ncalls tottime percall cumtime percall filename:lineno(function)
         1 0.001 0.001 0.025 0.025 <string>:1(<module>)
         1 0.000 0.000 0.007 0.007 _methods.py:133(_std)
         1 0.000 0.000 0.000 0.000 _methods.py:43(_count_reduce_items)
         1 0.006 0.006 0.007 0.007 _methods.py:86(_var)
         1 0.001 0.001 0.008 0.008 fromnumeric.py:2912(std)
         2 0.000 0.000 0.000 0.000 numeric.py:534(asanyarray)
         1 0.000 0.000 0.025 0.025 {built-in method builtins.exec}
         2 0.000 0.000 0.000 0.000 {built-in method builtins.hasattr}
         4 0.000 0.000 0.000 0.000 {built-in method builtins.isinstance}
         2 0.000 0.000 0.000 0.000 {built-in method builtins.issubclass}
         1 0.000 0.000 0.000 0.000 {built-in method builtins.max}
         2 0.000 0.000 0.000 0.000 {built-in method
numpy.core.multiarray.array}
         1 0.000 0.000 0.000 0.000 {method 'disable' of '_lsprof.Profiler'
objects}
         1 0.017 0.017 0.017 0.017 {method 'rand' of 'mtrand.RandomState'
objects}
         2 0.001 0.001 0.001 0.001 {method 'reduce' of 'numpy.ufunc'
objects}
```

23 function calls are executed in 0.025 seconds and most of the time is spent generating random numbers and calculating the standard deviation, as you would expect.

There is a great library called snakeviz that can be used to visualize cProfile output. Create a file named profiler_example_1.py and add the following code:

```
import numpy as np

np.std(np.random.rand(1000000))
```

In your terminal, navigate to the folder where you have your profiler_example_1.py and run the following command:

```
python -m cProfile -o profiler_output -s cumulative profiler_example_1.py
```

This will create a file called profiler_output and you can now use snakeviz to create a visualization

Visualizing performance statistics

Snakeviz is browser based and it will allow you to interact with performance metrics. `snakeviz` will use the file produced by the profiler named `profiler_output` to create visualizations:

```
snakeviz profiler_output
```

This command is going to run a small web server on `127.0.0.1:8080` and it will provide you the address where you can find your visualization, such as `http://127.0.0.1:8080/snakeviz/.../2FAutomated_Machine_Learning%2FCh4_Au tomated_Algorithm_Selection%2Fprofiler_output`.

Here, you can see the **Sunburst** style chart with various settings, such as **Depth** and **Cutoff**:

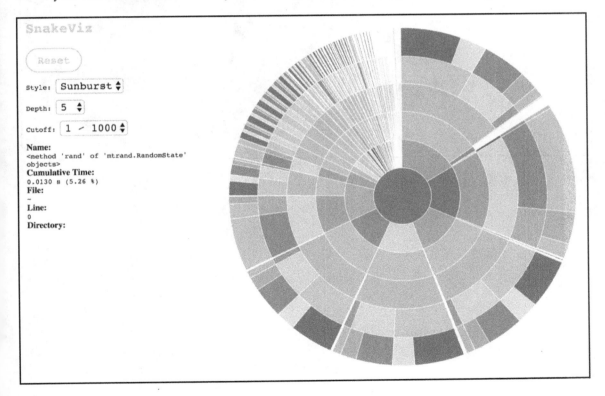

You can hover your mouse over it and it will show you the name of function, cumulative time, file, line, and directory. You can drill down to specific regions and see the details.

If you select the **Icicle** style, you will have a different visualization:

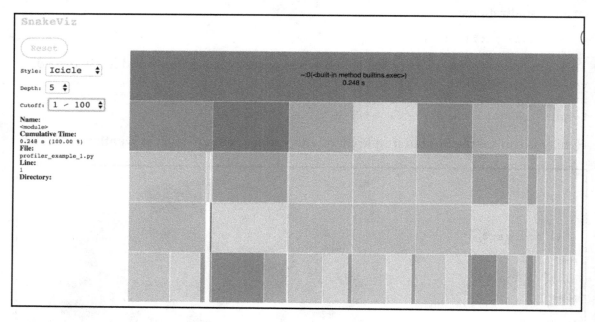

You can play with **Style**, **Depth**, and **Cutoff** to see which settings work best for you.

If you scroll down to the bottom, there will be a table similar to the following screenshot:

ncalls	tottime	percall	cumtime	percall	filename:lineno(function)
1	0.01301	0.01301	0.01301	0.01301	~:0(<method 'rand' of 'mtrand.RandomState' objects>)
19/18	0.09413	0.005229	0.09708	0.005393	~:0(<built-in method _imp.create_dynamic>)
1	0.004191	0.004191	0.005431	0.005431	_methods.py:86(_var)
127/1	0.003218	0.003218	0.2475	0.2475	~:0(<built-in method builtins.exec>)
1	0.000907	0.000907	0.2475	0.2475	profiler_example_1.py:1(<module>)
153/1	0.000865	0.000865	0.2282	0.2282	<frozen importlib._bootstrap>:958(_find_and_load)
141/1	0.000748	0.000748	0.228	0.228	<frozen importlib._bootstrap>:641(_load_unlocked)
153/1	0.000661	0.000661	0.2281	0.2281	<frozen importlib._bootstrap>:931(_find_and_load_unlocked)
2	0.001205	0.0006025	0.001205	0.0006025	~:0(<method 'reduce' of 'numpy.ufunc' objects>)
118/1	0.000446	0.000446	0.2279	0.2279	<frozen importlib._bootstrap_external>:672(exec_module)
1	0.00027	0.00027	0.01092	0.01092	random.py:38(<module>)
1	0.000261	0.000261	0.2273	0.2273	__init__.py:106(<module>)
118	0.02956	0.0002505	0.02956	0.0002505	~:0(<method 'read' of '_io.FileIO' objects>)
1	0.00023	0.00023	0.00023	0.00023	~:0(<function Random.seed at 0x105472510>)
1	0.000224	0.000224	0.000967	0.000967	getlimits.py:3(<module>)
1	0.000221	0.000221	0.001721	0.001721	core.py:21(<module>)
14	0.002977	0.0002126	0.002977	0.0002126	~:0(<built-in method posix.listdir>)

If you sort these values according to the `percall` column, you will see that the `rand` method of `mtrand.RandomState` objects and the `_var` method are among the most time-consuming calls.

You can examine anything that you run this way and this is a good first step to better understand and diagnose your code.

Implementing k-NN from scratch

You have already seen the k-NN algorithm in action; let's look at a very simple implementation. Save the following code block as `knn_prediction.py`:

```
import numpy as np
import operator

# distance module includes various distance functions
# You will use euclidean distance function to calculate distances between
scoring input and training dataset.
from scipy.spatial import distance
```

```
# Decorating function with @profile to get run statistics
@profile
def nearest_neighbors_prediction(x, data, labels, k):

    # Euclidean distance will be calculated between example to be predicted
and examples in data
    distances = np.array([distance.euclidean(x, i) for i in data])

    label_count = {}
    for i in range(k):
        # Sorting distances starting from closest to our example
        label = labels[distances.argsort()[i]]
        label_count[label] = label_count.get(label, 0) + 1
    votes = sorted(label_count.items(), key=operator.itemgetter(1),
reverse=True)

    # Return the majority vote
    return votes[0][0]

# Setting seed to make results reproducible
np.random.seed(23)

# Creating dataset, 20 x 5 matrix which means 20 examples with 5 features
for each
data = np.random.rand(100).reshape(20,5)

# Creating labels
labels = np.random.choice(2, 20)

# Scoring input
x = np.random.rand(5)

# Predicting class for scoring input with k=2
pred = nearest_neighbors_prediction(x, data, labels, k=2)
# Output is '0' in my case
```

You will profile this function to see how long it takes for each line to execute.

Profiling your Python script line by line

Go to your Terminal and run the following command:

```
$ pip install line_profiler
```

Once installation is finished, you can save the preceding snippet to a filename
`knn_prediction.py`.

As you have noticed, `nearest_neighbors_prediction` is decorated as follows:

```
@profile
def nearest_neighbors_prediction(x, data, labels, k):
    ...
```

It allows `line_profiler` to know which function to profile. Run the following command to save the profile results:

```
$ kernprof -l knn_prediction.py
```

The output will be as follows:

```
Start
Wrote profile results to knn_prediction.py.lprof
```

You can view the profiler results as follows:

```
$ python -m line_profiler knn_prediction.py.lprof
Timer unit: 1e-06 s

Total time: 0.001079 s
File: knn_prediction.py
Function: nearest_neighbors_prediction at line 24

Line # Hits Time Per Hit % Time Line Contents
==============================================================
    24 @profile
    25 def nearest_neighbors_prediction(x, data, labels, k):
    26
    27 # Euclidean distance will be calculated between example to be
predicted and examples in data
    28 1 1043.0 1043.0 96.7 distances = np.array([distance.euclidean(x, i)
for i in data])
    29
    30 1 2.0 2.0 0.2 label_count = {}
    31 3 4.0 1.3 0.4 for i in range(k):
    32 # Sorting distances starting from closest to our example
    33 2 19.0 9.5 1.8 label = labels[distances.argsort()[i]]
    34 2 3.0 1.5 0.3 label_count[label] = label_count.get(label, 0) + 1
    35 1 8.0 8.0 0.7 votes = sorted(label_count.items(),
key=operator.itemgetter(1), reverse=True)
    36
    37 # Return the majority vote
    38 1 0.0 0.0 0.0 return votes[0][0]
```

The most time-consuming part is calculating distances, as you would have expected.

In terms of big O notation, the complexity of the k-NN algorithm is `O(nm + kn)`, where `n` is the number of examples, `m` is the number of features, and `k` is the algorithm's hyperparameter. You can think about the reason as an exercise for now.

Every algorithm has similar properties that you should be aware of that will affect the training and scoring time of algorithms. These limitations become especially important for production use cases.

Linearity versus non-linearity

Another consideration is decision boundaries. Some algorithms, such as logistic regression or **Support Vector Machine** (**SVM**), can learn linear decision boundaries while others, such as tree-based algorithms, can learn non-linear decision boundaries. While linear decision boundaries are relatively easy to calculate and interpret, you should be aware of errors that linear algorithms will generate in the presence of non-linear relationships.

Drawing decision boundaries

The following code snippet will allow you to examine the decision boundaries of different types of algorithms:

```
import matplotlib.cm as cm

# This function will scale training datatset and train given classifier.
# Based on predictions it will draw decision boundaries.

def draw_decision_boundary(clf, X, y, h = .01, figsize=(9,9),
boundary_cmap=cm.winter, points_cmap=cm.cool):

    # After you apply StandardScaler, feature means will be removed and all
features will have unit variance.
    from sklearn.preprocessing import StandardScaler
    X = StandardScaler().fit_transform(X)

    # Splitting dataset to train and test sets.
    X_train, X_test, y_train, y_test = train_test_split(X, y, test_size=.4,
random_state=42)

    # Training given estimator on training dataset by invoking fit
function.
    clf.fit(X_train, y_train)
```

```
# Each estimator has a score function.
# Score will show you estimator's performance by showing metric
suitable to given classifier.
# For example, for linear regression, it will output coefficient of
determination R^2 of the prediction.
# For logistic regression, it will output mean accuracy.

score = clf.score(X_test, y_test)
print("Score: %0.3f" % score)

# Predict function of an estimator, will predict using trained model
pred = clf.predict(X_test)

# Figure is a high-level container that contains plot elements
figure = plt.figure(figsize=figsize)

# In current figure, subplot will create Axes based on given arguments
(nrows, ncols, index)
ax = plt.subplot(1, 1, 1)

# Calculating min/max of axes
x_min, x_max = X[:, 0].min() - 1, X[:, 0].max() + 1
y_min, y_max = X[:, 1].min() - 1, X[:, 1].max() + 1

# Meshgrid is usually used to evaluate function on grid.
# It will allow you to create points to represent the space you operate
xx, yy = np.meshgrid(np.arange(x_min, x_max, h), np.arange(y_min,
y_max, h))

# Generate predictions for all the point-pair created by meshgrid
Z = clf.predict(np.c_[xx.ravel(), yy.ravel()])
Z = Z.reshape(xx.shape)

# This will draw boundary
ax.contourf(xx, yy, Z, cmap=boundary_cmap)

# Plotting training data
ax.scatter(X_train[:, 0], X_train[:, 1], c=y_train, cmap=points_cmap,
edgecolors='k')

# Potting testing data
ax.scatter(X_test[:, 0], X_test[:, 1], c=y_test, cmap=points_cmap,
alpha=0.6, edgecolors='k')

# Showing your masterpiece
figure.show()
```

Decision boundary of logistic regression

You can start with logistic regression to test this function:

```
import numpy as np
import matplotlib.pyplot as plt
from matplotlib import cm

# sklearn.linear_model includes regression models where target variable is
a linear combination of input variables
from sklearn.linear_model import LogisticRegression

# make_moons is another useful function to generate sample data
from sklearn.datasets import make_moons
from sklearn.model_selection import train_test_split

X, y = make_moons(n_samples=1000, noise=0.1, random_state=0)

# Plot sample data
plt.scatter(X[:,0], X[:,1], c=y, cmap=cm.cool)
plt.show()
```

We get the following plot:

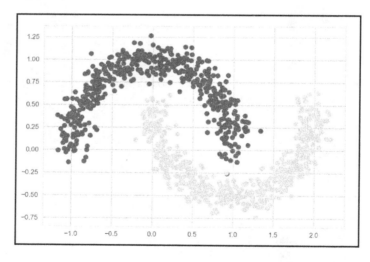

Now, you can use the `draw_decision_boundary` function to visualize the decision boundary for `LogisticRegression`:

```
draw_decision_boundary(LogisticRegression(), X, y)
```

It will output the following plot:

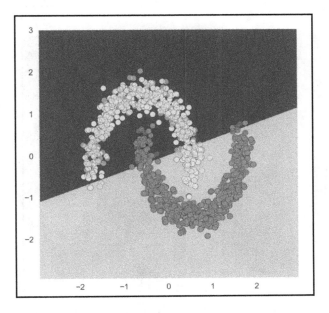

Logistic regression is a member of the generalized linear models and it produces a linear decision boundary. A linear decision boundary is not able to separate classes for such datasets. Logistic regression's output is calculated based on the weighted sum of its inputs. Since output doesn't depend on the product or quotient of its parameters, it will produce a linear decision boundary. There are ways to overcome this problem, such as regularization and feature mapping, but you can use other algorithms in such cases that are able to work with non-linear data.

The decision boundary of random forest

Random forest is a meta estimator, that will build many different models and aggregate their predictions to come up with a final prediction. Random forest is able to produce non-linear decision boundaries, since there's no linear relationship between inputs and outputs. It has many hyperparameters to play with but for the sake of simplicity, you will use the default configuration:

```
from sklearn.ensemble import RandomForestClassifier

draw_decision_boundary(RandomForestClassifier(), X, y)
```

We get the following plot from the preceding code:

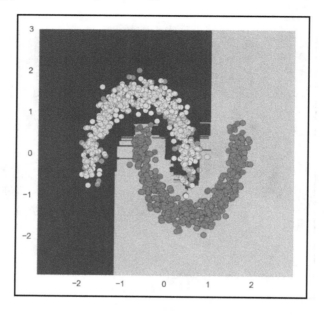

Not looking too bad at all! Every algorithm will provide you with different decision boundaries, based on their inner workings, and you should definitely experiment with different estimators to better understand their behavior.

Commonly used machine learning algorithms

As an exercise, the following is a list of commonly used supervised and unsupervised algorithms; scikit-learn has most of them:

- Supervised algorithms:
    - Linear regression
    - Logistic regression
    - k-NN
    - Random forest
    - Boosting algorithms (GBM, XGBoost, and LightGBM)
    - SVM
    - Neural networks

- Unsupervised algorithms:
  - K-means
  - Hierarchical clustering
  - Principal Component Analysis
  - Mixture models
  - Autoencoders

Necessary feature transformations

As you may have noticed, features are scaled in the previous section before training machine learning algorithms. Feature transformations are usually necessary for ML algorithms to work properly. For example, as a rule of thumb, for ML algorithms that use regularization, normalization is usually applied to features.

The following is a list of use cases where you should transform your features to prepare your dataset to be ready for ML algorithms:

- SVM expects its inputs to be in the standard range. You should normalize your variables before feeding them into the algorithm.
- **Principal Component Analysis (PCA)** helps you to project your features to another space based on variance maximization. You can then select the components cover most of the variance in your dataset, leaving the rest out to reduce dimensionality. When you are working with PCA, you can apply normalization, since some features may seem to explain almost all the variance due to differences in scale. You can eliminate the differences in scale by normalizing your features, as you will see in some examples in the following section.
- If you are working with regularized regression, which is usually the case with high-dimensional datasets, you will normalize your variables to control the scale, since regularization is not scale invariant.
- To work with the Naive Bayes algorithm, where features and label columns are expected to be categorical, you should transform your continuous variables to make them discretized by applying binning.
- In a time series, you usually apply log transformation to deal with exponentially increasing trends in order to have a linear trend and constant variance.
- When working with variables that are not numeric, such as categorical data, you will encode them into numerical features by applying transformations such as one-hot encoding, dummy coding, or feature hashing.

Supervised ML

Apart from feature transformations mentioned in the previous section, each ML algorithm has its own hyperparameter space to be optimized. You can think of searching the best ML pipeline as going through your configuration space and trying out your options in a smart way to find the best performing ML pipeline.

Auto-sklearn is very helpful in achieving that goal and the example that you have seen in the introductory chapter showed you the ease of use of the library. This section will explain what's happening under the hood to make this implementation successful.

Auto-sklearn uses *meta learning* to select promising data/feature processors and ML algorithms based on properties of the given dataset. Please refer to the following links for the list of preprocessing methods, classifiers, and regressors:

- Classifiers (`https://github.com/automl/auto-sklearn/tree/master/autosklearn/pipeline/components/classification`)
- Regressors (`https://github.com/automl/auto-sklearn/tree/master/autosklearn/pipeline/components/regression`)
- Preprocessors (`https://github.com/automl/auto-sklearn/tree/master/autosklearn/pipeline/components/feature_preprocessing`)

Meta learning mimics the experience of data scientists by analyzing the performance of ML pipelines across different datasets and matches those findings with new datasets to make recommendations for initial configurations.

Once meta learning creates an initial configuration, Bayesian optimization will deal with tuning the hyperparameters of different pipelines and top ranking pipelines will be used to create an ensemble that will likely outperform any of its members and also help to avoid over-fitting.

Default configuration of auto-sklearn

When you create an `AutoSklearnClassifier` object, which you will do shortly by the way, there are some default configurations that you need to be aware of; you can see them by running the following code:

```
from autosklearn.classification import AutoSklearnClassifier
AutoSklearnClassifier?
```

In Python, adding ? after a function will output very useful information, such as the signature, docstring, an explanation of the parameters, the attributes, and the file location.

If you look at the signature, you will see the default values:

```
Init signature: AutoSklearnClassifier(time_left_for_this_task=3600,
per_run_time_limit=360, initial_configurations_via_metalearning=25,
ensemble_size=50, ensemble_nbest=50, seed=1, ml_memory_limit=3072,
include_estimators=None, exclude_estimators=None,
include_preprocessors=None, exclude_preprocessors=None,
resampling_strategy='holdout', resampling_strategy_arguments=None,
tmp_folder=None, output_folder=None,
delete_tmp_folder_after_terminate=True,
delete_output_folder_after_terminate=True, shared_mode=False,
disable_evaluator_output=False, get_smac_object_callback=None,
smac_scenario_args=None)
```

For example, `time_left_for_this_task` is set to 60 minutes. If you are working on a rather complex dataset, you should set this parameter to a higher value to increase your chances of finding better ML pipelines.

Another one is `per_run_time_limit`, which is set to six minutes. Many ML algorithms will have their training time proportional to input data size, plus the training time will be affected also by the algorithm's complexity. You should set this parameter accordingly.

`ensemble_size` and `ensemble_nbest` are ensemble-related parameters that set size and the number of best models to be included in the ensemble.

`ml_memory_limit` is an important parameter since, if your algorithm will need more memory, training will be cancelled.

You can include/exclude specific data preprocessors or estimators in your ML pipeline by providing a list using the following parameters: `include_estimators`, `exclude_estimators`, `include_preprocessors`, and `exclude_preprocessors`

`resampling_strategy` will give you options to decide how to handle overfitting.

You can go through the rest of the parameters in the signature and see if you need to make any specific adjustments to your environment.

Finding the best ML pipeline for product line prediction

Let's write a small wrapper function first to prepare a dataset by encoding categorical variables:

```
# Importing necessary variables
import numpy as np
import pandas as pd
from autosklearn.classification import AutoSklearnClassifier
from autosklearn.regression import AutoSklearnRegressor
from sklearn.model_selection import train_test_split
from sklearn.metrics import accuracy_score
from sklearn.preprocessing import LabelEncoder
import wget
import pandas as pd

# Machine learning algorithms work with numerical inputs and you need to
transform all non-numerical inputs to numerical ones
# Following snippet encode the categorical variables

link_to_data =
'https://apsportal.ibm.com/exchange-api/v1/entries/8044492073eb964f46597b4b
e06ff5ea/data?accessKey=9561295fa407698694b1e254d0099600'
filename = wget.download(link_to_data)

print(filename)
# GoSales_Tx_NaiveBayes.csv

df = pd.read_csv('GoSales_Tx_NaiveBayes.csv')
df.head()
```

This will output the first five records of the DataFrame:

```
# PRODUCT_LINE GENDER AGE MARITAL_STATUS PROFESSION
# 0 Personal Accessories M 27 Single Professional
# 1 Personal Accessories F 39 Married Other
# 2 Mountaineering Equipment F 39 Married Other
# 3 Personal Accessories F 56 Unspecified Hospitality
# 4 Golf Equipment M 45 Married Retired
```

There are four features (GENDER, AGE, MARITAL_STATUS, and PROFESSION) and one label (PRODUCT_LINE) column in this dataset. Goal is to predict the product line that customers will be interested in.

You will need to encode textual data both for features and the label. You can apply
`LabelEncoder`:

```
df = df.apply(LabelEncoder().fit_transform)
df.head()
```

This will encode the `label` column:

```
#    PRODUCT_LINE GENDER AGE MARITAL_STATUS PROFESSION
# 0  4 1 27 1 3
# 1  4 0 39 0 2
# 2  2 0 39 0 2
# 3  4 0 56 2 1
# 4  1 1 45 0 5
```

As you can see, all categorical columns are encoded. Keep in mind that, in auto-sklearn's
API, you have the `feat_type` argument that allows you to specify columns either as
`Categorical` or `Numerical`:

```
feat_type : list, optional (default=None)
```

List of `str` of `len(X.shape[1])` describing the attribute type. Possible types are
`Categorical` and `Numerical`. Categorical attributes will be automatically one-hot
encoded. The values used for a categorical attribute must be integers obtained, for example,
by `sklearn.preprocessing.LabelEncoder`.

However, you can also use the `apply` function of the pandas DataFrame in this example.

The following wrapper functions will process input data and run experiments using auto-
classification or auto-regression algorithms of auto-sklearn:

```
# Function below will encode the target variable if needed
def encode_target_variable(df=None, target_column=None, y=None):

    # Below section will encode target variable if given data is pandas
dataframe
    if df is not None:
        df_type = isinstance(df, pd.core.frame.DataFrame)

        # Splitting dataset as train and test data sets
        if df_type:

            # If column data type is not numeric then labels are encoded
            if not np.issubdtype(df[target_column].dtype, np.number):
                le = preprocessing.LabelEncoder()
                df[target_column] = le.fit_transform(df[target_column])
```

```
                    return df[target_column]

            return df[target_column]
    # Below section will encode numpy array.
    else:

        # numpy array's data type is not numeric then labels are encoded
        if not np.issubdtype(y.dtype, np.number):
            le = preprocessing.LabelEncoder()
            y = le.fit_transform(y)
            return y

        return y


# Create a wrapper function where you can specify the type of learning
problem
def supervised_learner(type, X_train, y_train, X_test, y_test):

    if type == 'regression':
        # You can play with time related arguments for discovering more
pipelines
        automl = AutoSklearnRegressor(time_left_for_this_task=7200,
per_run_time_limit=720)
    else:
        automl = AutoSklearnClassifier(time_left_for_this_task=7200,
per_run_time_limit=720)

    # Training estimator based on learner type
    automl.fit(X_train, y_train)

    # Predicting labels on test data
    y_hat = automl.predict(X_test)

    # Calculating accuracy_score
    metric = accuracy_score(y_test, y_hat)

    # Return model, labels and metric
    return automl, y_hat, metric

# In function below, you need to provide numpy array or pandas dataframe
together with the name of the target column as arguments
def supervised_automl(data, target_column=None, type=None, y=None):

    # First thing is to check whether data is pandas dataframe
    df_type = isinstance(data, pd.core.frame.DataFrame)

    # Based on data type, you will split dataset as train and test data
```

```
sets
    if df_type:
        # This is where encode_target_variable function is used before data
split
        data[target_column] = encode_target_variable(data, target_column)
        X_train, X_test, y_train, y_test = \
            train_test_split(data.loc[:, data.columns != target_column],
data[target_column], random_state=1)
    else:
        y_encoded = encode_target_variable(y=y)
        X_train, X_test, y_train, y_test = train_test_split(X, y_encoded,
random_state=1)

    # If learner type is given, then you invoke supervied_learner
    if type != None:
        automl, y_hat, metric = supervised_learner(type, X_train, y_train,
X_test, y_test)

    # If type of learning problem is not given, you need to infer it
    # If there are more than 10 unique numerical values, problem will be
treated as regression problem,
    # Otherwise, classification problem

    elif len(df[target_column].unique()) > 10:
            print("""There are more than 10 uniques numerical values in
target column.
            Treating it as regression problem.""")
            automl, y_hat, metric = supervised_learner('regression',
X_train, y_train, X_test, y_test)
    else:
            automl, y_hat, metric = supervised_learner('classification',
X_train, y_train, X_test, y_test)

    # Return model, labels and metric
    return automl, y_hat, metric
```

You can now run it to see the results:

```
automl, y_hat, metric = supervised_automl(df, target_column='PRODUCT_LINE')
```

The following output shows the selected model with its parameters:

```
automl.get_models_with_weights()
  [(1.0,
   SimpleClassificationPipeline({'balancing:strategy': 'none',
'categorical_encoding:__choice__': 'no_encoding', 'classifier:__choice__':
'gradient_boosting', 'imputation:strategy': 'most_frequent',
'preprocessor:__choice__': 'feature_agglomeration', 'rescaling:__choice__':
```

```
  'robust_scaler', 'classifier:gradient_boosting:criterion': 'friedman_mse',
  'classifier:gradient_boosting:learning_rate': 0.6019977814828193,
  'classifier:gradient_boosting:loss': 'deviance',
  'classifier:gradient_boosting:max_depth': 5,
  'classifier:gradient_boosting:max_features': 0.4884281825655421,
  'classifier:gradient_boosting:max_leaf_nodes': 'None',
  'classifier:gradient_boosting:min_impurity_decrease': 0.0,
  'classifier:gradient_boosting:min_samples_leaf': 20,
  'classifier:gradient_boosting:min_samples_split': 7,
  'classifier:gradient_boosting:min_weight_fraction_leaf': 0.0,
  'classifier:gradient_boosting:n_estimators': 313,
  'classifier:gradient_boosting:subsample': 0.3242201709371377,
  'preprocessor:feature_agglomeration:affinity': 'cosine',
  'preprocessor:feature_agglomeration:linkage': 'complete',
  'preprocessor:feature_agglomeration:n_clusters': 383,
  'preprocessor:feature_agglomeration:pooling_func': 'mean',
  'rescaling:robust_scaler:q_max': 0.75, 'rescaling:robust_scaler:q_min':
  0.25},
    dataset_properties={
      'task': 1,
      'sparse': False,
      'multilabel': False,
      'multiclass': False,
      'target_type': 'classification',
      'signed': False})))]
```

You may see that a gradient-boosting algorithm is usually selected, and this is for a good reason. Currently, in the ML community, boosting-based algorithms are state-of-the-art and the most popular ones are **XGBoost**, **LightGBM**, and **CatBoost**.

Auto-sklearn offers support for the `GradientBoostingClassifier` of sklearn and XGBoost is currently disabled due to integration problems, but it's expected to be added back soon.

Finding the best machine learning pipeline for network anomaly detection

Let's run this pipeline on another dataset that is popular in the ML community. KDDCUP 99 dataset is tcpdump portions of the 1998 DARPA Intrusion Detection System Evaluation dataset and goal is to detect network intrusions. It includes numerical features hence it will be easier to set-up our AutoML pipeline:

```
# You can import this dataset directly from sklearn
from sklearn.datasets import fetch_kddcup99
```

```
# Downloading subset of whole dataset
dataset = fetch_kddcup99(subset='http', shuffle=True, percent10=True)
# Downloading https://ndownloader.figshare.com/files/5976042
# [INFO] [17:43:19:sklearn.datasets.kddcup99] Downloading
https://ndownloader.figshare.com/files/5976042

X = dataset.data
y = dataset.target

# 58725 examples with 3 features
X.shape
# (58725, 3)

y.shape
(58725,)

# 5 different classes to represent network anomaly
from pprint import pprint
pprint(np.unique(y))
# array([b'back.', b'ipsweep.', b'normal.', b'phf.', b'satan.'],
dtype=object)

automl, y_hat, metric = supervised_automl(X, y=y, type='classification')
```

Unsupervised AutoML

When your dataset doesn't have a target variable, you can use clustering algorithms to explore it, based on different characteristics. These algorithms group examples together, so that each group will have examples as similar as possible to each other, but dissimilar to examples in other groups.

Since you mostly don't have labels when you are performing such analysis, there is a performance metric that you can use to examine the quality of the resulting separation found by the algorithm.

It is called the **Silhouette Coefficient**. The Silhouette Coefficient will help you to understand two things:

- **Cohesion**: Similarity within clusters
- **Separation**: Dissimilarity among clusters

It will give you a value between 1 and -1, with values close to 1 indicating well-formed clusters.

If you have labels in your training data, you can also use other metrics, such as homogenity and completeness, which you will see later in the chapter.

Clustering algorithms are used to tackle many different tasks such as finding similar users, songs, or images, detecting key trends and changes in patterns, understanding community structures in social networks.

Commonly used clustering algorithms

There are two types of commonly used clustering algorithms: distance-based and probabilistic models. For example, k-means and **Density-Based Spatial Clustering of Applications with Noise (DBSCAN)** are distance-based algorithms, whereas the Gaussian mixture model is probabilistic.

Distance-based algorithms may use a variety of distance measures where Euclidean distance metrics are usually used.

Probabilistic algorithms will assume that there is a generative process with a mixture of probability distributions with unknown parameters and the goal is to calculate these parameters from the data.

Since there are many clustering algorithms, picking the right one depends on the characteristics of your data. For example, k-means will work with centroids of clusters and this requires clusters in your data to be evenly sized and convexly shaped. This means that k-means will not work well on elongated clusters or irregularly shaped manifolds. When your clusters in your data are not evenly sized or convexly shaped, you many want to use DBSCAN to cluster areas of any shape.

Knowing a thing or two about your data will bring you closer to finding the right algorithms, but what if you don't know much about your data? Many times when you are performing exploratory analysis, it might be hard to get your head around what's happening. If you find yourself in this kind of situation, an automated unsupervised ML pipeline can help you to understand the characteristics of your data better.

Be careful when you perform this kind of analysis, though; the actions you will take later will be driven by the results you will see and this could quickly send you down the wrong path if you are not cautious.

Creating sample datasets with sklearn

In `sklearn`, there are some useful ways to create sample datasets for testing algorithms:

```python
# Importing necessary libraries for visualization
import matplotlib.pyplot as plt
import seaborn as sns

# Set context helps you to adjust things like label size, lines and various
elements
# Try "notebook", "talk" or "paper" instead of "poster" to see how it
changes
sns.set_context('poster')

# set_color_codes will affect how colors such as 'r', 'b', 'g' will be
interpreted
sns.set_color_codes()

# Plot keyword arguments will allow you to set things like size or line
width to be used in charts.
plot_kwargs = {'s': 10, 'linewidths': 0.1}

import numpy as np
import pandas as pd

# Pprint will better output your variables in console for readability
from pprint import pprint


# Creating sample dataset using sklearn samples_generator
from sklearn.datasets.samples_generator import make_blobs
from sklearn.preprocessing import StandardScaler

# Make blobs will generate isotropic Gaussian blobs
# You can play with arguments like center of blobs, cluster standard
deviation
centers = [[2, 1], [-1.5, -1], [1, -1], [-2, 2]]
cluster_std = [0.1, 0.1, 0.1, 0.1]

# Sample data will help you to see your algorithms behavior
X, y = make_blobs(n_samples=1000,
                  centers=centers,
                  cluster_std=cluster_std,
                  random_state=53)
```

```
# Plot generated sample data
plt.scatter(X[:, 0], X[:, 1], **plot_kwargs)
plt.show()
```

We get the following plot from the preceding code:

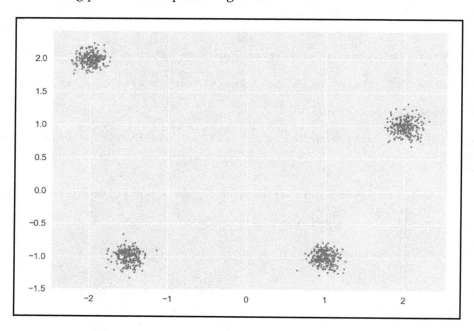

`cluster_std` will affect the amount of dispersion. Change it to `[0.4, 0.5, 0.6, 0.5]` and try again:

```
cluster_std = [0.4, 0.5, 0.6, 0.5]

X, y = make_blobs(n_samples=1000,
                  centers=centers,
                  cluster_std=cluster_std,
                  random_state=53)

plt.scatter(X[:, 0], X[:, 1], **plot_kwargs)
plt.show()
```

We get the following plot from the preceding code:

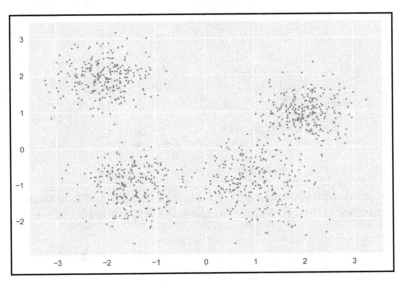

Now it looks more realistic!

Let's write a small class with helpful methods to create unsupervised experiments. First, you will use the `fit_predict` method to apply one or more clustering algorithms on the sample dataset:

```
class Unsupervised_AutoML:

    def __init__(self, estimators=None, transformers=None):
        self.estimators = estimators
        self.transformers = transformers
        pass
```

`Unsupervised_AutoML` class will initialize with a set of estimators and transformers. The second class method will be `fit_predict`:

```
def fit_predict(self, X, y=None):
    """
    fit_predict will train given estimator(s) and predict cluster
membership for each sample
    """

    # This dictionary will hold predictions for each estimator
    predictions = []
    performance_metrics = {}
```

```
    for estimator in self.estimators:
        labels = estimator['estimator'](*estimator['args'],
**estimator['kwargs']).fit_predict(X)
        estimator['estimator'].n_clusters_ = len(np.unique(labels))
        metrics =
self._get_cluster_metrics(estimator['estimator'].__name__,
estimator['estimator'].n_clusters_, X, labels, y)
        predictions.append({estimator['estimator'].__name__: labels})
        performance_metrics[estimator['estimator'].__name__] = metrics

    self.predictions = predictions
    self.performance_metrics = performance_metrics

    return predictions, performance_metrics
```

The `fit_predict` method uses the `_get_cluster_metrics` method to get the performance metrics, which is defined in the following code block:

```
# Printing cluster metrics for given arguments
def _get_cluster_metrics(self, name, n_clusters_, X, pred_labels,
true_labels=None):
    from sklearn.metrics import homogeneity_score, \
        completeness_score, \
        v_measure_score, \
        adjusted_rand_score, \
        adjusted_mutual_info_score, \
        silhouette_score

    print("""################# %s metrics ####################""" % name)
    if len(np.unique(pred_labels)) >= 2:

        silh_co = silhouette_score(X, pred_labels)

        if true_labels is not None:

            h_score = homogeneity_score(true_labels, pred_labels)
            c_score = completeness_score(true_labels, pred_labels)
            vm_score = v_measure_score(true_labels, pred_labels)
            adj_r_score = adjusted_rand_score(true_labels, pred_labels)
            adj_mut_info_score = adjusted_mutual_info_score(true_labels,
pred_labels)

            metrics = {"Silhouette Coefficient": silh_co,
                       "Estimated number of clusters": n_clusters_,
                       "Homogeneity": h_score,
                       "Completeness": c_score,
                       "V-measure": vm_score,
```

```
                    "Adjusted Rand Index": adj_r_score,
                    "Adjusted Mutual Information": adj_mut_info_score}

        for k, v in metrics.items():
            print("\t%s: %0.3f" % (k, v))

        return metrics

    metrics = {"Silhouette Coefficient": silh_co,
               "Estimated number of clusters": n_clusters_}

    for k, v in metrics.items():
        print("\t%s: %0.3f" % (k, v))

    return metrics

    else:
        print("\t# of predicted labels is {}, can not produce metrics.
\n".format(np.unique(pred_labels)))
```

The _get_cluster_metrics method calculates metrics, such as homogeneity_score, completeness_score, v_measure_score, adjusted_rand_score, adjusted_mutual_info_score, and silhouette_score. These metrics will help you to assess how well the clusters are separated and also measure the similarity within and between clusters.

K-means algorithm in action

You can now apply the KMeans algorithm to see how it works:

```
from sklearn.cluster import KMeans

estimators = [{'estimator': KMeans, 'args':(), 'kwargs':{'n_clusters': 4}}]

unsupervised_learner = Unsupervised_AutoML(estimators)
```

You can see the estimators:

```
unsupervised_learner.estimators
```

These will output the following:

```
[{'args': (),
  'estimator': sklearn.cluster.k_means_.KMeans,
  'kwargs': {'n_clusters': 4}}]
```

You can now invoke `fit_predict` to obtain `predictions` and `performance_metrics`:

```
predictions, performance_metrics = unsupervised_learner.fit_predict(X, y)
```

Metrics will be written to the console:

```
################# KMeans metrics ####################
    Silhouette Coefficient: 0.631
    Estimated number of clusters: 4.000
    Homogeneity: 0.951
    Completeness: 0.951
    V-measure: 0.951
    Adjusted Rand Index: 0.966
    Adjusted Mutual Information: 0.950
```

You can always print metrics later:

```
pprint(performance_metrics)
```

This will output the name of the estimator and its metrics:

```
{'KMeans': {'Silhouette Coefficient': 0.9280431207593165, 'Estimated number
of clusters': 4, 'Homogeneity': 1.0, 'Completeness': 1.0, 'V-measure': 1.0,
'Adjusted Rand Index': 1.0, 'Adjusted Mutual Information': 1.0}}
```

Let's add another class method to plot the clusters of the given estimator and predicted labels:

```
# plot_clusters will visualize the clusters given predicted labels
def plot_clusters(self, estimator, X, labels, plot_kwargs):

    palette = sns.color_palette('deep', np.unique(labels).max() + 1)
    colors = [palette[x] if x >= 0 else (0.0, 0.0, 0.0) for x in labels]

    plt.scatter(X[:, 0], X[:, 1], c=colors, **plot_kwargs)
    plt.title('{} Clusters'.format(str(estimator.__name__)), fontsize=14)
    plt.show()
```

Let's see the usage:

```
plot_kwargs = {'s': 12, 'linewidths': 0.1}
unsupervised_learner.plot_clusters(KMeans,
                                   X,
unsupervised_learner.predictions[0]['KMeans'],
                                   plot_kwargs)
```

You get the following plot from the preceding block:

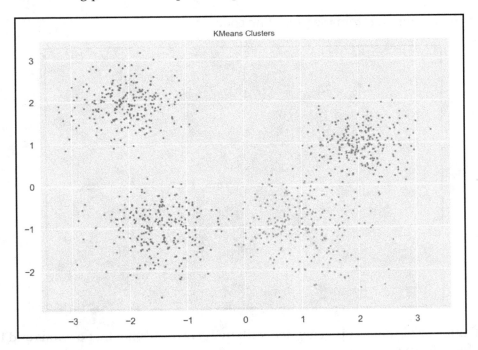

In this example, clusters are evenly sized and clearly separate from each other but, when you are doing this kind of exploratory analysis, you should try different hyperparameters and examine the results.

You will write a wrapper function later in this chapter to apply a list of clustering algorithms and their hyperparameters to examine the results. For now, let's see one more example with k-means where it does not work well.

When clusters in your dataset have different statistical properties, such as differences in variance, k-means will fail to identify clusters correctly:

```
X, y = make_blobs(n_samples=2000, centers=5, cluster_std=[1.7, 0.6, 0.8,
1.0, 1.2], random_state=220)

# Plot sample data
plt.scatter(X[:, 0], X[:, 1], **plot_kwargs)
plt.show()
```

We get the following plot from the preceding code:

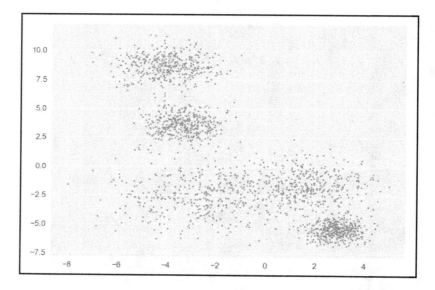

Although this sample dataset is generated with five centers, it's not that obvious and there might be four clusters, as well:

```
from sklearn.cluster import KMeans

estimators = [{'estimator': KMeans, 'args':(), 'kwargs':{'n_clusters': 4}}]

unsupervised_learner = Unsupervised_AutoML(estimators)

predictions, performance_metrics = unsupervised_learner.fit_predict(X, y)
```

Metrics in the console are as follows:

```
################## KMeans metrics ####################
   Silhouette Coefficient: 0.549
   Estimated number of clusters: 4.000
   Homogeneity: 0.729
   Completeness: 0.873
   V-measure: 0.795
   Adjusted Rand Index: 0.702
   Adjusted Mutual Information: 0.729
```

KMeans clusters are plotted as follows:

```
plot_kwargs = {'s': 12, 'linewidths': 0.1}
unsupervised_learner.plot_clusters(KMeans,
                                   X,
unsupervised_learner.predictions[0]['KMeans'],
                                   plot_kwargs)
```

We get the following plot from the preceding code:

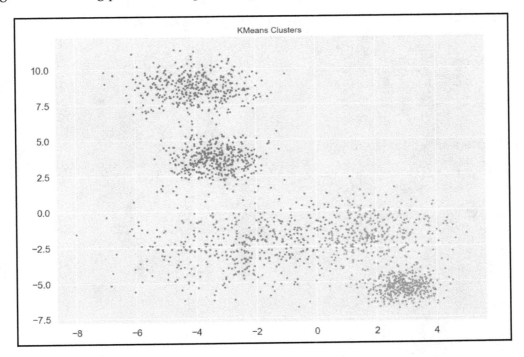

In this example, points between red (dark gray) and bottom-green clusters (light gray) seem to form one big cluster. K-means is calculating the centroid based on the mean value of points surrounding that centroid. Here, you need to have a different approach.

The DBSCAN algorithm in action

DBSCAN is one of the clustering algorithms that can deal with non-flat geometry and uneven cluster sizes. Let's see what it can do:

```
from sklearn.cluster import DBSCAN

estimators = [{'estimator': DBSCAN, 'args':(), 'kwargs':{'eps': 0.5}}]

unsupervised_learner = Unsupervised_AutoML(estimators)

predictions, performance_metrics = unsupervised_learner.fit_predict(X, y)
```

Metrics in the console are as follows:

```
################## DBSCAN metrics ###################
   Silhouette Coefficient: 0.231
   Estimated number of clusters: 12.000
   Homogeneity: 0.794
   Completeness: 0.800
   V-measure: 0.797
   Adjusted Rand Index: 0.737
   Adjusted Mutual Information: 0.792
```

DBSCAN clusters are plotted as follows:

```
plot_kwargs = {'s': 12, 'linewidths': 0.1}
unsupervised_learner.plot_clusters(DBSCAN,
                                   X,
       unsupervised_learner.predictions[0]['DBSCAN'],
                                   plot_kwargs)
```

We get the following plot from the preceding code:

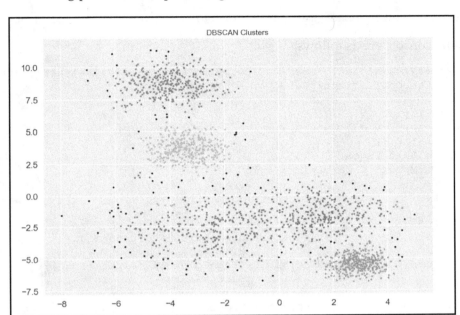

Conflict between red (dark gray) and bottom-green (light gray) clusters from the k-means case seems to be gone, but what's interesting here is that some small clusters appeared and some points were not assigned to any cluster based on their distance.

DBSCAN has the `eps(epsilon)` hyperparameter, which is related to proximity for points to be in same neighborhood; you can play with that parameter to see how the algorithm behaves.

When you are doing this kind of exploratory analysis where you don't know much about the data, visual clues are always important, because metrics can mislead you since not every clustering algorithm can be assessed using similar metrics.

Agglomerative clustering algorithm in action

Our last try will be with an agglomerative clustering algorithm:

```
from sklearn.cluster import AgglomerativeClustering

estimators = [{'estimator': AgglomerativeClustering, 'args':(),
'kwargs':{'n_clusters': 4, 'linkage': 'ward'}}]
```

```
unsupervised_learner = Unsupervised_AutoML(estimators)

predictions, performance_metrics = unsupervised_learner.fit_predict(X, y)
```

Metrics in the console are as follows:

```
################### AgglomerativeClustering metrics ####################
    Silhouette Coefficient: 0.546
    Estimated number of clusters: 4.000
    Homogeneity: 0.751
    Completeness: 0.905
    V-measure: 0.820
    Adjusted Rand Index: 0.719
    Adjusted Mutual Information: 0.750
```

`AgglomerativeClustering` clusters are plotted as follows:

```
plot_kwargs = {'s': 12, 'linewidths': 0.1}
unsupervised_learner.plot_clusters(AgglomerativeClustering,
                                   X,
unsupervised_learner.predictions[0]['AgglomerativeClustering'],
                                   plot_kwargs)
```

We get the following plot from the preceding code:

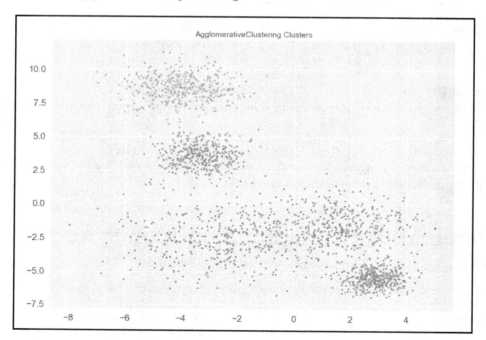

`AgglomerativeClustering` behaved like k-means in this example, with slight differences.

Simple automation of unsupervised learning

You should automate this whole discovery process to try different clustering algorithms with different hyperparameter settings. The following code will show you a simple way of doing that:

```
# You will create a list of algorithms to test
from sklearn.cluster import MeanShift, estimate_bandwidth,
SpectralClustering
from hdbscan import HDBSCAN

# bandwidth estimate for MeanShift algorithm to work properly
bandwidth = estimate_bandwidth(X, quantile=0.3, n_samples=100)

estimators = [{'estimator': KMeans, 'args': (), 'kwargs': {'n_clusters':
5}},
                    {'estimator': DBSCAN, 'args': (), 'kwargs':
{'eps': 0.5}},
                    {'estimator': AgglomerativeClustering, 'args': (),
'kwargs': {'n_clusters': 5, 'linkage': 'ward'}},
                    {'estimator': MeanShift, 'args': (), 'kwargs':
{'cluster_all': False, "bandwidth": bandwidth, "bin_seeding": True}},
                    {'estimator': SpectralClustering, 'args': (),
'kwargs': {'n_clusters':5}},
                    {'estimator': HDBSCAN, 'args': (), 'kwargs':
{'min_cluster_size':15}}]


unsupervised_learner = Unsupervised_AutoML(estimators)

predictions, performance_metrics = unsupervised_learner.fit_predict(X, y)
```

You will see the following metrics in the console:

```
################## KMeans metrics ####################
   Silhouette Coefficient: 0.592
   Estimated number of clusters: 5.000
   Homogeneity: 0.881
   Completeness: 0.882
   V-measure: 0.882
   Adjusted Rand Index: 0.886
   Adjusted Mutual Information: 0.881

################## DBSCAN metrics ####################
```

```
    Silhouette Coefficient: 0.417
    Estimated number of clusters: 5.000
    ...
################## AgglomerativeClustering metrics ###################
    Silhouette Coefficient: 0.581
    Estimated number of clusters: 5.000
    ...
################## MeanShift metrics ####################
    Silhouette Coefficient: 0.472
    Estimated number of clusters: 3.000
    ...
################## SpectralClustering metrics ####################
    Silhouette Coefficient: 0.420
    Estimated number of clusters: 5.000
    ...
################## HDBSCAN metrics ####################
    Silhouette Coefficient: 0.468
    Estimated number of clusters: 6.000
    ...
```

You can print labels and metrics later, since you have a label and metrics for each algorithm:

```
pprint(predictions)
[{'KMeans': array([3, 1, 4, ..., 0, 1, 2], dtype=int32)},
 {'DBSCAN': array([ 0, 0, 0, ..., 2, -1, 1])},
 {'AgglomerativeClustering': array([2, 4, 0, ..., 3, 2, 1])},
 {'MeanShift': array([0, 0, 0, ..., 1, 0, 1])},
 {'SpectralClustering': array([4, 2, 1, ..., 0, 1, 3], dtype=int32)},
 {'HDBSCAN': array([ 4, 2, 3, ..., 1, -1, 0])}]

pprint(performance_metrics)
{'AgglomerativeClustering': {'Adjusted Mutual Information':
0.8989601162598674,
                              'Adjusted Rand Index': 0.9074196173180163,
                              ...},
 'DBSCAN': {'Adjusted Mutual Information': 0.5694008711591612,
            'Adjusted Rand Index': 0.4685215791890368,
            ...},
 'HDBSCAN': {'Adjusted Mutual Information': 0.7857262723310214,
             'Adjusted Rand Index': 0.7907512089039799,
             ...},
 'KMeans': {'Adjusted Mutual Information': 0.8806038790635883,
            'Adjusted Rand Index': 0.8862210038915361,
            ...},
 'MeanShift': {'Adjusted Mutual Information': 0.45701704058584275,
               'Adjusted Rand Index': 0.4043364504640998,
               ...},
 'SpectralClustering': {'Adjusted Mutual Information': 0.7628653432724043,
```

```
'Adjusted Rand Index': 0.7111907598912597,
...}}
```

You can visualize the predictions in the same way by using the `plot_clusters` method.
Let's write another class method, that will plot clusters for all the estimators you have used
in your experiment:

```
def plot_all_clusters(self, estimators, labels, X, plot_kwargs):

    fig = plt.figure()

    for i, algorithm in enumerate(labels):

        quotinent = np.divide(len(estimators), 2)

        # Simple logic to decide row and column size of the figure
        if isinstance(quotinent, int):
            dim_1 = 2
            dim_2 = quotinent
        else:
            dim_1 = np.ceil(quotinent)
            dim_2 = 3

        palette = sns.color_palette('deep',
np.unique(algorithm[estimators[i]['estimator'].__name__]).max() + 1)
        colors = [palette[x] if x >= 0 else (0.0, 0.0, 0.0) for x in
                  algorithm[estimators[i]['estimator'].__name__]]

        plt.subplot(dim_1, dim_2, i + 1)
        plt.scatter(X[:, 0], X[:, 1], c=colors, **plot_kwargs)
        plt.title('{}
Clusters'.format(str(estimators[i]['estimator'].__name__)), fontsize=8)

    plt.show()
```

Let's see the usage:

```
plot_kwargs = {'s': 12, 'linewidths': 0.1}
unsupervised_learner.plot_all_clusters(estimators,
unsupervised_learner.predictions, X, plot_kwargs)
```

We get the following plot from the preceding code block:

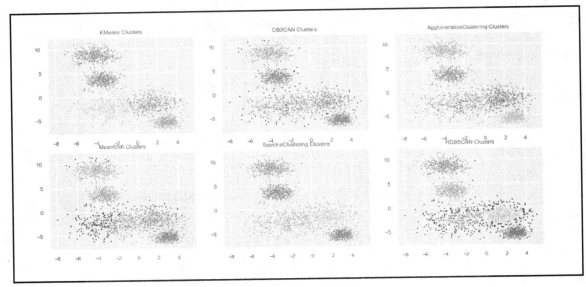

Top row, starting from left: KMeans, DBSCAN, AgglomerativeClustering

Bottom row, starting from left: MeanShift, SpectralClustering, HDBSCAN

Visualizing high-dimensional datasets

What about visually inspecting datasets that have more than three dimensions? In order to visually inspect your dataset, you need to have a maximum of three dimensions; if not, you need to use specific methods to reduce dimensionality. This is usually achieved by applying a **Principal Component Analysis (PCA)** or t-SNE algorithm.

The following code will load the `Breast Cancer Wisconsin Diagnostic` dataset, which is commonly used in ML tutorials:

```
# Wisconsin Breast Cancer Diagnostic Dataset
from sklearn.datasets import load_breast_cancer
import pandas as pd

data = load_breast_cancer()
X = data.data

df = pd.DataFrame(data.data, columns=data.feature_names)
df.head()
```

Output in the console is as follows:

```
   mean radius mean texture mean perimeter mean area mean smoothness \
0  17.99 10.38 122.80 1001.0 0.11840
1  20.57 17.77 132.90 1326.0 0.08474
2  19.69 21.25 130.00 1203.0 0.10960
3  11.42 20.38 77.58 386.1 0.14250
4  20.29 14.34 135.10 1297.0 0.10030


...

   mean fractal dimension ... worst radius \
0  0.07871 ... 25.38
1  0.05667 ... 24.99
2  0.05999 ... 23.57
3  0.09744 ... 14.91
4  0.05883 ... 22.54


...

   worst fractal dimension
0  0.11890
1  0.08902
2  0.08758
3  0.17300
4  0.07678
```

You have thirty different features to use to understand the different characteristics of a tumor in the given patient.

df.describe() will show you descriptive statistics for each feature:

```
df.describe()

       mean radius mean texture mean perimeter mean area \
count  569.000000 569.000000 569.000000 569.000000
mean   14.127292 19.289649 91.969033 654.889104
std    3.524049 4.301036 24.298981 351.914129
min    6.981000 9.710000 43.790000 143.500000
25%    11.700000 16.170000 75.170000 420.300000
50%    13.370000 18.840000 86.240000 551.100000
75%    15.780000 21.800000 104.100000 782.700000
max    28.110000 39.280000 188.500000 2501.000000


...

       mean symmetry mean fractal dimension ... \
```

```
count 569.000000 569.000000 ...
mean 0.181162 0.062798 ...
std 0.027414 0.007060 ...
min 0.106000 0.049960 ...
25% 0.161900 0.057700 ...
50% 0.179200 0.061540 ...
75% 0.195700 0.066120 ...
max 0.304000 0.097440 ...


...

        worst concave points worst symmetry worst fractal dimension
count 569.000000 569.000000 569.000000
mean 0.114606 0.290076 0.083946
std 0.065732 0.061867 0.018061
min 0.000000 0.156500 0.055040
25% 0.064930 0.250400 0.071460
50% 0.099930 0.282200 0.080040
75% 0.161400 0.317900 0.092080
max 0.291000 0.663800 0.207500
[8 rows x 30 columns]
```

Let's see the results before and after scaling. The following code snippet will fit the PCA to the original data.

Principal Component Analysis in action

The following code block shows you how to apply PCA with two components and visualize the results:

```
# PCA
from sklearn.decomposition import PCA

pca = PCA(n_components=2, whiten=True)
pca = pca.fit_transform(df)

plt.scatter(pca[:, 0], pca[:, 1], c=data.target, cmap="RdBu_r",
edgecolor="Red", alpha=0.35)
plt.colorbar()
plt.title('PCA, n_components=2')
plt.show()
```

We get the following plot from the preceding code:

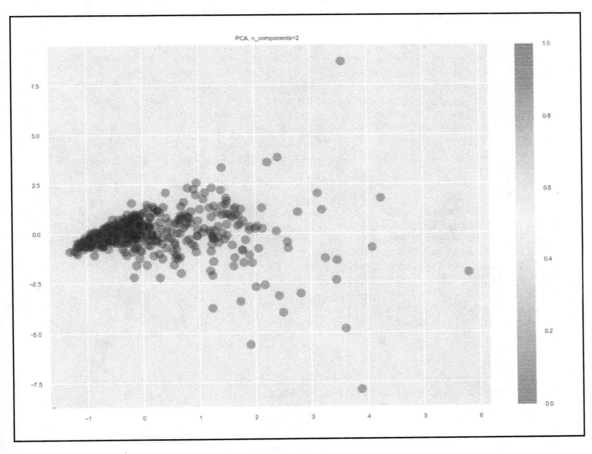

Plot of PCA, n_components=2

Here, you can see the red class (dark gray) is very condensed into one particular area and it's hard to separate classes. Differences in variances distort our view and scaling can help:

```
# Preprocess data.
scaler = StandardScaler()
scaler.fit(df)
preprocessed_data = scaler.transform(df)
scaled_features_df = pd.DataFrame(preprocessed_data, index=df.index,
columns=df.columns)
```

After preprocessing data by applying `StandardScaler`, the dataset has unit variance:

```
scaled_features_df.describe()

        mean radius mean texture mean perimeter mean area \
count 5.690000e+02 5.690000e+02 5.690000e+02 5.690000e+02
mean -3.162867e-15 -6.530609e-15 -7.078891e-16 -8.799835e-16
std 1.000880e+00 1.000880e+00 1.000880e+00 1.000880e+00
min -2.029648e+00 -2.229249e+00 -1.984504e+00 -1.454443e+00
25% -6.893853e-01 -7.259631e-01 -6.919555e-01 -6.671955e-01
50% -2.150816e-01 -1.046362e-01 -2.359800e-01 -2.951869e-01
75% 4.693926e-01 5.841756e-01 4.996769e-01 3.635073e-01
max 3.971288e+00 4.651889e+00 3.976130e+00 5.250529e+00


...

        mean symmetry mean fractal dimension ... \
count 5.690000e+02 5.690000e+02 ...
mean -1.971670e-15 -1.453631e-15 ...
std 1.000880e+00 1.000880e+00 ...
min -2.744117e+00 -1.819865e+00 ...
25% -7.032397e-01 -7.226392e-01 ...
50% -7.162650e-02 -1.782793e-01 ...
75% 5.307792e-01 4.709834e-01 ...
max 4.484751e+00 4.910919e+00 ...


...

        worst concave points worst symmetry worst fractal dimension
count 5.690000e+02 5.690000e+02 5.690000e+02
mean -1.412656e-16 -2.289567e-15 2.575171e-15
std 1.000880e+00 1.000880e+00 1.000880e+00
min -1.745063e+00 -2.160960e+00 -1.601839e+00
25% -7.563999e-01 -6.418637e-01 -6.919118e-01
50% -2.234689e-01 -1.274095e-01 -2.164441e-01
75% 7.125100e-01 4.501382e-01 4.507624e-01
max 2.685877e+00 6.046041e+00 6.846856e+00
[8 rows x 30 columns]
```

Apply PCA to see whether the first two principal components are enough to separate labels:

```
# PCA
from sklearn.decomposition import PCA

pca = PCA(n_components=2, whiten=True)
pca = pca.fit_transform(scaled_features_df)

plt.scatter(pca[:, 0], pca[:, 1], c=data.target, cmap="RdBu_r",
```

```
edgecolor="Red", alpha=0.35)
plt.colorbar()
plt.title('PCA, n_components=2')
plt.show()
```

We get the following output from the preceding code:

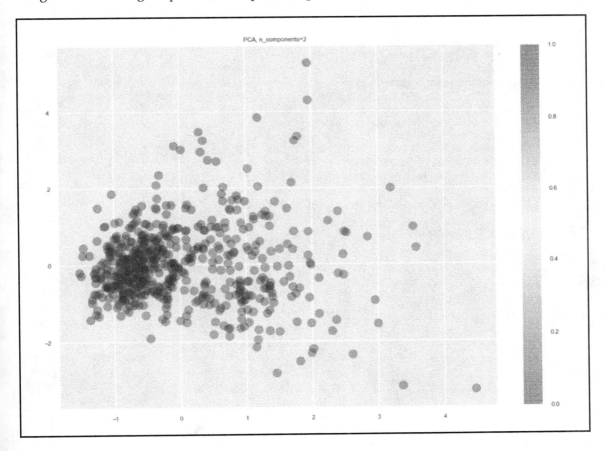

PCA, n_components=2, after scaling

This seems interesting, as examples with different labels are mostly separated using the first two principal components.

t-SNE in action

You can also try t-SNE to visualize high-dimensional data. First, TSNE will be applied to the original data:

```
# TSNE
from sklearn.manifold import TSNE

tsne = TSNE(verbose=1, perplexity=40, n_iter=4000)
tsne = tsne.fit_transform(df)
```

Output in the console is as follows:

```
[t-SNE] Computing 121 nearest neighbors...
[t-SNE] Indexed 569 samples in 0.000s...
[t-SNE] Computed neighbors for 569 samples in 0.010s...
[t-SNE] Computed conditional probabilities for sample 569 / 569
[t-SNE] Mean sigma: 33.679703
[t-SNE] KL divergence after 250 iterations with early exaggeration:
48.886528
[t-SNE] Error after 1600 iterations: 0.210506
```

Plotting the results is as follows:

```
plt.scatter(tsne[:, 0], tsne[:, 1], c=data.target, cmap="winter",
edgecolor="None", alpha=0.35)
plt.colorbar()
plt.title('t-SNE')
plt.show()
```

We get the following output from the preceding code:

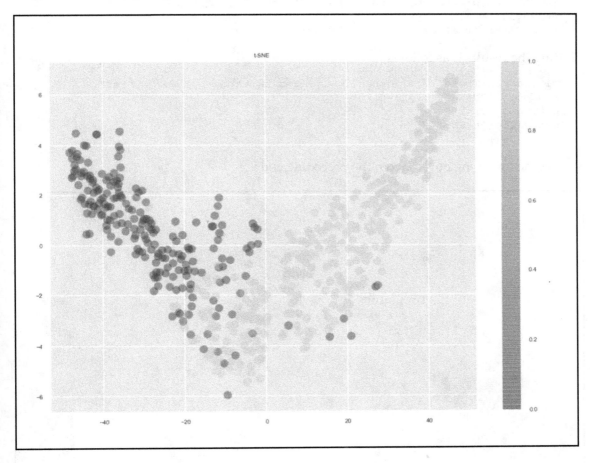

Plot of TSNE

Applying TSNE on scaled data is as follows:

```
tsne = TSNE(verbose=1, perplexity=40, n_iter=4000)
tsne = tsne.fit_transform(scaled_features_df)
```

Output in the console is as follows:

```
[t-SNE] Computing 121 nearest neighbors...
[t-SNE] Indexed 569 samples in 0.001s...
[t-SNE] Computed neighbors for 569 samples in 0.018s...
[t-SNE] Computed conditional probabilities for sample 569 / 569
```

```
[t-SNE] Mean sigma: 1.522404
[t-SNE] KL divergence after 250 iterations with early exaggeration:
66.959343
[t-SNE] Error after 1700 iterations: 0.875110
```

Plotting the results is as follows:

```
plt.scatter(tsne[:, 0], tsne[:, 1], c=data.target, cmap="winter",
edgecolor="None", alpha=0.35)
plt.colorbar()
plt.title('t-SNE')
plt.show()
```

We get the following output from the preceding code:

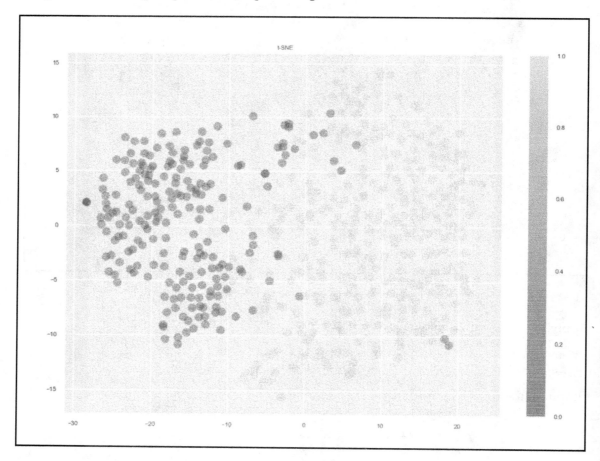

TSNE after scaling

Adding simple components together to improve the pipeline

Let's make some adjustments to the `fit_predict` method to include a decomposer in your pipeline, so that you can visualize high-dimensional data if necessary:

```python
def fit_predict(self, X, y=None, scaler=True, decomposer={'name': PCA,
'args':[], 'kwargs': {'n_components': 2}}):
    """
    fit_predict will train given estimator(s) and predict cluster
membership for each sample
    """

    shape = X.shape
    df_type = isinstance(X, pd.core.frame.DataFrame)

    if df_type:
        column_names = X.columns
        index = X.index

    if scaler == True:
        from sklearn.preprocessing import StandardScaler
        scaler = StandardScaler()
        X = scaler.fit_transform(X)

        if df_type:
            X = pd.DataFrame(X, index=index, columns=column_names)

    if decomposer is not None:
        X = decomposer['name'](*decomposer['args'],
**decomposer['kwargs']).fit_transform(X)

        if df_type:
            if decomposer['name'].__name__ == 'PCA':
                X = pd.DataFrame(X, index=index, columns=['component_' +
str(i + 1) for i in
range(decomposer['kwargs']['n_components'])])
            else:
                X = pd.DataFrame(X, index=index, columns=['component_1',
'component_2'])

        # if dimensionality reduction is applied, then n_components will be
set accordingly in hyperparameter configuration
        for estimator in self.estimators:
            if 'n_clusters' in estimator['kwargs'].keys():
                if decomposer['name'].__name__ == 'PCA':
```

```
                            estimator['kwargs']['n_clusters'] =
decomposer['kwargs']['n_components']
                    else:
                        estimator['kwargs']['n_clusters'] = 2

    # This dictionary will hold predictions for each estimator
    predictions = []
    performance_metrics = {}

    for estimator in self.estimators:
        labels = estimator['estimator'](*estimator['args'],
**estimator['kwargs']).fit_predict(X)
        estimator['estimator'].n_clusters_ = len(np.unique(labels))
        metrics =
self._get_cluster_metrics(estimator['estimator'].__name__,
estimator['estimator'].n_clusters_, X, labels, y)
        predictions.append({estimator['estimator'].__name__: labels})
        performance_metrics[estimator['estimator'].__name__] = metrics

    self.predictions = predictions
    self.performance_metrics = performance_metrics

    return predictions, performance_metrics
```

Now, you can apply `fit_predict` to your datasets. The following code block shows you an example of the usage:

```
from sklearn.cluster import KMeans, DBSCAN, AgglomerativeClustering,
MeanShift, estimate_bandwidth, SpectralClustering
from hdbscan import HDBSCAN

from sklearn.datasets import load_breast_cancer

data = load_breast_cancer()
X = data.data
y = data.target

# Necessary for bandwidth
bandwidth = estimate_bandwidth(X, quantile=0.1, n_samples=100)

estimators = [{'estimator': KMeans, 'args': (), 'kwargs': {'n_clusters':
5}},
                            {'estimator': DBSCAN, 'args': (), 'kwargs':
{'eps': 0.3}},
                            {'estimator': AgglomerativeClustering, 'args': (),
'kwargs': {'n_clusters': 5, 'linkage': 'ward'}},
                            {'estimator': MeanShift, 'args': (), 'kwargs':
```

```
{'cluster_all': False, "bandwidth": bandwidth, "bin_seeding": True}},
                          {'estimator': SpectralClustering, 'args': (),
'kwargs': {'n_clusters':5}},
                          {'estimator': HDBSCAN, 'args': (), 'kwargs':
{'min_cluster_size':15}}]

unsupervised_learner = Unsupervised_AutoML(estimators)

predictions, performance_metrics = unsupervised_learner.fit_predict(X, y,
decomposer=None)
```

Automated unsupervised learning is a highly experimental process, especially if you don't know much about your data. As an exercise, you can extend the Unsupervised_AutoML class to try with more than one hyperparameter set for each algorithm and visualize the results.

Summary

In this chapter, you learned about many different aspects when it comes to choosing a suitable ML pipeline for a given problem.

Computational complexity, differences in training and scoring time, linearity versus non-linearity, and algorithm, specific feature transformations are valid considerations and it's useful to look at your data from these perspectives.

You gained a better understanding of selecting suitable models and how machine learning pipelines work by practicing various use cases. You are starting to scratch the surface and this chapter was a good starting point to extend these skills.

In the next chapter, you will learn about optimizing hyperparameters and will be introduced to more advanced concepts, such as Bayesian-based hyperparameter optimization.

Hyperparameter Optimization

5

The auto-sklearn library uses **Bayesian optimization** to tune the hyperparameters of **machine learning** (**ML**) pipelines. You will learn the inner workings of Bayesian optimization, but let's first review the basics of mathematical optimization.

In simple terms, optimization deals with selecting the best values to minimize or maximize a given function. A function is called a **loss function** or a **cost function** if our objective is minimization. If you are trying to maximize it, then it's called a **utility function** or a **fitness function**. For example, when you are building ML models, a loss function helps you to minimize the prediction error during the training phase.

When you look at this whole process from a wider angle, there are many variables that come into play.

First, you may work on a system to decide the type of problem, such as an unsupervised, supervised, semi-supervised, or reinforcement learning problem. You may decide on a hardware and software configuration depending on the data size and complexity. Then you may choose the suitable languages or libraries to use in your experiments. From a set of available transformers and estimators, you may choose a subset of them to be used during the training, validation, and testing phases.

All of these could be called **configuration parameters** to set the scene for developing ML pipelines.

Second, transformers and estimators have their own parameters to figure out during the training phase, such as coefficients in linear models, or degree parameters to create polynomial and interaction features.

For example, ML algorithms are usually classified as parametric or non-parametric. If an algorithm has a fixed number of parameters, which means the function form is known, then it's a parametric; if not, then it's called a **non-parametric** and your data will shape the function's form.

Third, apart from parameters, you need to set hyperparameters before training starts to guide the estimation of transformer and estimator parameters.

Hyperparameters are particularly important because your pipeline's performance will depend on them, and since there are many hyperparameters where each can take a range of values, you quickly come to the realization that this is an optimization problem.

Given hyperparameters and the range of values that they can take, which is your search space, how can you efficiently find the best performing ML pipeline? In practice, the best performing ML pipeline is the one that has the best cross-validation score.

The following topics will be covered in this chapter:

- Configuration space for ML experiments
- ML model parameters and hyperparameters
- What is warm start and how it helps parameter optimization
- Bayesian-based hyperparameter tuning
- An example system

Technical requirements

You can find all the code examples in the `Chapter 05` folder of the book's repository.

Hyperparameters

In order to better understand this process, you will start simple with Branin function which has 3 global minima:

$$f(x) = a(x_2 - bx_1^2 + cx_1 - r)^2 + s(1 - t)\,cos(x_1) + s$$

The following code snippet shows you the minimization of the Branin function:

```
import numpy as np

def branin(x):

    # Branin function has 2 dimensions and it has 3 global mimima
    x1 = x[0]
    x2 = x[1]
```

```
    # Global minimum is f(x*)=0.397887 at points (-pi, 12.275), (pi,2.275)
and (9.42478, 2.475)

    # Recommended values of a, b, c, r, s and t for Branin function
    a = 1
    b = 5.1 / (4 * np.pi**2)
    c = 5. / np.pi
    r = 6.
    s = 10.
    t = 1 / (8 * np.pi)

    # Calculating separate parts of the function first for verbosity
    p1 = a * (x2 - (b * x1**2) + (c * x1) - r)**2
    p2 = s * (1-t) * np.cos(x1)
    p3 = s

    # Calculating result
    ret = p1 + p2 + p3

    return ret

# minimize function from scipy.optimize will minimize a scalar function
with one or more variables
from scipy.optimize import minimize

x = [5.6, 3.2]

res = minimize(branin, x)

print(res)
```

Executing the previous code snippet will result in the following output:

```
fun: 0.3978873577297417
hess_inv: array([[0.10409341, -0.0808961],
[-0.0808961, 0.56160622]])
jac: array([3.57627869e-07, -1.19209290e-07])
message: 'Optimization terminated successfully.'
nfev: 36
nit: 5
njev: 9
status: 0
success: True
x: array([3.14159268, 2.27499994])
```

Optimization is successfully terminated and the global minima can be found at (3.14159268, 2.27499994) of the Branin function. There are many solvers to use for your optimization problems, such as **BFGS**, **L-BFGS-B**, and **SLSQP**, and these will have different characteristics, such as consistency and complexity. Practicing through examples will get you familiar with some of them and will open space for further exploration.

Let's review the basics of optimization for ML problems. The following formula shows what most ML problems reduce to:

$$L = \sum_{i=1}^{N}(y_i - f(x_i|w,b))^2 + \alpha \sum_{j=1}^{D} w_j^2 + \beta \sum_{j=1}^{D} |w_j|$$

In this equation, you have loss function and regularization terms to prevent overfitting. Weights, denoted by w, are what you are trying to learn during the training process and these are previously mentioned parameters of the learning algorithm. Apart from these parameters, you generally need to define hyperparameters, such as learning rate and early stopping condition, which will affect the learning behavior.

Have you also noticed α and β in the loss function? These are the parameters that you need to set before training, and they are also hyperparameters.

Hyperparameters help you to keep a healthy balance between model bias and model variance.

Let's look at a brief example of estimator parameters in `sklearn`:

```
from sklearn.linear_model import LogisticRegression

log_reg = LogisticRegression()
log_reg.get_params()
```

The output will look as follows:

```
{'C': 1.0,
 'class_weight': None,
 'dual': False,
 'fit_intercept': True,
 'intercept_scaling': 1,
 'max_iter': 100,
 'multi_class': 'ovr',
 'n_jobs': 1,
 'penalty': 'l2',
 'random_state': None,
```

```
'solver': 'liblinear',
'tol': 0.0001,
'verbose': 0,
'warm_start': False}
```

You have 14 hyperparameters here and if you think about the possible combinations, you will realize how big the search space can be. Your goal is to get a best cross-validation score out of all the sets of hyperparameters.

One of the important hyperparameters of `LogisticRegression` is C and it controls the strength of regularization. Value is inversely affecting the regularization strength, which means higher values indicate weaker regularization.

Even if you are an expert of the algorithm that you are working with, setting hyperparameters correctly is experimental and subjective to the experience of the practitioner. You need to find better ways than your heuristic approach to find a near-optimal or optimal set of hyperparameters.

For example, you can use `GridSearchCV` or `RandomizedSearchCV` to search the hyperparameter space in `sklearn`:

- `GridSearchCV` generates candidate sets from given hyperparameters and a range of values that they can take. Suppose you have the following parameter grid:

  ```
  # Hyperparameters
  param_grid = [ {'C': [0.001, 0.01, 0.1, 1, 10, 20, 50, 100],
                  'penalty': ['l1', 'l2']} ]
  ```

Then `GridSearhCV` will generate the following parameters:

```
'params': [{'C': 0.001, 'penalty': 'l1'},
  {'C': 0.001, 'penalty': 'l2'},
  {'C': 0.01, 'penalty': 'l1'},
  {'C': 0.01, 'penalty': 'l2'},
  {'C': 0.1, 'penalty': 'l1'},
  {'C': 0.1, 'penalty': 'l2'},
  {'C': 1, 'penalty': 'l1'},
  {'C': 1, 'penalty': 'l2'},
  {'C': 10, 'penalty': 'l1'},
  {'C': 10, 'penalty': 'l2'},
  {'C': 20, 'penalty': 'l1'},
  {'C': 20, 'penalty': 'l2'},
  {'C': 50, 'penalty': 'l1'},
  {'C': 50, 'penalty': 'l2'},
  {'C': 100, 'penalty': 'l1'},
```

```
                    {'C': 100, 'penalty': 'l2'}]
```

It will perform an exhaustive search to find a best cross-validation score.

- `RandomizedSearchCV` performs its search differently to `GridSearchCV`. Instead of searching the hyperparameter space exhaustively, it samples parameter settings from specified distributions. You should construct your parameter grid in the following way:

```
# Hyperparameters
param_grid = {'C': sp_randint(1, 100),
              'penalty': ['l1', 'l2']}
```

Have you noticed `sp_randint`? It will allow `RandomizedSearchCV` to draw random variables from uniform distribution and parameters will be created as follows:

```
'params': [{'C': 6, 'penalty': 'l2'},
    {'C': 97, 'penalty': 'l2'},
    {'C': 92, 'penalty': 'l2'},
    {'C': 62, 'penalty': 'l1'},
    {'C': 63, 'penalty': 'l2'},
    {'C': 5, 'penalty': 'l2'},
    {'C': 7, 'penalty': 'l1'},
    {'C': 45, 'penalty': 'l1'},
    {'C': 77, 'penalty': 'l2'},
    {'C': 12, 'penalty': 'l1'},
    {'C': 72, 'penalty': 'l2'},
    {'C': 28, 'penalty': 'l1'},
    {'C': 7, 'penalty': 'l2'},
    {'C': 65, 'penalty': 'l1'},
    {'C': 32, 'penalty': 'l1'},
    {'C': 84, 'penalty': 'l1'},
    {'C': 27, 'penalty': 'l1'},
    {'C': 12, 'penalty': 'l1'},
    {'C': 21, 'penalty': 'l1'},
    {'C': 65, 'penalty': 'l1'}],
```

Let's look at an example of the usage, both for `GridSearchCV` and `RandomizedSearchCV`.

The following snippet shows you `GridSearchCV`:

```
from sklearn.linear_model import LogisticRegression

log_reg = LogisticRegression()

# Hyperparameters
```

```
param_grid = {'C': [0.001, 0.01, 0.1, 1, 10, 20, 50, 100],
              'penalty': ['l1', 'l2']}

from sklearn.model_selection import GridSearchCV

n_folds = 5
estimator = GridSearchCV(log_reg,param_grid, cv=n_folds)

from sklearn import datasets
iris = datasets.load_iris()
X = iris.data
Y = iris.target

estimator.fit(X, Y)
```

You will see the following output:

```
GridSearchCV(cv=5, error_score='raise',
        estimator=LogisticRegression(C=1.0, class_weight=None, dual=False,
fit_intercept=True,
            intercept_scaling=1, max_iter=100, multi_class='ovr', n_jobs=1,
            penalty='l2', random_state=None, solver='liblinear', tol=0.0001,
            verbose=0, warm_start=False),
        fit_params=None, iid=True, n_jobs=1,
        param_grid=[{'C': [0.001, 0.01, 0.1, 1, 10, 20, 50, 100], 'penalty':
['l1', 'l2']}],
        pre_dispatch='2*n_jobs', refit=True, return_train_score=True,
        scoring=None, verbose=0)
```

Once training is done, you can see the best performing estimator settings:

```
estimator.best_estimator_
```

The preceding code will generate the following output:

```
LogisticRegression(C=10, class_weight=None, dual=False, fit_intercept=True,
intercept_scaling=1, max_iter=100, multi_class='ovr', n_jobs=1,
penalty='l1', random_state=None, solver='liblinear', tol=0.0001,
verbose=0, warm_start=False)
```

You can also see the best score:

```
estimator.best_score_
```

With the following output:

```
0.98
```

You can also see all results by checking `cv_results_`:

```
estimator.cv_results_
```

This will give you various metrics for each training run:

```
{'mean_fit_time': array([0.00039144, 0.00042701, 0.00036378, 0.00043044,
0.00145531,
        0.00046387, 0.00670047, 0.00056334, 0.00890565, 0.00064907,
        0.00916181, 0.00063758, 0.01110044, 0.00076027, 0.01196856,
        0.00084472]),
 'mean_score_time': array([0.00017729, 0.00018134, 0.00016704, 0.00016623,
0.00017071,
        0.00016556, 0.00024438, 0.00017123, 0.00020232, 0.00018559,
        0.00020504, 0.00016532, 0.00024428, 0.00019045, 0.00023465,
        0.00023274]),
 'mean_test_score': array([0.33333333, 0.40666667, 0.33333333, 0.66666667,
0.77333333,
        0.82 , 0.96 , 0.96 , 0.98 , 0.96666667,
        0.96666667, 0.96666667, 0.96666667, 0.97333333, 0.96 ,
        0.98 ]),
 'mean_train_score': array([0.33333333, 0.40166667, 0.33333333, 0.66666667,
0.775 ,
        0.83166667, 0.96333333, 0.96333333, 0.97333333, 0.97333333,
        0.97333333, 0.97666667, 0.975 , 0.97833333, 0.975 ,
        0.98 ]),
 'param_C': masked_array(data=[0.001, 0.001, 0.01, 0.01, 0.1, 0.1, 1, 1,
10, 10, 20,
                   20, 50, 50, 100, 100],
             mask=[False, False, False, False, False, False, False, False,
                   False, False, False, False, False, False, False,
False],
        fill_value='?',
             dtype=object),
 'param_penalty': masked_array(data=['l1', 'l2', 'l1', 'l2', 'l1', 'l2',
'l1', 'l2', 'l1',
                   'l2', 'l1', 'l2', 'l1', 'l2', 'l1', 'l2'],
             mask=[False, False, False, False, False, False, False, False,
                   False, False, False, False, False, False, False,
False],
        fill_value='?',
             dtype=object),
 'params': [{'C': 0.001, 'penalty': 'l1'},
  {'C': 0.001, 'penalty': 'l2'},
```

```
    {'C': 0.01, 'penalty': 'l1'},
    {'C': 0.01, 'penalty': 'l2'},
    {'C': 0.1, 'penalty': 'l1'},
    {'C': 0.1, 'penalty': 'l2'},
    {'C': 1, 'penalty': 'l1'},
    {'C': 1, 'penalty': 'l2'},
    {'C': 10, 'penalty': 'l1'},
    {'C': 10, 'penalty': 'l2'},
    {'C': 20, 'penalty': 'l1'},
    {'C': 20, 'penalty': 'l2'},
    {'C': 50, 'penalty': 'l1'},
    {'C': 50, 'penalty': 'l2'},
    {'C': 100, 'penalty': 'l1'},
    {'C': 100, 'penalty': 'l2'}],
 'rank_test_score': array([15, 14, 15, 13, 12, 11, 8, 8, 1, 4, 4, 4, 4, 3,
8, 1],
       dtype=int32),
 'split0_test_score': array([0.33333333, 0.36666667, 0.33333333,
0.66666667, 0.7 ,
        0.76666667, 1. , 1. , 1. , 1. ,
        1. , 1. , 1. , 1. , 0.96666667,
        1. ]),
 'split0_train_score': array([0.33333333, 0.41666667, 0.33333333,
0.66666667, 0.775 ,
        0.825 , 0.95 , 0.95 , 0.95 , 0.96666667,
        0.95 , 0.975 , 0.95833333, 0.975 , 0.95833333,
        0.975 ]),
 'split1_test_score': array([0.33333333, 0.46666667, 0.33333333,
0.66666667, 0.8 ,
        0.86666667, 0.96666667, 0.96666667, 1. , 1. ,
        0.96666667, 1. , 0.96666667, 1. , 0.96666667,
        1. ]),
 'split1_train_score': array([0.33333333, 0.35833333, 0.33333333,
0.66666667, 0.775 ,
        0.825 , 0.95833333, 0.96666667, 0.975 , 0.96666667,
        0.975 , 0.975 , 0.975 , 0.975 , 0.975 ,
        0.975 ]),
 'split2_test_score': array([0.33333333, 0.36666667, 0.33333333,
0.66666667, 0.8 ,
        0.83333333, 0.93333333, 0.93333333, 0.96666667, 0.93333333,
        0.93333333, 0.93333333, 0.93333333, 0.93333333, 0.93333333,
        0.96666667]),
 'split2_train_score': array([0.33333333, 0.41666667, 0.33333333,
0.66666667, 0.76666667,
        0.83333333, 0.96666667, 0.96666667, 0.975 , 0.975 ,
        0.975 , 0.98333333, 0.975 , 0.98333333, 0.975 ,
        0.98333333]),
 'split3_test_score': array([0.33333333, 0.46666667, 0.33333333,
```

```
    0.66666667, 0.8 ,
           0.83333333, 0.9 , 0.9 , 0.93333333, 0.9 ,
           0.93333333, 0.9 , 0.93333333, 0.93333333, 0.93333333,
           0.93333333]),
   'split3_train_score': array([0.33333333, 0.39166667, 0.33333333,
    0.66666667, 0.775 ,
           0.84166667, 0.975 , 0.975 , 0.99166667, 0.98333333,
           0.99166667, 0.98333333, 0.99166667, 0.98333333, 0.99166667,
           0.99166667]),
   'split4_test_score': array([0.33333333, 0.36666667, 0.33333333,
    0.66666667, 0.76666667,
           0.8 , 1. , 1. , 1. , 1. ,
           1. , 1. , 1. , 1. , 1. ,
           1. ]),
   'split4_train_score': array([0.33333333, 0.425 , 0.33333333, 0.66666667,
    0.78333333,
           0.83333333, 0.96666667, 0.95833333, 0.975 , 0.975 ,
           0.975 , 0.96666667, 0.975 , 0.975 , 0.975 ,
           0.975 ]),
   'std_fit_time': array([7.66660734e-05, 3.32198455e-05, 1.98168153e-05,
    6.91923414e-06,
           4.74922317e-04, 2.65661212e-05, 1.03221712e-03, 3.79795334e-05,
           1.86899641e-03, 8.53752397e-05, 1.93386463e-03, 2.95752073e-05,
           2.91377734e-03, 5.70420424e-05, 3.59721435e-03, 9.67829087e-05]),
   'std_score_time': array([1.28883712e-05, 2.39771817e-05, 4.81959487e-06,
    2.47955322e-06,
           1.34236224e-05, 2.41545203e-06, 5.64869920e-05, 8.94803700e-06,
           4.10209125e-05, 3.35513820e-05, 3.04168290e-05, 2.87924369e-06,
           4.91685012e-05, 1.62987656e-05, 4.23611246e-05, 7.26868455e-05]),
   'std_test_score': array([0. , 0.04898979, 0. , 0. , 0.03887301,
           0.03399346, 0.03887301, 0.03887301, 0.02666667, 0.0421637 ,
           0.02981424, 0.0421637 , 0.02981424, 0.03265986, 0.02494438,
           0.02666667]),
   'std_train_score': array([0. , 0.02438123, 0. , 0. , 0.00527046,
           0.0062361 , 0.00849837, 0.00849837, 0.01333333, 0.0062361 ,
           0.01333333, 0.0062361 , 0.01054093, 0.00408248, 0.01054093,
           0.00666667])}
```

Let's see how it works for RandomizedSearchCV:

```
from sklearn.model_selection import RandomizedSearchCV
from scipy.stats import randint as sp_randint

# Hyperparameters
param_grid = {'C': sp_randint(1, 100),
                 'penalty': ['l1', 'l2']}

n_iter_search = 20
```

```
n_folds = 5
estimator = RandomizedSearchCV(log_reg, param_distributions=param_grid,
n_iter=n_iter_search, cv=n_folds)

estimator.fit(X, Y)
```

The preceding code generates the following output similar to `GridSearchCV`:

```
RandomizedSearchCV(cv=5, error_score='raise',
          estimator=LogisticRegression(C=1.0, class_weight=None,
dual=False, fit_intercept=True,
          intercept_scaling=1, max_iter=100, multi_class='ovr', n_jobs=1,
          penalty='l2', random_state=None, solver='liblinear', tol=0.0001,
          verbose=0, warm_start=False),
          fit_params=None, iid=True, n_iter=20, n_jobs=1,
          param_distributions={'C':
<scipy.stats._distn_infrastructure.rv_frozen object at 0x1176d4c88>,
'penalty': ['l1', 'l2']},
          pre_dispatch='2*n_jobs', random_state=None, refit=True,
          return_train_score=True, scoring=None, verbose=0)
```

Let's also see `best_estimator_`:

```
estimator.best_estimator_
```

The preceding code generates the following output:

```
LogisticRegression(C = 95, class_weight=None, dual=False,
fit_intercept=True,
          intercept_scaling=1, max_iter=100, multi_class='ovr', n_jobs=1,
          penalty ='l2', random_state=None, solver='liblinear', tol=0.0001,
          verbose = 0, warm_start=False)
```

The `estimator.best_score_` shows the following output:

```
0.98
```

`RandomizedSearchCV` has the same best score but one thing to note here is that the best performing estimator settings has `C = 95`, a value which is hard to find since people generally try round values such as 10, 100, or 1000 when constructing the parameter grid manually.

You can similarly check results of cross-validation with `estimator.cv_results_`:

```
{'mean_fit_time': array([0.0091342 , 0.00065241, 0.00873041, 0.00068126,
0.00082703,
          0.01093817, 0.00067267, 0.00961967, 0.00883713, 0.00069351,
```

```
        0.01048965, 0.00068388, 0.01074204, 0.0090354 , 0.00983639,
        0.01081419, 0.01014266, 0.00067706, 0.01015086, 0.00067825]),
 'mean_score_time': array([0.00026116, 0.0001647 , 0.00020576, 0.00017738,
0.00022368,
        0.00023923, 0.00016236, 0.00017295, 0.00026078, 0.00021319,
        0.00028219, 0.00018024, 0.00027289, 0.00025878, 0.00020723,
        0.00020337, 0.00023756, 0.00017438, 0.00028505, 0.0001936 ]),
 'mean_test_score': array([0.96666667, 0.97333333, 0.97333333, 0.98 ,
0.97333333,
        0.96666667, 0.97333333, 0.96666667, 0.98 , 0.97333333,
        0.96666667, 0.98 , 0.96666667, 0.96666667, 0.96666667,
        0.96666667, 0.96666667, 0.98 , 0.96666667, 0.96666667]),
 'mean_train_score': array([0.97333333, 0.97833333, 0.97333333, 0.98 ,
0.97833333,
        0.975 , 0.97833333, 0.975 , 0.97333333, 0.97833333,
        0.975 , 0.98 , 0.975 , 0.97333333, 0.975 ,
        0.975 , 0.975 , 0.97833333, 0.975 , 0.97666667]),
 'param_C': masked_array(data=[20, 53, 5, 95, 50, 71, 41, 43, 8, 30, 70,
91, 53, 15,
                    35, 41, 56, 82, 90, 27],
            mask=[False, False, False, False, False, False, False, False,
                  False, False, False, False, False, False, False, False,
                  False, False, False, False],
        fill_value='?',
            dtype=object),
 'param_penalty': masked_array(data=['l1', 'l2', 'l1', 'l2', 'l2', 'l1',
'l2', 'l1', 'l1',
                    'l2', 'l1', 'l2', 'l1', 'l1', 'l1', 'l1', 'l1', 'l2',
                    'l1', 'l2'],
            mask=[False, False, False, False, False, False, False, False,
                  False, False, False, False, False, False, False, False,
                  False, False, False, False],
        fill_value='?',
            dtype=object),
 'params': [{'C': 20, 'penalty': 'l1'},
  {'C': 53, 'penalty': 'l2'},
  {'C': 5, 'penalty': 'l1'},
  {'C': 95, 'penalty': 'l2'},
  {'C': 50, 'penalty': 'l2'},
  {'C': 71, 'penalty': 'l1'},
  {'C': 41, 'penalty': 'l2'},
  {'C': 43, 'penalty': 'l1'},
  {'C': 8, 'penalty': 'l1'},
  {'C': 30, 'penalty': 'l2'},
  {'C': 70, 'penalty': 'l1'},
  {'C': 91, 'penalty': 'l2'},
  {'C': 53, 'penalty': 'l1'},
  {'C': 15, 'penalty': 'l1'},
```

```
        {'C': 35, 'penalty': 'l1'},
        {'C': 41, 'penalty': 'l1'},
        {'C': 56, 'penalty': 'l1'},
        {'C': 82, 'penalty': 'l2'},
        {'C': 90, 'penalty': 'l1'},
        {'C': 27, 'penalty': 'l2'}],
 'rank_test_score': array([10, 5, 5, 1, 5, 10, 5, 10, 1, 5, 10, 1, 10, 10,
10, 10, 10,
            1, 10, 10], dtype=int32),
 'split0_test_score': array([1., 1., 1., 1., 1., 1., 1., 1., 1., 1., 1.,
1., 1., 1., 1., 1., 1.,
            1., 1., 1.]),
 'split0_train_score': array([0.95 , 0.975 , 0.95833333, 0.975 , 0.975,
        0.95833333, 0.975 , 0.95833333, 0.95833333, 0.975 ,
        0.95833333, 0.975 , 0.95833333, 0.95 , 0.95833333,
        0.95833333, 0.95833333, 0.975 , 0.95833333, 0.975 ]),
 'split1_test_score': array([0.96666667, 1. , 1. , 1. , 1. ,
        0.96666667, 1. , 0.96666667, 1. , 1. ,
        0.96666667, 1. , 0.96666667, 0.96666667, 0.96666667,
        0.96666667, 0.96666667, 1. , 0.96666667, 1. ]),
 'split1_train_score': array([0.975, 0.975, 0.975, 0.975, 0.975, 0.975,
0.975, 0.975, 0.975,
        0.975, 0.975, 0.975, 0.975, 0.975, 0.975, 0.975, 0.975, 0.975,
        0.975, 0.975]),
 'split2_test_score': array([0.93333333, 0.93333333, 0.93333333,
0.96666667, 0.93333333,
        0.93333333, 0.93333333, 0.93333333, 0.96666667, 0.93333333,
        0.93333333, 0.96666667, 0.93333333, 0.93333333, 0.93333333,
        0.93333333, 0.93333333, 0.96666667, 0.93333333, 0.93333333]),
 'split2_train_score': array([0.975 , 0.98333333, 0.975 , 0.98333333,
0.98333333,
        0.975 , 0.98333333, 0.975 , 0.975 , 0.98333333,
        0.975 , 0.98333333, 0.975 , 0.975 , 0.975 ,
        0.975 , 0.975 , 0.98333333, 0.975 , 0.98333333]),
 'split3_test_score': array([0.93333333, 0.93333333, 0.93333333,
0.93333333, 0.93333333,
        0.93333333, 0.93333333, 0.93333333, 0.93333333, 0.93333333,
        0.93333333, 0.93333333, 0.93333333, 0.93333333, 0.93333333,
        0.93333333, 0.93333333, 0.93333333, 0.93333333, 0.9 ]),
 'split3_train_score': array([0.99166667, 0.98333333, 0.98333333,
0.99166667, 0.98333333,
        0.99166667, 0.98333333, 0.99166667, 0.98333333, 0.98333333,
        0.99166667, 0.99166667, 0.99166667, 0.99166667, 0.99166667,
        0.99166667, 0.99166667, 0.98333333, 0.99166667, 0.98333333]),
 'split4_test_score': array([1., 1., 1., 1., 1., 1., 1., 1., 1., 1., 1.,
1., 1., 1., 1., 1., 1.,
            1., 1., 1.]),
 'split4_train_score': array([0.975 , 0.975 , 0.975 , 0.975 , 0.975 ,
```

```
        0.975 , 0.975 , 0.975 , 0.975 , 0.975 ,
        0.975 , 0.975 , 0.975 , 0.975 , 0.975 ,
        0.975 , 0.975 , 0.975 , 0.975 , 0.96666667]),
 'std_fit_time': array([2.16497645e-03, 5.39653699e-05, 1.00355397e-03,
4.75298306e-05,
        9.75692490e-05, 2.63689357e-03, 7.04799517e-05, 2.52499464e-03,
        1.92020413e-03, 6.05031761e-05, 1.78589024e-03, 5.85074724e-05,
        2.28621528e-03, 2.19771432e-03, 1.96957384e-03, 3.06769107e-03,
        1.15194163e-03, 2.10475943e-05, 1.33958298e-03, 4.09795418e-05]),
 'std_score_time': array([4.62378644e-05, 1.66142000e-06, 3.40806829e-05,
1.73623737e-05,
        5.26490415e-05, 4.75790783e-05, 1.48510089e-06, 7.53432889e-06,
        3.86445261e-05, 8.16042958e-05, 4.98746594e-05, 1.93474877e-05,
        2.82650630e-05, 2.54787261e-05, 2.55031663e-05, 3.09080976e-05,
        2.99830109e-05, 7.89824294e-06, 2.02431836e-05, 4.25877252e-05]),
 'std_test_score': array([0.02981424, 0.03265986, 0.03265986, 0.02666667,
0.03265986,
        0.02981424, 0.03265986, 0.02981424, 0.02666667, 0.03265986,
        0.02981424, 0.02666667, 0.02981424, 0.02981424, 0.02981424,
        0.02981424, 0.02981424, 0.02666667, 0.02981424, 0.0421637 ]),
 'std_train_score': array([0.01333333, 0.00408248, 0.00816497, 0.00666667,
0.00408248,
        0.01054093, 0.00408248, 0.01054093, 0.00816497, 0.00408248,
        0.01054093, 0.00666667, 0.01054093, 0.01333333, 0.01054093,
        0.01054093, 0.01054093, 0.00408248, 0.01054093, 0.0062361 ])}
```

Cross-validation results may look messy but you can import them to `pandas` DataFrame:

```
import pandas as pd

df = pd.DataFrame(estimator.cv_results_)

df.head()
```

We can see a couple of records as follows:

```
  mean_fit_time mean_score_time mean_test_score mean_train_score param_C \
0 0.009134 0.000261 0.966667 0.973333 20
1 0.000652 0.000165 0.973333 0.978333 53
2 0.008730 0.000206 0.973333 0.973333 5
3 0.000681 0.000177 0.980000 0.980000 95
4 0.000827 0.000224 0.973333 0.978333 50
  param_penalty params rank_test_score \
0 l1 {'C': 20, 'penalty': 'l1'} 10
1 l2 {'C': 53, 'penalty': 'l2'} 5
2 l1 {'C': 5, 'penalty': 'l1'} 5
3 l2 {'C': 95, 'penalty': 'l2'} 1
4 l2 {'C': 50, 'penalty': 'l2'} 5
```

```
       split0_test_score split0_train_score ... split2_test_score \
0 1.0 0.950000 ... 0.933333
1 1.0 0.975000 ... 0.933333
2 1.0 0.958333 ... 0.933333
3 1.0 0.975000 ... 0.966667
4 1.0 0.975000 ... 0.933333
       split2_train_score split3_test_score split3_train_score \
0 0.975000 0.933333 0.991667
1 0.983333 0.933333 0.983333
2 0.975000 0.933333 0.983333
3 0.983333 0.933333 0.991667
4 0.983333 0.933333 0.983333
       split4_test_score split4_train_score std_fit_time std_score_time \
0 1.0 0.975 0.002165 0.000046
1 1.0 0.975 0.000054 0.000002
2 1.0 0.975 0.001004 0.000034
3 1.0 0.975 0.000048 0.000017
4 1.0 0.975 0.000098 0.000053
     std_test_score std_train_score
0 0.029814 0.013333
1 0.032660 0.004082
2 0.032660 0.008165
3 0.026667 0.006667
4 0.032660 0.004082
[5 rows x 22 columns]
```

You can filter DataFrame to see where `mean_test_score` is at its maximum:

```
df[df['mean_test_score'] == df['mean_test_score'].max()]
```

This outputs the following:

```
       mean_fit_time mean_score_time mean_test_score mean_train_score param_C
\
3 0.000681 0.000177 0.98 0.980000 95
8 0.008837 0.000261 0.98 0.973333 8
11 0.000684 0.000180 0.98 0.980000 91
17 0.000677 0.000174 0.98 0.978333 82
     param_penalty params rank_test_score \
3 l2 {'C': 95, 'penalty': 'l2'} 1
8 l1 {'C': 8, 'penalty': 'l1'} 1
11 l2 {'C': 91, 'penalty': 'l2'} 1
17 l2 {'C': 82, 'penalty': 'l2'} 1
       split0_test_score split0_train_score ... split2_test_score \
3 1.0 0.975000 ... 0.966667
8 1.0 0.958333 ... 0.966667
11 1.0 0.975000 ... 0.966667
17 1.0 0.975000 ... 0.966667
```

```
      split2_train_score split3_test_score split3_train_score \
3  0.983333 0.933333 0.991667
8  0.975000 0.933333 0.983333
11 0.983333 0.933333 0.991667
17 0.983333 0.933333 0.983333
      split4_test_score split4_train_score std_fit_time std_score_time \
3  1.0 0.975 0.000048 0.000017
8  1.0 0.975 0.001920 0.000039
11 1.0 0.975 0.000059 0.000019
17 1.0 0.975 0.000021 0.000008
      std_test_score std_train_score
3  0.026667 0.006667
8  0.026667 0.008165
11 0.026667 0.006667
17 0.026667 0.004082
[4 rows x 22 columns]
```

As an exercise, you can create a parameter grid for `GradientBoostingClassifier` with the following hyperparameters, to experiment with both `GridSearchCV` and `RandomizedSearchCV`:

- `learning_rate` (default=0.1)—Boosting learning rate
- `n_estimators` (default=100)—Number of boosted trees to fit
- `max_depth` (default=3)—Maximum tree depth

Warm start

In terms of **Automated ML (AutoML)** pipelines, hyperparameter search space can grow really quickly and an exhaustive search becomes impracticable with limited time and finite resources. You need smarter ways to perform this task, especially if you have a large dataset with a complex model working on it. If you find yourself in this kind of situation, a `GridSeachCV` instances exhaustive search won't be feasible, or random parameter draws of `RandomizedSearchCV` might not give you the best results given limited time.

The basic idea of warm start is to use the information gained from previous training runs to identify smarter starting points for the next training run.

For example, `LogisticRegression` has a `warm_start` parameter, which is set to `False` by default. The following example shows you the training time the first time, and after the parameter update when it's set to `False`:

```
from sklearn.linear_model import LogisticRegression
```

```
log_reg = LogisticRegression(C=10, tol=0.00001)

from sklearn import datasets
iris = datasets.load_iris()
X = iris.data
Y = iris.target

from time import time
start = time()
log_reg.fit(X, Y)
end = time()
print("Time: {}".format(end - start))
# Time: 0.0009272098541259766

log_reg.set_params(C=20)
# LogisticRegression(C=100, class_weight=None, dual=False,
fit_intercept=True,
# intercept_scaling=1, max_iter=100, multi_class='ovr', n_jobs=1,
# penalty='12', random_state=None, solver='liblinear', tol=0.0001,
# verbose=0, warm_start=False)

start = time()
log_reg.fit(X, Y)
end = time()
print("Time: {}".format(end - start))
# Time: 0.0012941360473632812
```

The default solver for `LogisticRegression` is `liblinear`, which will re-initialize the weights before every new fit, but other solvers such as `lbfgs`, `newton-cg`, `sag`, and `saga` can take advantage of the `warm_start` and reduce the computational time by using the information from previous fits.

The following code snippet shows you a small example of how it works in practice:

```
log_reg = LogisticRegression(C=10, solver='sag', warm_start=True,
max_iter=10000)

start = time()
log_reg.fit(X, Y)
end = time()
print("Time: {}".format(end - start))
# Time: 0.043714046478271484

log_reg.set_params(C=20)

start = time()
log_reg.fit(X, Y)
```

```
end = time()
print("Time: {}".format(end - start))
# Time: 0.020781755447387695
```

Bayesian-based hyperparameter tuning

There are a couple of approaches to be used when it comes to model-based hyperparameter tuning and these approaches come together under **Sequential Model-based Global Optimization (SMBO)**.

When you think about `GridSearchCV` or `RandomizedSearchCV`, you may rightfully feel that the way they cross validate hyperparameters is not very smart. Both pre-define sets of hyperparameters to be validated during training time and are not designed to benefit from the information that they might get during training. If you could find a way to learn from previous iterations of hyperparameter validation based on model performance, then you would have an idea about which hyperparameter set is likely to give a better performance in the next iteration.

SMBO approaches emanated from this reasoning and Bayesian-based hyperparameter optimization is one of these approaches.

Sequential Model-based Algorithm Configuration (SMAC) is a great library that uses Bayesian optimization to configure hyperparameters of a given ML algorithm, and it's very easy to use.

The following snippet shows you how to optimize the `branin` function that you used at the beginning with SMAC:

```
from smac.facade.func_facade import fmin_smac

x, cost, _ = fmin_smac(func=branin, # function
                       x0=[3.2, 4.5], # default configuration
                       bounds=[(-5, 10), (0, 15)], # limits
                       maxfun=500, # maximum number of evaluations
                       rng=3) # random seed


print(x, cost)
# [3.12848204 2.33810374] 0.4015064637498025
```

An example system

In this section, you will write a wrapper function to optimize the XGBoost algorithm hyperparameters to improve performance on the `Breast Cancer Wisconsin` dataset:

```
# Importing necessary libraries
import numpy as np
from xgboost import XGBClassifier
from sklearn import datasets
from sklearn.model_selection import cross_val_score

# Importing ConfigSpace and different types of parameters
from smac.configspace import ConfigurationSpace
from ConfigSpace.hyperparameters import CategoricalHyperparameter, \
    UniformFloatHyperparameter, UniformIntegerHyperparameter
from ConfigSpace.conditions import InCondition

# Import SMAC-utilities
from smac.tae.execute_func import ExecuteTAFuncDict
from smac.scenario.scenario import Scenario
from smac.facade.smac_facade import SMAC

# Creating configuration space.
# Configuration space will hold all of your hyperparameters
cs = ConfigurationSpace()

# Defining hyperparameters and range of values that they can take
learning_rate = UniformFloatHyperparameter("learning_rate", 0.001, 0.1,
default_value=0.1)
n_estimators = UniformIntegerHyperparameter("n_estimators", 100, 200,
default_value=100)

# Adding hyperparameters to configuration space
cs.add_hyperparameters([learning_rate, n_estimators])

# Loading data set
wbc_dataset = datasets.load_breast_cancer()

# Creating function to cross validate XGBoost classifier given the
configuration space
def xgboost_from_cfg(cfg):
    """ Creates a XGBoost based on a configuration and evaluates it on the
    Wisconsin Breast Cancer-dataset using cross-validation.

    Parameters:
    -----------
    cfg: Configuration (ConfigSpace.ConfigurationSpace.Configuration)
```

```
            Configuration containing the parameters.
            Configurations are indexable!
        Returns:
        --------
        A crossvalidated mean score for the svm on the loaded data-set.
        """

        cfg = {k: cfg[k] for k in cfg if cfg[k]}

        clf = XGBClassifier(**cfg, eval_metric='auc', early_stopping_rounds=50,
random_state=42)

        scores = cross_val_score(clf, wbc_dataset.data, wbc_dataset.target,
cv=5)

        return 1 - np.mean(scores) # Minimize!


# Creating Scenario object
scenario = Scenario({"run_obj": "quality",
                     "runcount-limit": 200, # maximum function evaluations
                     "cs": cs, # configuration space
                     "deterministic": "true"
                     })



# SMAC object handles bayesian optimization loop
print("Please wait until optimization is finished")
smac = SMAC(scenario=scenario, rng=np.random.RandomState(42),
        tae_runner=xgboost_from_cfg)

incumbent = smac.optimize()

# Let's see the best performing hyperparameter values
print(incumbent)
# Configuration:
# learning_rate, Value: 0.08815217130807515
# n_estimators, Value: 196

# You can see the errpr rate of optimized hyperparameters
inc_value = xgboost_from_cfg(incumbent)

print("Optimized Value: %.2f" % (inc_value))
# 0.02
```

Great! Now you know how to create your configuration space, add your hyperparameter and define the value ranges for each of them. After configuration is done, you've seen how to create a scenario object and use SMAC to optimize hyperparameters of a given estimator.

You can use the SMAC object to get a run history and see the cost of each configuration:

```
param_1 = []
param_2 = []
costs = []

for k,v in smac.runhistory.config_ids.items():
    param_1.append(k._values['learning_rate'])
    param_2.append(k._values['n_estimators'])
    costs.append(smac.runhistory.cost_per_config[v])

print(len(param_1), len(param_2), len(costs))

import matplotlib.pyplot as plt
import matplotlib.cm as cm

sc = plt.scatter(param_1, param_2, c=costs)
plt.colorbar(sc)
plt.show()
```

The following diagram shows you different values that `learning_rate` and `n_estimators` took during optimization and their associated cost:

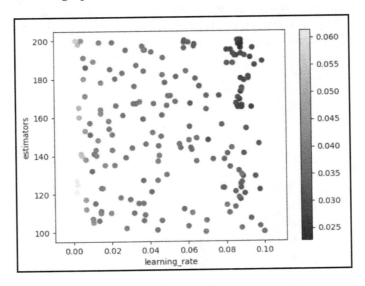

You can see that the best configurations were ~0.09 for `learning_rate` and ~200 for `n_estimators`.

Summary

In this chapter, you learned about model parameters, hyperparameters, and configuration space. Let's review them quickly:

- **Model parameters**: You can consider these as parameters to be learned during training time
- **Model hyperparameters**: These are the parameters that you should define before the training run starts
- **Configuration space parameters**: These parameters refer to any other parameter used for the environment that hosts your experiment

You have been introduced to common hyperparameter optimization methods, such as grid search and randomized search. Grid search and randomized search do not use the information produced from previous training runs and this is a disadvantage that Bayesian-based optimization methods address.

Bayesian-based optimization methods leverage the information of previous training runs to decide what will be the hyperparameter values for the next training run and navigate through the hyperparameter space in a smarter way. SMAC is what auto-sklearn uses under the hood to optimize hyperparameters of a given estimator and this chapter showed you how you can use this method with your own ML pipelines.

6
Creating AutoML Pipelines

The previous chapters focused on the different stages that are required to be executed in a **machine learning** (**ML**) project. Many moving parts have to be tied together for an ML model to execute and produce results successfully. This process of tying together different pieces of the ML process is known as **pipelines**. A pipeline is a generalized concept but very important concept for a Data Scientist. In software engineering, people build pipelines to develop software that is exercised from source code to deployment. Similarly, in ML, a pipeline is created to allow data flow from its raw format to some useful information. It provides mechanism to construct a multi-ML parallel pipeline system in order to compare the results of several ML methods.

Each stage of a pipeline is fed processed data from its preceding stage; that is, the output of a processing unit is supplied as an input to its next step. The data flows through the pipeline just as water flows in a pipe. Mastering the pipeline concept is a powerful way to create error-free ML models, and pipelines form a crucial element for building an AutoML system. In this chapter, we will work on the following topics:

- Introduction to ML pipelines
- Building a simple pipeline
- Function transformer
- Building a complex pipeline using weak learners and ensembles

We will begin with an introduction to ML pipelines in the next section.

Technical requirements

All the code examples can be found in the Chapter 06 folder in the GitHub link for this chapter.

An introduction to machine learning pipelines

Usually, an ML algorithm needs clean data to detect some patterns in the data and make predictions over a new dataset. However, in real-world applications, the data is often not ready to be directly fed into an ML algorithm. Similarly, the output from an ML model is just numbers or characters that need to be processed for performing some actions in the real world. To accomplish that, the ML model has to be deployed in a production environment. This entire framework of converting raw data to usable information is performed using a ML pipeline.

The following is a high-level illustration of an ML pipeline:

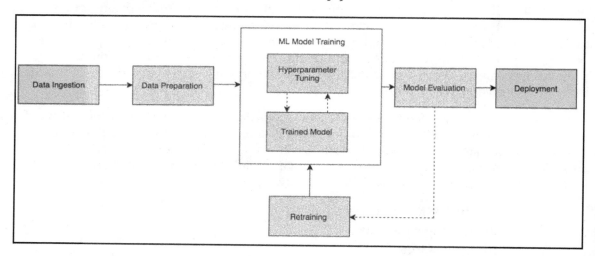

We will break down the blocks illustrated in the preceding figure as follows:

- **Data Ingestion**: It is the process of obtaining data and importing data for use. Data can be sourced from multiple systems, such as **Enterprise Resource Planning** (**ERP**) software, **Customer Relationship Management** (**CRM**) software, and web applications. The data extraction can be in the real time or batches. Sometimes, acquiring the data is a tricky part and is one of the most challenging steps as we need to have a good business and data understanding abilities.

- **Data Preparation**: We studied various data preparation techniques in Chapter 3, *Data Preprocessing*. There are several methods to preprocess the data to a suitable form for building models. Real-world data is often skewed—there is missing data, which is sometimes noisy. It is, therefore, necessary to preprocess the data to make it clean and transformed, so it's ready to be run through the ML algorithms.

- **ML model training**: It involves the use of various ML techniques to understand essential features in the data, make predictions, or derive insights out of it. Often, the ML algorithms are already coded and available as API or programming interfaces. The most important responsibility we need to take is to tune the hyperparameters. The use of hyperparameters and optimizing them to create a best-fitting model are the most critical and complicated parts of the model training phase.

- **Model Evaluation**: There are various criteria using which a model can be evaluated. It is a combination of statistical methods and business rules. In an AutoML pipeline, the evaluation is mostly based on various statistical and mathematical measures. If an AutoML system is developed for some specific business domain or use cases, then the business rules can also be embedded into the system to evaluate the correctness of a model.

- **Retraining**: The first model that we create for a use case is not often the best model. It is considered as a baseline model, and we try to improve the model's accuracy by training it repetitively.

- **Deployment**: The final step is to deploy the model that involves applying and migrating the model to business operations for their use. The deployment stage is highly dependent on the IT infrastructure and software capabilities an organization has.

As we see, there are several stages that we will need to perform to get results out of an ML model. The scikit-learn provides us a pipeline functionality that can be used to create several complex pipelines. While building an AutoML system, pipelines are going to be very complex, as many different scenarios have to be captured. However, if we know how to preprocess the data, utilizing an ML algorithm and applying various evaluation metrics, a pipeline is a matter of giving a shape to those pieces.

Let's design a very simple pipeline using scikit-learn.

A simple pipeline

We will first import a dataset known as `Iris`, which is already available in scikit-learn's sample dataset library (`http://scikit-learn.org/stable/auto_examples/datasets/plot_iris_dataset.html`). The dataset consists of four features and has 150 rows. We will be developing the following steps in a pipeline to train our model using the `Iris` dataset. The problem statement is to predict the species of an `Iris` data using four different features:

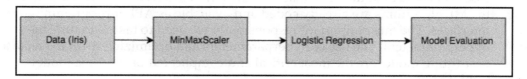

In this pipeline, we will use a `MinMaxScaler` method to scale the input data and logistic regression to predict the species of the `Iris`. The model will then be evaluated based on the accuracy measure:

1. The first step is to import various libraries from scikit-learn that will provide methods to accomplish our task. We have learn about all this in previous chapters. The only addition is the `Pipeline` method from `sklearn.pipeline`. This will provide us with necessary methods needed to create an ML pipeline:

```
from sklearn.datasets import load_iris
from sklearn.preprocessing import MinMaxScaler
from sklearn.linear_model import LogisticRegression
from sklearn.model_selection import train_test_split
from sklearn.pipeline import Pipeline
```

2. The next step is to load the `iris` data and split it into training and test dataset. In this example, we will use 80% of the dataset to train the model and the remaining 20% to test the accuracy of the model. We can use the `shape` function to view the dimension of the dataset:

```
# Load and split the data
iris = load_iris()
X_train, X_test, y_train, y_test = train_test_split(iris.data,
iris.target, test_size=0.2, random_state=42)
X_train.shape
```

3. The following result shows the training dataset having 4 columns and 120 rows, which equates to 80% of the `Iris` dataset and is as expected:

```
Out[22]:  (120, 4)
```

4. Next, we print the dataset to take a glance at the data:

```
print(X_train)
```

The preceding code provides the following output:

```
[[4.6 3.6 1.  0.2]
 [5.7 4.4 1.5 0.4]
 [6.7 3.1 4.4 1.4]
 [4.8 3.4 1.6 0.2]
 [4.4 3.2 1.3 0.2]
 [6.3 2.5 5.  1.9]
 [6.4 3.2 4.5 1.5]
 [5.2 3.5 1.5 0.2]
 [5.  3.6 1.4 0.2]
 [5.2 4.1 1.5 0.1]
 [5.8 2.7 5.1 1.9]
 [6.  3.4 4.5 1.6]
 [6.7 3.1 4.7 1.5]
 [5.4 3.9 1.3 0.4]
 [5.4 3.7 1.5 0.2]
```

5. The next step is to create a pipeline. The pipeline object is in the form of (key, value) pairs. Key is a string that has the name for a particular step, and value is the name of the function or actual method. In the following code snippet, we have named the `MinMaxScaler()` method as `minmax` and `LogisticRegression(random_state=42)` as `lr`:

```
pipe_lr = Pipeline([('minmax', MinMaxScaler()),
    ('lr', LogisticRegression(random_state=42))])
```

6. Then, we fit the pipeline object—`pipe_lr`—to the training dataset:

```
pipe_lr.fit(X_train, y_train)
```

7. When we execute the preceding code, we get the following output, which shows the final structure of the fitted model that was built:

```
Out[25]: Pipeline(memory=None,
         steps=[('minmax', MinMaxScaler(copy=True, feature_range=(0, 1))), ('clf', LogisticRegression(C=1.0, class_weight
    =None, dual=False, fit_intercept=True,
             intercept_scaling=1, max_iter=100, multi_class='ovr', n_jobs=1,
             penalty='l2', random_state=42, solver='liblinear', tol=0.0001,
             verbose=0, warm_start=False))])
```

8. The last step is to score the model on the `test` dataset using the `score` method:

```
score = pipe_lr.score(X_test, y_test)
print('Logistic Regression pipeline test accuracy: %.3f' % score)
```

As we can note from the following results, the accuracy of the model was `0.900`, which is 90%:

```
Logistic Regression pipeline test accuracy: 0.900
```

In the preceding example, we created a pipeline, which constituted of two steps, that is, `minmax` scaling and `LogisticRegression`. When we executed the `fit` method on the `pipe_lr` pipeline, the `MinMaxScaler` performed a `fit` and `transform` method on the input data, and it was passed on to the estimator, which is a logistic regression model. These intermediate steps in a pipeline are known as **transformers**, and the last step is an estimator.

Transformers are used for data preprocessing and has two methods, `fit` and `transform`. The `fit` method is used to find parameters from the training data, and the `transform` method is used to apply the data preprocessing techniques to the dataset.

Estimators are used for creating machine learning model and has two methods, `fit` and `predict`. The `fit` method is used to train a ML model, and the `predict` method is used to apply the trained model on a test or new dataset.

This concept is summarized in the following figure:

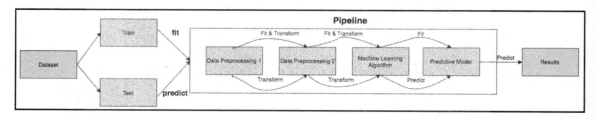

We have to call only the pipeline's **fit** method to train a model and call the **predict** method to create predictions. Rest all functions that is, **Fit** and **Transform** are encapsulated in the pipeline's functionality and executed as shown in the preceding figure.

Sometimes, we will need to write some custom functions to perform custom transformations. The following section is about function transformer that can assist us in implementing this custom functionality.

FunctionTransformer

A `FunctionTransformer` is used to define a user-defined function that consumes the data from the pipeline and returns the result of this function to the next stage of the pipeline. This is used for stateless transformations, such as taking the square or log of numbers, defining custom scaling functions, and so on.

In the following example, we will build a pipeline using the `CustomLog` function and the predefined preprocessing method `StandardScaler`:

1. We import all the required libraries as we did in our previous examples. The only addition here is the `FunctionTransformer` method from the `sklearn.preprocessing` library. This method is used to execute a custom transformer function and stitch it together to other stages in a pipeline:

```
import numpy as np
from sklearn.datasets import load_iris
from sklearn.model_selection import train_test_split
from sklearn import preprocessing
from sklearn.pipeline import make_pipeline
from sklearn.preprocessing import FunctionTransformer
from sklearn.preprocessing import StandardScaler
```

2. In the following code snippet, we will define a custom function, which returns the log of a number X:

```
def CustomLog(X):
    return np.log(X)
```

3. Next, we will define a data preprocessing function named `PreprocData`, which accepts the input data (X) and target (Y) of a dataset. For this example, the Y is not necessary, as we are not going to build a supervised model and just demonstrate a data preprocessing pipeline. However, in the real world, we can directly use this function to create a supervised ML model.

4. Here, we use a `make_pipeline` function to create a pipeline. We used the `pipeline` function in our earlier example, where we have to define names for the data preprocessing or ML functions. The advantage of using a `make_pipeline` function is that it generates the names or keys of a function automatically:

```
def PreprocData(X, Y):
pipe = make_pipeline(
 FunctionTransformer(CustomLog),StandardScaler()
 )
 X_train, X_test, Y_train, Y_test = train_test_split(X, Y)
 pipe.fit(X_train, Y_train)
 return pipe.transform(X_test), Y_test
```

5. As we are ready with the pipeline, we can load the `Iris` dataset. We print the input data `X` to take a look at the data:

```
iris = load_iris()
X, Y = iris.data, iris.target
print(X)
```

The preceding code prints the following output:

```
[[5.1 3.5 1.4 0.2]
 [4.9 3.  1.4 0.2]
 [4.7 3.2 1.3 0.2]
 [4.6 3.1 1.5 0.2]
 [5.  3.6 1.4 0.2]
 [5.4 3.9 1.7 0.4]
 [4.6 3.4 1.4 0.3]
 [5.  3.4 1.5 0.2]
 [4.4 2.9 1.4 0.2]
 [4.9 3.1 1.5 0.1]
 [5.4 3.7 1.5 0.2]
 [4.8 3.4 1.6 0.2]
 [4.8 3.  1.4 0.1]
 [4.3 3.  1.1 0.1]
 [5.8 4.  1.2 0.2]
 [5.7 4.4 1.5 0.4]
 [5.4 3.9 1.3 0.4]
 [5.1 3.5 1.4 0.3]
 [5.7 3.8 1.7 0.3]
```

6. Next, we will call the `PreprocData` function by passing the `iris` data. The result returned is a transformed dataset, which has been processed first using our `CustomLog` function and then using the `StandardScaler` data preprocessing method:

```
X_transformed, Y_transformed = PreprocData(X, Y)
print(X_transformed)
```

7. The preceding data transformation task yields the following transformed data results:

```
[[-0.2347759  -0.48960713  0.69581726  0.88662043]
 [ 0.00396322 -0.48960713  0.76352343  1.07005764]
 [ 0.34706281 -0.48960713  0.62528921  0.372669  ]
 [ 0.56654528 -0.25197392  0.92180958  0.7806152 ]
 [ 1.08613866  0.41464764  1.01013024  1.0272376 ]
 [ 1.18545964  0.19965017  0.76352343  1.0272376 ]
 [-0.11435918 -0.48960713  0.39414489  0.4532015 ]
 [ 0.9853462   0.19965017  0.51366007  0.52776295]
 [-0.48219832  0.82518858 -1.30762888 -0.73266584]
 [-0.3573624   1.02148788 -1.54981681 -1.43005448]
 [ 0.56654528 -0.73588342  0.69581726  0.7806152 ]
 [-0.7389596   0.82518858 -1.42439437 -1.43005448]
 [ 1.08613866 -0.48960713  0.66092059  0.52776295]
 [ 0.67368713  0.41464764  0.82862485  1.0272376 ]
 [-1.0057925  -1.82170004  0.02677876  0.18923179]
 [-1.0057925   0.82518858 -1.30762888 -1.43005448]
 [ 0.2346079  -0.02239764  0.66092059  0.7806152 ]
 [ 1.18545964  0.19965017  0.86025995  0.93570915]
 [ 0.67368713 -0.48960713  0.92180958  0.98251383]
 [ 0.12026292 -0.02239764  0.76352343  0.7806152 ]
 [-0.11435918 -0.02239764  0.43492827  0.372669  ]
 [ 0.00396322  1.92574265 -1.68528336 -1.43005448]]
```

We will now need to build various complex pipelines for an AutoML system. In the following section, we will create a sophisticated pipeline using several data preprocessing steps and ML algorithms.

A complex pipeline

In this section, we will determine the best classifier to predict the species of an Iris flower using its four different features. We will use a combination of four different data preprocessing techniques along with four different ML algorithms for the task. The following is the pipeline design for the job:

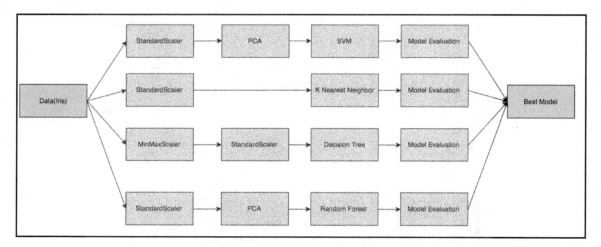

We will proceed as follows:

1. We start with importing the various libraries and functions that are required for the task:

```
from sklearn.datasets import load_iris
from sklearn.preprocessing import StandardScaler
from sklearn.decomposition import PCA
from sklearn.preprocessing import MinMaxScaler
from sklearn.model_selection import train_test_split
from sklearn.neighbors import KNeighborsClassifier
from sklearn.ensemble import RandomForestClassifier
from sklearn import svm
from sklearn import tree
from sklearn.pipeline import Pipeline
```

2. Next, we load the `Iris` dataset and split it into `train` and `test` datasets. The `X_train` and `Y_train` dataset will be used for training the different models, and `X_test` and `Y_test` will be used for testing the trained model:

```
# Load and split the data
iris = load_iris()
X_train, X_test, y_train, y_test = train_test_split(iris.data,
iris.target, test_size=0.2, random_state=42)
```

3. Next, we will create four different pipelines, one for each model. In the pipeline for the SVM model, `pipe_svm`, we will first scale the numeric inputs using `StandardScaler` and then create the principal components using **Principal Component Analysis (PCA)**. Finally, a **Support Vector Machine (SVM)** model is built using this preprocessed dataset.

4. Similarly, we will construct a pipeline to create the KNN model named `pipe_knn`. Only `StandardScaler` is used to preprocess the data before executing the `KNeighborsClassifier` to create the KNN model.

5. Then, we create a pipeline for building a decision tree model. We use the `StandardScaler` and `MinMaxScaler` methods to preprocess the data to be used by the `DecisionTreeClassifier` method.

6. The last model created using a pipeline is the random forest model, where only the `StandardScaler` is used to preprocess the data to be used by the `RandomForestClassifier` method.

The following is the code snippet for creating these four different pipelines used to create four different models:

```
# Construct svm pipeline

pipe_svm = Pipeline([('ss1', StandardScaler()),
        ('pca', PCA(n_components=2)),
        ('svm', svm.SVC(random_state=42))])
# Construct knn pipeline
pipe_knn = Pipeline([('ss2', StandardScaler()),
        ('knn', KNeighborsClassifier(n_neighbors=6,
metric='euclidean'))])

# Construct DT pipeline
pipe_dt = Pipeline([('ss3', StandardScaler()),
        ('minmax', MinMaxScaler()),
        ('dt', tree.DecisionTreeClassifier(random_state=42))])

# Construct Random Forest pipeline
num_trees = 100
```

```
max_features = 1
pipe_rf = Pipeline([('ss4', StandardScaler()),
        ('pca', PCA(n_components=2)),
        ('rf', RandomForestClassifier(n_estimators=num_trees,
max_features=max_features))])
```

7. Next, we will need to store the name of pipelines in a dictionary, which would be used to display results:

```
pipe_dic = {0: 'K Nearest Neighbours', 1: 'Decision Tree',
2:'Random Forest', 3:'Support Vector Machines'}
```

8. Then, we will list the four pipelines to execute those pipelines iteratively:

```
pipelines = [pipe_knn, pipe_dt,pipe_rf,pipe_svm]
```

9. Now, we are ready with the complex structure of the whole pipeline. The only things that remain are to fit the data to the pipeline, evaluate the results, and select the best model.

   In the following code snippet, we fit each of the four pipelines iteratively to the training dataset:

```
# Fit the pipelines
for pipe in pipelines:
  pipe.fit(X_train, y_train)
```

10. Once the model fitting is executed successfully, we will examine the accuracy of the four models using the following code snippet:

```
# Compare accuracies
for idx, val in enumerate(pipelines):
    print('%s pipeline test accuracy: %.3f' % (pipe_dic[idx],
val.score(X_test, y_test)))
```

11. We can note from the following results that the k-nearest neighbors and decision tree models lead the pack with a perfect accuracy of 100%. This is too good to believe and might be a result of using a small data set and/or overfitting:

```
K Nearest Neighbours pipeline test accuracy: 1.00
Decision Tree pipeline test accuracy: 1.00
Random Forest pipeline test accuracy: 0.90
Support Vector Machines pipeline test accuracy: 0.90
```

12. We can use any one of the two winning models, **k-nearest neighbors** (**KNN**) or decision tree model, for deployment. We can accomplish this using the following code snippet:

```
best_accuracy = 0
best_classifier = 0
best_pipeline = ''
for idx, val in enumerate(pipelines):
  if val.score(X_test, y_test) > best_accuracy:
  best_accuracy = val.score(X_test, y_test)
  best_pipeline = val
  best_classifier = idx
print('%s Classifier has the best accuracy of %.2f' %
(pipe_dic[best_classifier],best_accuracy))
```

13. As the accuracies were similar for k-nearest neighbor and decision tree, KNN was chosen to be the best model, as it was the first model in the pipeline. However, at this stage, we can also use some business rules or access the execution cost to decide the best model:

```
K Nearest Neighbours is the classifier has the best accuracy of 1.00
```

Summary

This chapter was a sketch of building pipelines for ML systems—it is just the tip of the iceberg. Building pipelines is very complicated. However, once developed, it makes the life of a developer more comfortable. It reduces the complexity of formulating different models and thus becomes an essential concept, which is required to create an AutoML system. The concepts that we described in this chapter give you a foundation for creating pipelines. You must have understood when you built the pipelines in this chapter how well-structured the model building process became with the use of pipelines.

The next chapter will summarize our learning so far. It will also provide you with several suggestions that would be useful in devising an AutoML system and executing data science projects successfully.

Dive into Deep Learning

7

The next step in **artificial intelligence** (**AI**) is more about automation. In this book, we have covered some of the fundamentals of **Automated machine learning** (**AutoML**). There is one more area of AI that has just begun showing up in multiple use cases and is required to be applied extremely for automation. This area of the AI landscape is known as **deep learning** (**DL**). DL is at the tipping point of what machines can do. It can do more than **machine learning** (**ML**), with ease and with better precision. A DL algorithm can learn the critical features of a dataset by itself, can adjust the weights to create a better model, and much more. The applications of DL networks are extensive.

With the advent of Deep learning, researchers and practitioners in the field of image, speech, and video recognition, are seeing some actionable results. It has helped AI to get close to its original goal of becoming the brains of the robot. It also has a role to play in the growing field of the **Internet of Things** (**IoT**). For enterprises, DL is already playing an important role in streamlining customer service and assisting in the automation of many human-intensive tasks. You might have, by now, encountered bots powered by DL trying to answer your product queries or helping you book your favorite pizza orders.

DL is also unleashing developments in the field of medicine and healthcare. Don't be surprised if machines start diagnosing your diseases by reading X-rays and MRI scans. It is expected that DL would solve many mysteries that humanity has and automate substantial manual tasks that were not possible before. Interesting, isn't it? Let's unveil some of the deep secrets of DL.

In this chapter, we will learn about:

- Feed-forward neural networks
- Autoencoders
- Deep convolutional networks

In this chapter, we will try to touch on some basic concepts of DL illustratively. Our focus here is not to discourage you from DL with equations, mathematical formulas, and derivatives. Though they are essential concepts, they can be overwhelming. Instead, we will walk you through the concepts in an illustrative way and help you to write your very first DL codes.

Neural networks are the precursors to DL networks, and they form the building blocks of the DL framework. The basic idea behind a neural network is to create a computing system that is modeled on the working of our biological brain.

Technical requirements

All the code examples can be found in the Chapter 07 folder in GitHub.

Overview of neural networks

The best definition of a neural network is provided by an inventor, Dr. Robert Hecht-Nielsen, one of the first neurocomputer scientists, in *Neural Network Primer: Part I* by Maureen Caudill, AI Expert, Feb. 1989:

> *...a computing system made up of a number of simple, highly interconnected processing elements, which process information by their dynamic state response to external inputs.*

The fundamental building blocks of neural networks are neurons, and they are organized in different layers. The tiered architecture has the neurons in each layer connected to neurons in the next layer. A neural network has, at a minimum, three layers. The input layer is connected to one or more hidden layers, where the connection is established through a system of **weighted** links. The last hidden layer is connected to the output layer which produces the results of a task.

The following diagram illustrates a three-layered neural network:

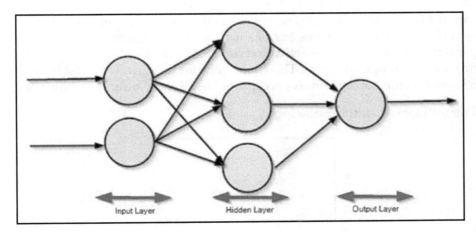

This network is also known as a fully connected artificial neural network or a **feed-forward neural network** (**FNN**). There is another kind of neural network architecture where the results are propagated back to learn and adjust the weights, known as a **feed-forward neural network** with backpropagation, as shown in the following diagram:

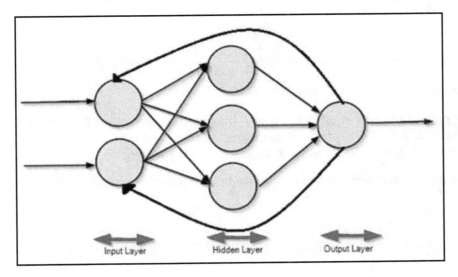

Let's examine each unit of a neural network in a comprehensive manner.

Neuron

Neurons are the basic unit of a neural network. Each neuron has a number of inputs, a processor, and an output. The processing of a neuron starts by accumulating all of its incoming inputs, and, based on the activation function, it fires a signal that is propagated to other neurons or as an output signal. This helps neurons to learn. The most basic form of a neuron is known as the **perceptron**. A perceptron has a binary output of either 0 or 1.

A typical neuron looks like the following:

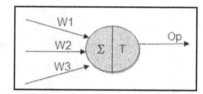

As we can see, neurons have several inputs. For each input connection, there is a weight associated with that specific connection. When the neuron is activated, the state is computed by adding the inputs multiplied by its corresponding connection's weight. Mathematically, it can be denoted by the following function:

$$\sum_{i=1}^{m} w_i x_i$$

Where x_i is the input value with bias included.

The bias is one more extra input, a neuron. A bias has its own connection weight, and the value of bias is always 1. This is there to make sure that even if there are no inputs, namely, the input value is 0, there is going to be an activation in the neuron.

Once the state is computed, the value is passed through an activation function to normalize the result.

Activation functions

Activation functions are used to produce non-linear decisions using the prior linear combination of weighted inputs. We will discuss four different types of activation functions that are predominantly used for DL applications:

- Step
- Sigmoid
- ReLU
- Tanh

The step function

In the step function, if the value of the weighted sum of inputs is greater than a certain threshold, the neuron is activated. Two options are as follows:

$$\varnothing(x) = \begin{cases} 1, if x \geq 0 \\ 0, if x < 0 \end{cases}$$

If x, namely the weighted sum of the input values, is greater than or equal to 0, 1 is activated, and 0 otherwise. The following figure illustrates the step function:

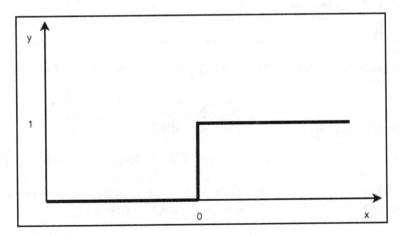

The next widely used activation function is the **sigmoid** function.

The sigmoid function

The sigmoid function is defined as:

$$\emptyset(x) = \frac{1}{1 + e^{-x}}$$

Here, x is the value of the weighted sum of the input values. We have seen this function in logistic regression. When x is below zero it drops off, and anything above zero it approximates towards one. Unlike a step function, it is a non-linear activation function. It is mostly used in output layers in a neural network, when we work on classification tasks trying to predict probabilities. The following figure illustrates the sigmoid function:

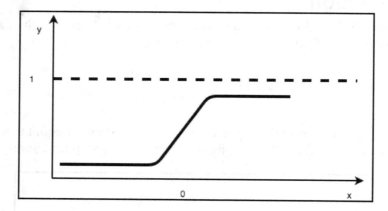

The next activation function we discuss is **ReLU**, which is widely used in the hidden layers of a neural network.

The ReLU function

Researchers have found out that a neural network using **Rectified Linear Unit (ReLU)** function, trains faster than other non-linear functions like sigmoid and tanh without a significant drop in accuracy. So, the **ReLU function** is one of the most important activation functions. It gives an output of x, if x is positive, and O otherwise.

It is defined as the following:

$$A(x) = max\ (0,x)$$

The ReLU function is as shown in the following figure:

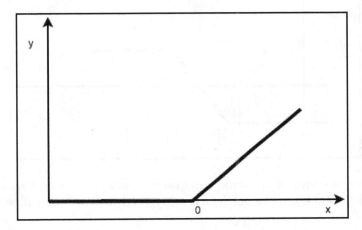

 ReLU is a non-linear function and the combination of ReLU functions are also non-linear. The range of ReLU is from 0 to infinity.

Next, we discuss the tanh function, which is very similar to the sigmoid function, but here the values go below 0.

The tanh function

The tanh function is also known as the **hyperbolic tangent function**. The values go from -1 to +1.

Its mathematical formula is as follows:

$$\varnothing(x) = \frac{1 - e^{-2x}}{1 + e^{-2x}}$$

The output of the tanh function is zero centered. It is also a non-linear function and so can be used to stack different layers. The tanh function is as shown in the following figure:

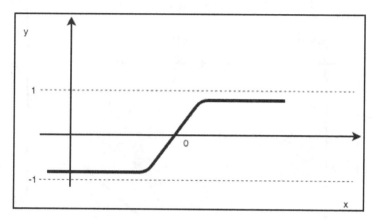

Now that we have some idea about what a neural network is, the structure of a neural network, and its different components, let's create a feed-forward neural network using Keras.

A feed-forward neural network using Keras

Keras is a DL library, originally built on Python, that runs over TensorFlow or Theano. It was developed to make DL implementations faster:

1. We call `install keras` using the following command in your operation system's Command Prompt:

   ```
   pip install keras
   ```

2. We start by importing the numpy and pandas library for data manipulation. Also, we set a seed that allows us to reproduce the script's results:

   ```
   import numpy as np
   import pandas as pd
   numpy.random.seed(8)
   ```

3. Next, the sequential model and dense layers are imported from `keras.models` and `keras.layers` respectively. Keras models are defined as a sequence of layers. The sequential construct allows the user to configure and add layers. The dense layer allows a user to build a fully connected network:

```
from keras.models import Sequential
from keras.layers import Dense
```

4. The HR attrition dataset is then loaded, which has 14,999 rows and 10 columns. The `salary` and `sales` attributes are one-hot encoded to be used by Keras for building a DL model:

```
#load hrdataset
hr_data = pd.read_csv('data/hr.csv', header=0)
# split into input (X) and output (Y) variables
data_trnsf = pd.get_dummies(hr_data, columns =['salary', 'sales'])
data_trnsf.columns
X = data_trnsf.drop('left', axis=1)
X.columns
```

The following is the output from the preceding code:

```
Out[16]: Index(['satisfaction_level', 'last_evaluation', 'number_project',
                'average_montly_hours', 'time_spend_company', 'Work_accident',
                'promotion_last_5years', 'salary_high', 'salary_low', 'salary_medium',
                'sales_IT', 'sales_RandD', 'sales_accounting', 'sales_hr',
                'sales_management', 'sales_marketing', 'sales_product_mng',
                'sales_sales', 'sales_support', 'sales_technical'],
              dtype='object')
```

5. The dataset is then split with a ratio of 70:30 to train and test the model:

```
from sklearn.model_selection import train_test_split

X_train, X_test, Y_train, Y_test = train_test_split(X,
data_trnsf.left, test_size=0.3, random_state=42)
```

6. Next, we start creating a fully connected neural network by defining a sequential model using three layers. The first layer is the input layer. In this layer, we define the the number of input features using the `input_dim` argument, the number of neurons, and the activation function. We set the `input_dim` argument to 20 for the 20 input features we have in our preprocessed dataset `X_train`. The number of neurons in the first layer is specified to be 12. The target is to predict the employee attrition which is a binary classification problem. So, we use the rectifier `activation` function in the first two layers to introduce non-linearity into the model and activate the neurons. The second layer, which is the hidden layer, is configured with 10 neurons. The third layer, which is the output layer, has one neuron with a `sigmoid` activation function. This ensures that the output is between 0 and 1 for the binary classification task:

```
# create model
model = Sequential()
model.add(Dense(12, input_dim=20, activation='relu'))
model.add(Dense(10, activation='relu'))
model.add(Dense(1, activation='sigmoid'))
```

7. Once we configure the model, the next step is to compile the model. During the compilation, we specify the `loss` function, the `optimizer`, and the `metrics`. Since we are dealing with a two class problem, we specify the `loss` function as `binary_crossentropy`. We declare `adam` as the optimizer to be used for this exercise. The choice of the optimization algorithm is crucial for the model's excellent performance. The `adam` optimizer is an extension to a stochastic gradient descent algorithm and is a widely used optimizer:

```
# Compile model
model.compile(loss='binary_crossentropy', optimizer='adam',
metrics=['accuracy'])
```

8. Next, we fit the model to the training set using the `fit` method. An epoch is used to specify the number of forward and backward passes. The `batch_size` parameter is used to declare the number of training examples to be used in each epoch. In our example, we specify the number of `epochs` to be 100 with a `batch_size` of 10:

```
# Fit the model
X_train = np.array(X_train)
model.fit(X_train, Y_train, epochs=100, batch_size=10)
```

9. Once we execute the preceding code snippet, the execution starts and we can see the progress, as in the following screenshot. The processing stops once it reaches the number of epochs that is specified in the model's `fit` method:

```
Epoch 1/100
10499/10499 [==============================] - 6s - loss: 0.6086 - acc: 0.7618
Epoch 2/100
10499/10499 [==============================] - 4s - loss: 0.5390 - acc: 0.7620
Epoch 3/100
10499/10499 [==============================] - 4s - loss: 0.5015 - acc: 0.7631
Epoch 4/100
10499/10499 [==============================] - 4s - loss: 0.4569 - acc: 0.7781
Epoch 5/100
10499/10499 [==============================] - 4s - loss: 0.3980 - acc: 0.8119
Epoch 6/100
10499/10499 [==============================] - 4s - loss: 0.3359 - acc: 0.8544
Epoch 7/100
10499/10499 [==============================] - 4s - loss: 0.3005 - acc: 0.8805
Epoch 8/100
10499/10499 [==============================] - 4s - loss: 0.2818 - acc: 0.8874
Epoch 9/100
10499/10499 [==============================] - 5s - loss: 0.2713 - acc: 0.8946
```

10. The final step is to evaluate the model. We specified accuracy earlier in the evaluation metrics. At the final step, we retrieve the model's accuracy using the following code snippet:

```
# evaluate the model
scores = model.evaluate(X_train, Y_train)
print("%s: %.4f%%" % (model.metrics_names[1], scores[1]*100))

X_test = np.array(X_test)

scores = model.evaluate(X_test, Y_test)
print("%s: %.4f%%" % (model.metrics_names[1], scores[1]*100))
```

The following result shows the model accuracy to be `93.56%` and test accuracy to be `93.20%`, which is a pretty good result. We might get slightly different results than those depicted as per the seed:

```
9024/10499 [=========================>.....] - ETA: 0s
acc: 93.56%
3072/4500 [===================>..........] - ETA: 0s
acc: 93.20%
```

Data scaling is often required to obtain good results from neural networks.

In the following section we discuss autoencoders, which is an unsupervised DL technique and widely used for non-linear dimensionality reduction.

Autoencoders

An autoencoder is a type of DL which can be used for unsupervised learning. It is similar to other dimensionality reduction techniques such as **Principal Component Analysis (PCA)** which we studied earlier. However, PCA projects data from higher dimensions to lower dimensions using linear transformation, but autoencoders use non-linear transformations.

In an autoencoder, there are two parts to its structure:

- **Encoder**: This part compresses the input into a fewer number of elements or bits. The input is compressed to the maximum point, which is known as **latent space** or **bottleneck**. These compressed bits are known as **encoded bits**.
- **Decoder**: The decoder tries to reconstruct the input based on the encoded bits. If the decoder can reproduce the exact input from the encoded bits, then we can say that there was a perfect encoding. However, it is an ideal case scenario and does not always happen. The reconstruction error provides a way to measure the reconstruction effort of the decoder and judge the accuracy of the autoencoder.

Now that we have a bit of understanding of the structure of an autoencoder, let's visualize it using the following figure:

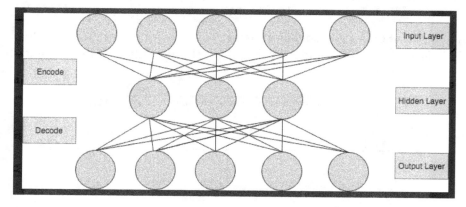

There are different types of autoencoders, such as:

- **Vanilla autoencoder**: It has two layers of neural network architecture, with one hidden layer.
- **Sparse autoencoder**: It is used to learn the sparse representation of data. Here, a constraint is imposed on its loss function to constraint the reconstruction of an autoencoder.
- **Denoising autoencoder**: In these autoencoders, partially corrupted inputs are introduced. This is done to prevent the autoencoder from simply learning the structure of inputs and forces the network to discover more robust features to learn the input patterns.

Anomaly detection is one of the most widely used use cases for autoencoders. It is a process to detect the unknown from the knowns. In an anomaly detection exercise, the input data always has one class which is *known*. As an autoencoder learns the pattern of the data by reconstructing the input data, it tends to discover the unknown patterns which might be the anomalies in the data:

1. As we did for the previous example, here we import the required libraries using the following code snippet:

```
%matplotlib inline
import numpy as np
import pandas as pd
import matplotlib.pyplot as plt
from sklearn.model_selection import train_test_split
from keras.models import Model, load_model
from keras.layers import Input, Dense
np.random.seed(8)
```

2. Next, the dataset used for building the anomaly detector using an autoencoder is loaded. The data used for the demo was extracted from the 1974 Motor Trend US magazine; it comprises fuel consumption and 10 aspects of automobile design and performance for 32 automobiles (1973–74 models). The dataset was modified a bit to introduce some data anomalies:

```
# load autodesign
auto_data = pd.read_csv('data/auto_design.csv')
# split into input (X) and output (Y) variables
X =auto_data.drop('Unnamed: 0', 1)
from sklearn.model_selection import train_test_split
X_train, X_test = train_test_split(X, test_size=0.3,
random_state=42)
```

```
print(X_train)
X_train.shape
```

We get the following output for the preceding code:

	mpg	cyl	disp	hp	drat	wt	qsec	vs	am	gear	carb	ID
4	18.7	8	360.0	175	3.15	3.440	17.02	0	0	3	2	5
16	14.7	8	440.0	230	3.23	5.345	17.42	0	0	3	4	17
5	18.1	6	225.0	105	2.76	3.460	20.22	1	0	3	1	6
13	15.2	8	275.8	180	3.07	3.780	18.00	0	0	3	3	14
11	16.4	8	275.8	180	3.07	4.070	17.40	0	0	3	3	12
23	13.3	8	350.0	245	3.73	3.840	15.41	0	0	3	4	24
1	21.0	6	160.0	110	3.90	2.875	17.02	0	1	4	4	2
2	22.8	4	108.0	93	3.85	2.320	18.61	1	1	4	1	3
26	26.0	4	120.3	91	4.43	2.140	16.70	0	1	5	2	27
3	21.4	6	258.0	110	3.08	3.215	19.44	1	0	3	1	4
21	15.5	8	318.0	150	2.76	3.520	16.87	0	0	3	2	22
27	30.4	4	95.1	113	3.77	1.513	16.90	1	1	5	2	28
22	15.2	8	304.0	150	3.15	3.435	17.30	0	0	3	2	23
18	80.4	10	75.7	100	4.93	1.615	150.52	1	1	4	2	19
31	21.4	4	121.0	109	4.11	2.780	18.60	1	1	4	2	32
20	21.5	4	120.1	97	3.70	2.465	20.01	1	0	3	1	21
7	24.4	4	146.7	62	3.69	3.190	20.00	1	0	4	2	8
10	17.8	6	167.6	210	800.0	900.000	1000.00	1	0	4	4	11
14	10.4	8	472.0	205	2.93	5.250	17.98	0	0	3	4	15
28	15.8	8	351.0	264	4.22	3.170	14.50	0	1	5	4	29
19	33.9	4	71.1	65	4.22	1.835	19.90	1	1	4	1	20
6	14.3	8	360.0	245	3.21	3.570	15.84	0	0	3	4	7

3. Next, the input dimension is defined. As there are 12 different input features, and as we plan to use all the features in the autoencoder, we define the number of input neurons to be 12. This is embedded in an input layer, as shown in the following code snippet:

```
input_dim = X_train.shape[1]
encoding_dim = 12
input_layer = Input(shape=(input_dim, ))
```

4. Next, we create an encoder and decoder. The ReLU function, which is a non-linear activation function, is used in the encoder. The encoded layer is passed on to the decoder, where it tries to reconstruct the input data pattern:

```
encoded = Dense(encoding_dim, activation='relu')(input_layer)
decoded = Dense(12, activation='linear')(encoded)
```

5. The following model maps the input to its reconstruction, which is done in the decoder layer, decoded. Next, the optimizer and loss function is defined using the compile method. The adadelta optimizer uses exponentially-decaying gradient averages and is a highly-adaptive learning rate method. The reconstruction is a linear process and is defined in the decoder using the linear activation function. The loss is defined as mse, which is mean squared error, and which we studied in Chapter 2, *Introduction to Machine Learning Using Python*:

```
autoencoder = Model(input_layer, decoded)
autoencoder.compile(optimizer='adadelta', loss='mse')
```

6. Next, the training data, X_train, is fitted into the autoencoder. Let's train our autoencoder for 100 epochs with a batch_size of 4 and observe if it reaches a stable train or test loss value:

```
X_train = np.array(X_train)
autoencoder.fit(X_train, X_train,epochs=100,batch_size=4)
```

7. Once we execute the preceding code snippet, the execution starts, and we can see the progress in the following screenshot. The processing stops once it reaches the number of epochs that is specified in the model's fit method:

```
Epoch 1/100
22/22 [==============================] - 0s - loss: 28985.7149
Epoch 2/100
22/22 [==============================] - 0s - loss: 28571.5341
Epoch 3/100
22/22 [==============================] - 0s - loss: 28183.4400
Epoch 4/100
22/22 [==============================] - 0s - loss: 27798.2921
Epoch 5/100
22/22 [==============================] - 0s - loss: 27422.6434
Epoch 6/100
22/22 [==============================] - 0s - loss: 27080.4889
Epoch 7/100
22/22 [==============================] - 0s - loss: 26722.0817
Epoch 8/100
22/22 [==============================] - 0s - loss: 26391.1487
Epoch 9/100
22/22 [==============================] - 0s - loss: 26058.9774
Epoch 10/100
```

8. Once the model is fitted, we predict the input values by passing the same X_train dataset to the autoencoder's `predict` method. Next, we calculate the `mse` values to know whether the autoencoder was able to reconstruct the dataset correctly and how much the reconstruction error was:

```
predictions = autoencoder.predict(X_train)
mse = np.mean(np.power(X_train - predictions, 2), axis=1)
```

9. We can plot the `mse` to view the reconstruction error and the index of input data which it was not able to reconstruct properly:

```
plt.plot(mse)
```

10. We can observe from the following plot that the autoencoder was not able to reconstruct the 16th record of the dataset properly. The reconstruction error is too high for that record and it is an anomaly. The 13th record also has a small reconstruction error, which might be an anomaly as well:

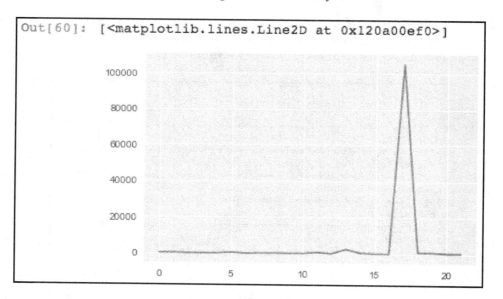

In the following section, we will focus on **Convolutional Neural Networks (CNN)**, which are extensively used for image processing and image recognition.

Convolutional Neural Networks

This section will focus on the CNN's architecture. Though CNN is a topic that might not be covered fully in a single chapter, we will focus on the important elements that a CNN has for you to get started with CNNs easily. During our discussion, we will use the Keras package to create a CNN using the sample MNIST dataset that the package has.

The question that comes to mind when we hear the term CNN is, *why CNN?* We will try to answer this question with a short explanation.

Why CNN?

We discussed feed-forward neural networks in an earlier section. Though they are powerful, one of their main disadvantages is that an FNN ignores the structure of the input data. All data feed to the network has to be first converted into a 1D numerical array. However, for higher-dimensional arrays such as in an image, it gets difficult to deal with such conversion. It is essential to preserve the structure of images, as there is a lot of hidden information stored inside the, this is where a CNN comes into the picture. A CNN considers the structure of the images while processing them.

The next question that we have is the difficult term-convolution. What is it?

What is convolution?

Convolution is a special kind of mathematical operation that involves the multiplication of two functions, f and g, to produce a new modified function (f * g). For example, the convolution between an image (let's say function f) with a filter function, g, will produce a new version of the image.

We just discussed filters, so let's try to understand what filters are.

What are filters?

A CNN uses filters to identify features in an image, such as edges, lines, or arches. They search for certain important patterns or features in an image. Filters are designed to search for certain characteristics in an image and detect whether or not the image contains those characteristics. A filter is applied at different positions in an image, until it covers the whole image. Filters form a critical element in a convolution layer, an important step in a CNN.

There are mainly four different layers in a CNN:

- Convolution layer
- ReLU layer
- Pooling layer
- Fully connected layer

Let's discuss the convolution layer, which is the first stage in a CNN.

The convolution layer

This is the layer where the convolution operation takes place between the input image and the filters that we just discussed. This step is carried out to reduce the overall size of the image, so that it is easier to process the image in the next layers. Let's understand the function of this layer with a simple question, *how do we identify a dog or a cat?* It comes naturally to us within a second when we see them. We don't analyze all their features to determine whether a dog is a dog or a cat is a cat.

We recognize the important features, such as their eyes, ear, or tail, and then identify the creature. This is what is also done in a convolution layer. In this layer, the important features are identified and the rest are all ignored. The filters are moved across the image to detect the essential features in the image. The process of moving the filters are called **strides**.

The results of the convolution layer are then passed through a non-linear activation function, such as the ReLU function.

The ReLU layer

This additional step is applied to the convoluted layer to introduce non-linearity in the convoluted feature map. We learned about the ReLU function in the earlier section. The images have a highly non-linear pattern. When we apply convolution, there is a risk that it might become linear as there are linear operations like multiplication and summations. So, a non-linear activation function, such as ReLU, is used to preserve the non-linearity in the images.

The next stage in a CNN is the pooling layer.

The pooling layer

The pooling layer further reduces the size of the feature representation by applying a pooling function. There are different kinds of pooling functions, such as `average`, `min`, and `max`. Max pooling is widely used as it tends to keep the `max` values of a feature map for each stride. This is similar to the convolution layer where we have a sliding window and the window slides over the feature map to find the `max` value within each stride. The window size in a pooling layer is typically less than that used in the convolution layer.

The pooled feature map is then flattened to a 1D representation to be used in a fully connected layer.

The fully connected layer

There can be multiple convolution, ReLU, and pooling operations in a CNN. However, there is always a last single stage which is a fully connected layer. The fully connected layer is the feed-forward neural network that we discussed earlier. The purpose of this step is to make different predictions on the `image` dataset, such as classifying images.

The following diagram illustrates the final picture of a CNN's basic architecture:

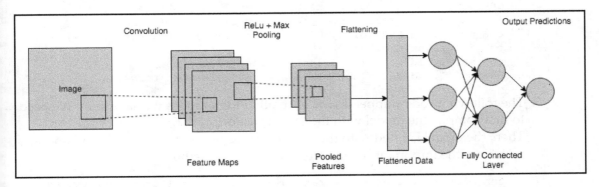

Now that we understand some basics about CNNs, let's create a CNN using Keras. We will use the `MNIST` dataset that is present in Keras itself. The `MNIST` dataset is a well-known dataset of written digits. The dataset is already segregated into a train and test set. It has around 70,000 images. Each image has a gray scale dimension of 28 * 28.

The full code for this section can be found in the book's code repository. We will demonstrate the vital code sections.

We start building a Keras DL model, by defining a sequential model:

1. As discussed, the sequential methods enable us to add one layer over the others that are executed in sequence. The first layer that is added is the convolution layer defined by the `Conv2D` method. As the `MNIST` dataset consists of 2D images, we add a 2D convolution layer. The `kernel_size` parameter is used to define the size of the filter, and the strides are for defining the moving window.

2. There is no different ReLU layer in Keras. However, we can define the activation function in the convolution layer itself. The activation function we choose for this task is ReLU.

3. The third step is to add a max pooling layer using the `MaxPooling2D` method. The `pool_size` is defined to be 2 * 2 and the stride for the pooling layer is 2 * 2.

4. The fourth step of flattening the data is done by adding a `Flatten2D` method. The last layer, which is the fully connected layer, is defined similarly to the feed-forward neural network:

```
#Model Definition
cnn_model = Sequential()
cnn_model.add(Conv2D(32, kernel_size=(5, 5), strides=(1,
1),activation='relu',input_shape=input))
cnn_model.add(MaxPooling2D(pool_size=(2, 2), strides=(2, 2)))
cnn_model.add(Flatten())
cnn_model.add(Dense(1000, activation='relu'))
cnn_model.add(Dense(num_classes, activation='softmax'))
```

5. The following code snippet is similar to other Keras codes we have seen. We need to first compile the model with the `loss` function, `optimizer`, and `metrics`. Then, the model is fitted with the training set using the `batch_size` and `epochs`, which are the important parameters in a model fit method:

```
cnn_model.compile(loss=keras.losses.categorical_crossentropy,
 optimizer=keras.optimizers.Adam(),
 metrics=['accuracy'])
cnn_model.fit(x_train, y_train,
batch_size=10,
epochs=10,
verbose=1,
validation_data=(x_test, y_test))
```

6. Once we execute the preceding code, we need to wait for some time for the results. It takes a lot of time to complete just 10 epochs as the training dataset is huge and images are complex:

```
Train on 60000 samples, validate on 10000 samples
Epoch 1/10
60000/60000 [==============================] - 566s - loss: 0.0994 - acc: 0.9697 - val_loss: 0.0685 - val_acc: 0.9779
Epoch 2/10
60000/60000 [==============================] - 533s - loss: 0.0406 - acc: 0.9879 - val_loss: 0.0501 - val_acc: 0.9835
Epoch 3/10
60000/60000 [==============================] - 554s - loss: 0.0240 - acc: 0.9925 - val_loss: 0.0451 - val_acc: 0.9877
Epoch 4/10
60000/60000 [==============================] - 577s - loss: 0.0172 - acc: 0.9945 - val_loss: 0.0551 - val_acc: 0.9872
Epoch 5/10
60000/60000 [==============================] - 558s - loss: 0.0152 - acc: 0.9960 - val_loss: 0.0580 - val_acc: 0.9877
Epoch 6/10
60000/60000 [==============================] - 692s - loss: 0.0121 - acc: 0.9968 - val_loss: 0.0787 - val_acc: 0.9851
Epoch 7/10
60000/60000 [==============================] - 59789s - loss: 0.0108 - acc: 0.9974 - val_loss: 0.0739 - val_acc: 0.98
78
Epoch 8/10
60000/60000 [==============================] - 561s - loss: 0.0101 - acc: 0.9976 - val_loss: 0.0855 - val_acc: 0.9866
Epoch 9/10
60000/60000 [==============================] - 1463s - loss: 0.0083 - acc: 0.9979 - val_loss: 0.0983 - val_acc: 0.985
5
Epoch 10/10
60000/60000 [==============================] - 537s - loss: 0.0098 - acc: 0.9980 - val_loss: 0.0924 - val_acc: 0.9875
<keras.callbacks.History at 0x11c954898>
```

7. When the training is completed, we can evaluate the accuracy of the model using the following code snippet:

```
model_score = cnn_model.evaluate(x_test, y_test, verbose=0)
print('Loss on the test data:', model_score[0])
print('Model accuracy on the test data:', model_score[1])
```

The model has an impressive accuracy of 0.9875, which is 98.75%, on the test data:

```
Loss on the test data: 0.09238649257670754
Model accuracy on the test data: 0.9875
```

Summary

In this chapter, we introduced you to the world of neural networks and deep learning. We discussed different activation functions, the structure of a neural network, and demonstrated a feed-forward neural network using Keras.

Deep learning is a topic in itself, and there are several deep learning books with an in-depth focus. The objective of this chapter was to provide you with a head start in exploring deep learning, as it is the next frontier in machine learning automation. We witnessed the power of autoencoders for dimensionality reduction. Also, the CNNs, with their robust feature-processing mechanism, are an essential component for building the automated systems of the future.

We will end our discussion in the next chapter, where we review what we have covered so far, the next steps, and the necessary skills to create a complete machine learning system.

Critical Aspects of ML and Data Science Projects

8

If you have made it this far, give yourself a pat on the shoulder. This is not to think of yourself as a **machine learning** (**ML**) expert, but rather to acknowledge the work that you have done to learn **Automated ML** (**AutoML**) workflows. You are now ready to apply these techniques to solve your problems!

In this chapter, you are going to review what you have learned throughout the chapters and put your learning into a broader perspective.

We will be covering the following topics in our discussion:

- Machine learning as a search
- Trade-offs in ML
- An engagement model for a typical data science project
- The phases of an engagement model

Machine learning as a search

Throughout the previous chapters, you have seen many different techniques applied to modeling problems and most of those techniques, although they seem simple, include many parameters that ultimately affect the outcome of your efforts. Many modeling problems require AutoML to be represented as a search problem and in the majority of cases, there are only sub-optimal solutions to be found.

In a broader sense, modeling is just a mapping between your input data and output data. As a result, you will be able to infer the output where new input data arrives with unknown output. In order to achieve your objective, you need to think about your experiment design and configure your environment accordingly, since you really don't know what will be the best-performing ML pipeline—but let's stop for a second and step back.

Implementing performant systems really starts from some fundamental choices about the system architecture that will allow you to design and deliver successful data science solutions. One of the things you should start thinking about is your system configuration for hardware and software, such as the type of server, CPU or GPU-specific requirements, memory and disk requirements, software requirements and similar. As you will work on larger datasets, your configuration will be more important. The choices you make at this point will determine the performance of your data science stack, which will likely contain some of the following software frameworks and libraries:

- Specific software distributions such as Anaconda
- Data-processing frameworks such as Hadoop, Apache Spark, Kafka
- Task-specific libraries such as scikit-learn, XGBoost, TensorFlow/Keras, PyTorch
- Data management systems such as MongoDB, Neo4j, Apache Cassandra, and MySQL

This is not an exhaustive list but, even with such limited scope, this is a lot of information to digest. You should ideally be familiar with at least the role each one plays in a typical architecture and, once you get into building systems, these choices will become clear as you implement systems for different use cases.

Once you have these pieces in place and working smoothly, you can start to think about how you will move data around and feed it into your ML pipeline.

When you are in the data processing and modeling phase, options are vast and, as mentioned previously, each and every method has its own set of parameters. The following shows you the typical flow of what you have practiced so far:

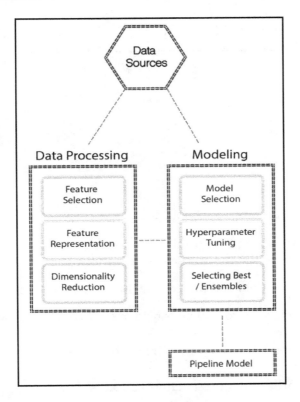

Let's consider a text processing pipeline for predicting financial market movements and see what each of these steps means in such a set up.

First, you will have various data sources; these may include data coming from:

- Financial exchanges
- Company announcement and filings
- News agencies that provide general and financial news
- Macro-economic data from government agencies
- Regulatory reports
- Social networks such as Twitter

The following diagram shows couple of different data sources:

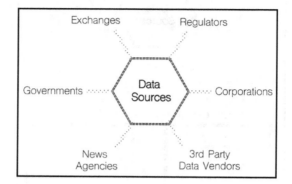

When you have such data stored, you need to process this data to be used in the modeling phase since ML models need numerical vectorized inputs.

The first step is feature selection, and this may include the following steps:

- Determine if every word will be considered as a different feature; this is commonly known as a **bag-of-words**
- Determine if noun phrases, verb phrases, or named entities could be used as features
- Categorize words into representative concepts
- Create n-grams, which are a contiguous sequence of items

The following figure helps us to understand the different feature selections:

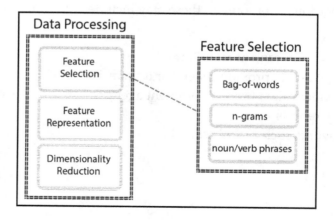

Once you have decided what features you are going to use, you will think about reducing the number of dimensions to avoid the curse of dimensionality. This phase may include the following steps:

- Simple filtering operations, such as only including the top 100 concepts
- Setting thresholds to include only words that occur more than the given threshold
- Using pre-defined dictionaries, created by domain experts, to filter input data
- Standard operations, such as removing stop words and lemmatization

The following figure helps you to understand the different approaches for feature selection and representation:

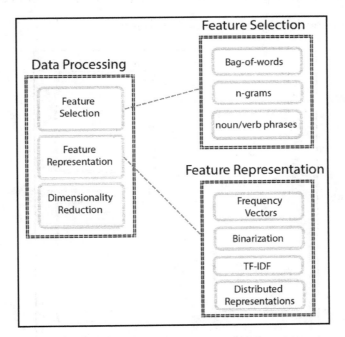

Dimensionality reduction is also a phase which you could come back to after feature representation. Once you have numerical feature vectors, you could apply methods such as **Principal Component Analysis (PCA)** to further reduce dimensionality. Let's look at typical operations for feature representation:

- Representing the words in a vocabulary as frequency vectors, where each word will be assigned to a number of its occurrence
- Binarizing frequency vectors so that every value will be either 0 or 1
- Using **term frequency-inverse document frequency (tf-idf)** encoding to represent words as their relative importance to the whole document in a collection of documents, namely **corpus**
- Using distributed representations such as Word2Vec or Doc2Vec

As a result, you have the full figure explained as follows:

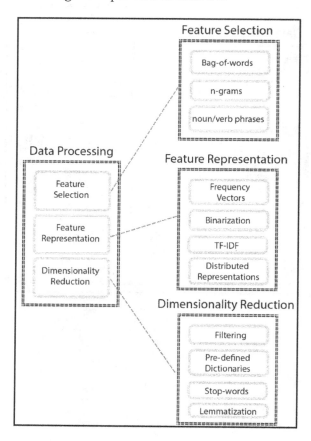

Once you are done with the data processing part you can start modeling, and in this case you will have many different algorithms to choose from. In text mining, the following are the most commonly used algorithms:

- Deep neural networks, particularly **Long Short-Term Memory (LSTM)** networks, which are a special type of **recurrent neural networks (RNNs)**
- Support Vector Machines
- Decision trees
- Ensembles
- Regression algorithms
- Naive Bayes

The following figure shows couple of different algorithms which can be used:

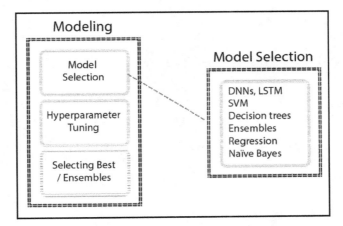

Each algorithm will have its own parameter space, and parameters are mainly two types:

- Hyperparameters which are set before training starts
- Model parameters which are learned during training

The goal is to optimize hyperparameters so that your model parameters will give you the best generalization performance. Search space is usually very large and you have seen some methods, such as Bayesian optimization, which explore the space in efficient ways.

For example, let's take a look at only the parameters of the XGBoost algorithm, which dominates the ML applications.

If you run the following lines, you will see the explanations for model parameters:

```
import xgboost as xgb
classifier = xgb.XGBClassifier()

classifier?
```

This gives you the following output:

```
Type: XGBClassifier
String form:
XGBClassifier(base_score=0.5, booster='gbtree', colsample_bylevel=1,
  colsample_bytree=1, g <...> reg_alpha=0, reg_lambda=1, scale_pos_weight=1,
seed=None,
  silent=True, subsample=1)
File: ~/anaconda/lib/python3.6/site-packages/xgboost/sklearn.py
Docstring:
Implementation of the scikit-learn API for XGBoost classification.
 Parameters
 ----------
max_depth : int
 Maximum tree depth for base learners.
learning_rate : float
 Boosting learning rate (xgb's "eta")
n_estimators : int
 Number of boosted trees to fit.
silent : boolean
 Whether to print messages while running boosting.
objective : string or callable
 Specify the learning task and the corresponding learning objective or
 a custom objective function to be used (see note below).
booster: string
 Specify which booster to use: gbtree, gblinear or dart.
nthread : int
 Number of parallel threads used to run xgboost. (Deprecated, please use
n_jobs)
n_jobs : int
 Number of parallel threads used to run xgboost. (replaces nthread)
gamma : float
 Minimum loss reduction required to make a further partition on a leaf node
of the tree.
min_child_weight : int
 Minimum sum of instance weight(hessian) needed in a child.
max_delta_step : int
 Maximum delta step we allow each tree's weight estimation to be.
```

```
subsample : float
 Subsample ratio of the training instance.
colsample_bytree : float
 Subsample ratio of columns when constructing each tree.
colsample_bylevel : float
 Subsample ratio of columns for each split, in each level.
reg_alpha : float (xgb's alpha)
 L1 regularization term on weights
reg_lambda : float (xgb's lambda)
 L2 regularization term on weights
scale_pos_weight : float
 Balancing of positive and negative weights.
base_score:
 The initial prediction score of all instances, global bias.
seed : int
 Random number seed. (Deprecated, please use random_state)
random_state : int
 Random number seed. (replaces seed)
missing : float, optional
 Value in the data which needs to be present as a missing value. If
 None, defaults to np.nan.
**kwargs : dict, optional
 Keyword arguments for XGBoost Booster object. Full documentation of
parameters can
 be found here:
https://github.com/dmlc/xgboost/blob/master/doc/parameter.md.
 Attempting to set a parameter via the constructor args and **kwargs dict
simultaneously
 will result in a TypeError.
 Note:
 **kwargs is unsupported by Sklearn. We do not guarantee that parameters
passed via
 this argument will interact properly with Sklearn.
```

To optimize hyperparameters such as XGBoost's, you need to select an approach such as grid search, random search, Bayesian optimization, or evolutionary optimization. In practice, Bayesian optimization yields good results for optimizing the hyperparameters of ML algorithms.

The following addition to the flow shows common hyperparameters and approaches used in optimization:

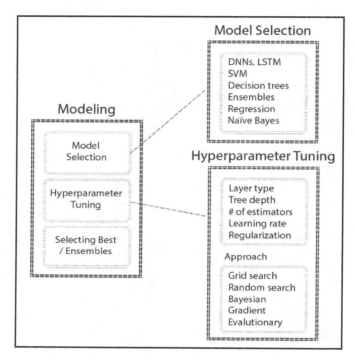

Ultimately, you can select the best-performing ML pipeline or you can create your own ensemble to leverage multiple pipelines.

Mastering these pipelines requires you to get familiar with each step and properly navigate the whole search space to end up with acceptable, near-optimal solutions.

Trade-offs in machine learning

There are mainly two aspects to consider:

- Training time
- Scoring time

Both will act as constraints as you are developing your pipelines.

Let's think about the limitations that training and scoring time bring to the table. Requirements for training time will usually determine the algorithms that you will include in your candidate list. For example, logistic regression and **Support Vector Machines (SVMs)** are fast-to-train algorithms, and this might be important to you, especially if you are prototyping ideas quickly using big data. They are also fast when it comes to scoring. There are different implementations for both, and also different options are available for solvers, which make these two convenient for many ML use cases.

However, for something like a deep neural network, training and scoring time are very limiting constraints as you may not be able to tolerate a week-long training time or more than a second scoring time. You can improve training and scoring time by having more powerful hardware resources, but that may cause your bills to sky rocket, depending on the complexity of your network. Apart from the selection of algorithms, training time also highly depends on your hyperparameter space as it may cause it to be much longer.

Another concern is scalability, which is related to your data size, and you need to ensure that your pipeline's scalability matches the speed of growth of your data. At this point, you should look at factors such as support for multithreaded, multicore, parallel, or distributed training.

Engagement model for a typical data science project

When you start to learn anything new, or build on your existing knowledge, it's important to understand the background of things and how the story has evolved over time, knowing that the current trends were a natural evolution of conventional reporting, **business intelligence (BI)**, and analytics. That's why the initial chapters walked you through the background and fundamentals of ML pipelines, such as data preprocessing, automated algorithm selection, and hyperparameter optimization.

Due to the highly experimental nature of AutoML pipelines, there were many concepts explained together with their practical examples.

The ideas that advanced analytics and ML use to solve problems are not necessarily new, but they are only usable now as people have easy access to cheaper hardware and software resources. More advanced technologies are at your disposal to address some of the issues that you were not able to address before.

In this book, you have learned various aspects of developing ML pipelines. However, in real-world projects, developing ML pipelines is just one of the variables. Operationalizing ML pipelines is crucially important since you can only benefit from well-developed pipelines if you successfully deploy and monitor these pipelines. Many companies have **Software as a Service** (**SaaS**) offerings for ML, and they aim to abstract away the low-level complexities of managing ML pipelines in production environments.

In the following section, we will discuss the different phases of data science projects so that you can understand exactly where modeling falls when you are dealing with the successful delivery of end-to-end data science projects.

The phases of an engagement model

A very well-known modeling process is CRISP-DM for data mining and predictive analytics projects, and it involves six steps:

1. Business understanding
2. Data understanding
3. Data preparation
4. Modeling
5. Evaluation
6. Deployment

Each of these phases follows each other, and some of them happen in a recursive fashion by providing feedback to the preceding phase. The deployment phase is particularly important in terms of model monitoring and maintenance, which is the focus of this chapter.

Let's quickly look at each of these phases and their purpose in the overall process.

Business understanding

This is the phase where you fully focus on the business objectives in terms of project goals, scope, resources, limitations, iterations, and checkpoints.

You try to understand the whole picture in business terms and frame the problem technically. There might be competing objectives between different internal stakeholders in your organization, and you should be aware of them and find the sweet spot. For example, in supply chain management, product supply organizations try to keep their inventory at optimum levels, while sales organization would like to build an excessive inventory for upcoming product launches based on very optimistic sales forecasts. You should know who will benefit from the ML and data science capability that you will implement.

In this phase, you are typically trying to address the following items:

- Getting familiar with current decision making processes and splitting them further into separate use cases for different scenarios.
- Having agreed on human resources, identifying the data sources to be used (for example data extracts, data lakes, operational DBs, and so on).
- Finding out the assumptions and trying to validate them with available data, and separating facts from opinions/intuitions before moving on.
- Agreeing on deliverables and the tools/technologies to be used to deliver them throughout the project.
- Deciding which evaluation metrics/KPIs will be used for both ML models and business outcomes. You should always be in line with business objectives.
- Identifying the risks that might cause delays or project failure, and making these clear to the stakeholders. The success of a ML project is inherently probabilistic, not like the BI work which most people are used to work with.

Data understanding

This is the phase where you develop an understanding of the data sources that you will use throughout the project.

In this phase, you are typically trying to address the following items:

- Clearing data access and authorization issues.
- Loading data into a platform of preference for initial analysis.
- Being aware of sensitive information and performing necessary operations, such as anonymizing or deletion of sensitive data.
- Identifying datasets to be used.
- Identifying data schema and getting field descriptions.

- Determining the quantity for each dataset and identifying discrepancies. For example, you check if the variables that are present in different tables have the same datatype, for example, a variable could be an integer type in one table and a decimal type in another.
- Exploring sample datasets, such as producing basic including count, mean, standard deviation, percentiles, and checking variable distributions.
- Getting familiar with how data is collected to see if there are possible measurement errors during data collection.
- Studying correlations while keeping the stats proverb in mind—*correlation does not imply causation.*
- Detecting noise, such as outliers, and agreeing on how you will treat them.
- Ensuring the sample dataset represents the population by checking different properties of the dataset. For example, whether there is any skewness towards a different category of data due to the data availability.
- Performing multiple quality checks in a timely manner to ensure data quality. For example, you can identify and clarify erroneous and missing values, such as a value of 100,000,000,000 in the date column, or a value of 25,000 where the mean value is 23.4.
- Deciding on the amount of data to be used as test data and keeping it separate from your training data.

Ultimately, these kind of practices will lead you to create an automated data preparation flow and data quality reports after a few engagements.

Data preparation

This is the phase where you will create your final dataset to be used in the modeling phase by joining different data sources, cleaning, formatting, and engineering features.

In this phase, you are typically trying to address the following items:

- Identifying relevant datasets for model building.
- Documenting data joins and aggregations to construct the final dataset.
- Writing functions with useful arguments to have flexibility later in the project for cleaning and formatting datasets, such as removing outliers by x%, or imputing missing values with mean, median, or most frequent.
- Treating outliers accordingly.
- Playing with feature engineering methods.

- Selecting the features. In general, there are three main methods for feature selection:
  - Filter methods
  - Wrapper methods
  - Embedded methods
- Determining feature importance, listing reasons for including/excluding features.
- Agreeing on the data transformation pipelines to be constructed.
- Writing custom transformers for specific operations, such as extracting paragraphs, sentences, and words from a given corpus by extending Apache Spark's or scikit-learn's transformer class, and similar for the estimators.
- Properly versioning datasets and writing additional commentary, explaining the steps involved with preparation.

Modeling

This is the phase where you consider your options for modeling the final dataset that you have created in the previous phases.

In this phase, you are typically trying to address the following items:

- Determining the type of ML problem, such as supervised, semi-supervised, unsupervised, and reinforcement learning.
- Shortlisting ML models which would fit the bill.
- Agreeing on evaluation metrics and paying attention to important points, such as class imbalance as it tricks metrics such as accuracy. If the dataset is imbalanced, you can refer to sampling techniques to obtain a balanced dataset.
- Identifying the level of tolerance for false negatives and false positives.
- Thinking about how you would properly set up the cross-validation.
- Analyzing the most important features of performant models.
- Analyzing the model sensitivity with respect to each feature. Different algorithms might rank features differently; this would help you to understand how models react if distributional properties of features change over time.
- Fine-tuning models.
- Determining the type of ML workload that would be suitable for deployment, such as online, batch, and streaming deployments.
- Taking the training and scoring time into consideration as computational complexity and data size are usually constraints when choosing an algorithm.

Evaluation

This is the phase where you review the process and make sure you have covered all the planned items.

In this phase, you are typically trying to address the following items:

- Reviewing all the phases and ensuring that the model pipeline to be deployed is properly addressing all the issues and steps performed previously
- Preparing a nice presentation, keeping it clean and simple, *simple* but not *simpler*
- Presenting the outcomes, sticking to the point, explaining how your model meets the business objectives
- Explaining the limitations and in what circumstances it can go south

Deployment

This is the phase where you start to operationalize your ML models.

In this phase, you are typically trying to address the following items:

- Having a short test drive in production
- Monitoring the performance
- Identifying the strategy to improve the model such as re-evaluation, a retraining loop, and a redeployment loop, when model performance starts to decay
- Preparing the final report and deliverables

You can definitely extend the list of items that you are going to address for each phase, but this list should give you an overall idea of what you need to cover.

There will be numerous times when you will be joining a project team in the middle of a project's timeline. In these kinds of situations, you usually lack the project background and you need several meetings with key people to understand what's going on. Knowing these phases will help you to understand the current stage of the project and identify what has been missed or clarify the next steps.

When you are going through these steps, it's important to document your reasonings and findings for each step. Proper documentation will save you time when you need to redo some of the steps, as you might not remember how you performed some of the analysis or the data processing.

Summary

As in other things that you pursue in your life, practice is the only thing that will help you to improve your skills in developing ML pipelines. You need to spend a considerable amount of time with many different techniques and algorithms to deal with various problems and datasets.

Especially in real-word projects, where you may not come across similar problems, every project will require you to have a different approach. You will quickly realize that it's not only modeling that matters, but it's rather the understanding of how these technologies integrate with each other, and play nicely in enterprise software architectures.

By learning AutoML systems, you took a huge step forward and have a better understanding of AutoML pipelines. You should definitely strive to learn more about other aspects, such as the domain-specific applications in the areas of your interest, application architectures, production environments, and model maintenance techniques.

Thank you for taking the time to go through the content, and we sincerely hope that you have enjoyed reading this book as much as we did writing it!

Other Books You May Enjoy

If you enjoyed this book, you may be interested in these other books by Packt:

Python Machine Learning - Second Edition
Sebastian Raschka, Vahid Mirjalili

ISBN: 978-1-78712-593-3

- Understand the key frameworks in data science, machine learning, and deep learning
- Harness the power of the latest Python open source libraries in machine learning
- Master machine learning techniques using challenging real-world data
- Master deep neural network implementation using the TensorFlow library
- Ask new questions of your data through machine learning models and neural networks
- Learn the mechanics of classification algorithms to implement the best tool for the job
- Predict continuous target outcomes using regression analysis
- Uncover hidden patterns and structures in data with clustering
- Delve deeper into textual and social media data using sentiment analysis

Machine Learning with TensorFlow 1.x
Quan Hua, Shams Ul Azeem, Saif Ahmed

ISBN: 978-1-78646-296-1

- Explore how to use different machine learning models to ask different questions of your data
- Learn how to build deep neural networks using TensorFlow 1.x
- Cover key tasks such as clustering, sentiment analysis, and regression analysis using TensorFlow 1.x
- Find out how to write clean and elegant Python code that will optimize the strength of your algorithms
- Discover how to embed your machine learning model in a web application for increased accessibility
- Learn how to use multiple GPUs for faster training using AWS

Leave a review - let other readers know what you think

Please share your thoughts on this book with others by leaving a review on the site that you bought it from. If you purchased the book from Amazon, please leave us an honest review on this book's Amazon page. This is vital so that other potential readers can see and use your unbiased opinion to make purchasing decisions, we can understand what our customers think about our products, and our authors can see your feedback on the title that they have worked with Packt to create. It will only take a few minutes of your time, but is valuable to other potential customers, our authors, and Packt. Thank you!

Index

CPSIA information can be obtained
at www.ICGtesting.com
Printed in the USA
FSHW010026250220
67490FS

9 781788 629898